IDENTITY, CULTURE & COMMUNICATIONS
IN THE EARLY MODERN WORLD

Two other volumes currently available by Peter Burke from *EER:*

Secret History and Historical Consciousness.
From the Renaissance to Romanticism.

"Burke characteristically mixes seemingly opposing approaches
– historical truth and fiction, oral and print sources, elite and folk
tastes, mega- and micro history, symbolic and literal readings,
private and public knowledge – to reveal their coexistence and
interaction. He revisits received views with neglected or newly
discovered sources and aperçus, not to overturn but to enlighten
and amplify. Burke makes arcane topics of daunting complexity
relevant and readily accessible in remarkable feats of translation
from past to present. Familiarity with an extraordinary range
of multilingual sources is couched in graceful and self-effacing
prose, consistently instructive and entertaining."
        – **David Lowenthal**, *Times Literary Supplement,* 7 April 2017.

"*Secret History* is a timely collection in which Peter's Burke's
many strengths as a cultural historian are all on display:
intellectual independence, restless curiosity, a willingness to
seek out questions others have ignored, and a mastery of the
early modern period and its legacy. It's also beautifully written.
Anyone interested in intellectual history or the making of modern
Europe will find this a deeply rewarding read."
        – **James Shapiro**, Professor of English at Columbia University,
                and author of *1606: Shakespeare and the Year of Lear.*

"His erudition is enviable, and his lucid, effortless presentation
exemplary."
                – **John Pemble**, joint winner of the *Wolfson Prize*
                        for The Mediterranean Passion.

What is History Really About? Reflections on Theory and Practice.

AND ALSO FORTHCOMING…

Myths, Memories and The Representation of Identities.

IDENTITY, CULTURE & COMMUNICATIONS IN THE EARLY MODERN WORLD

Peter Burke

Emeritus Professor of Cultural History,
Emmanuel College, Cambridge.

EER

Edward Everett Root, Publishers, Brighton, 2018.

EER

Edward Everett Root Publishers, Co. Ltd.,
30 New Road, Brighton, Sussex, BN1 1BN, England.
www.eerpublishing.com

edwardeverettroot@yahoo.co.uk

Identity, Culture & Communications in the Early Modern World
Peter Burke

First published in England in 2018.
© Peter Burke 2018.
This edition © Edward Everett Root Publishers 2018.

ISBN: 978-1-912224-14-2 Paperback.
ISBN: 978-1-912224-13-5 Hardcover.
ISBN: 978-1-912224-73-9 Ebook.

Cover designed by Pageset Limited, High Wycombe, Buckinghamshire.
Printed and bound in England by Lightning Source UK, Milton Keynes.

CONTENTS

ACKNOWLEDGEMENTS

The author and the publishers gratefully acknowledge the permission of those publications in which the original chapters previously appeared in books or in journals, as follows:

A Civil Tongue: Language and Politeness in Early Modern Europe, first published in P. Burke, B. Harrison and P. Slack (eds.), *Civil Histories: essays presented to Sir Keith Thomas*, Oxford, Oxford University Press, 2000, 31–48; Diglossia in Early Modern Europe, first published in V. Rjéoutski, G. Argent and D. Offord (eds.), *European Francophonie*, Oxford, P. Lang, 2014, 33–49; The Renaissance Translator as Go-Between, first published in Wernervon Koppenfels (ed.), *Renaissance Go-Betweens*, Berlin, De Gruyter, 2005, 18–31; The Jesuits and the Art of Translation in Early Modern Europe, first published in John O'Malley et al. (eds.), *The Jesuits, II: Cultures, Sciences and the Arts, 1540–1773*, Toronto, University of Toronto Press, 2006, 24–32; Early Modern Venice as a Centre of Information and Communication, first published in *Venice Reconsidered: the History and Civilization of an Italian City-State 1297–1799*, John Martin and Dennis Romano(eds.), Baltimore, Johns Hopkins University Press, 2000, 389–419; *The Age of the Baroque*, first published in Italian in *Storia Moderna*, Rome, Donzelli, 1998, 229–48. Not previously published in English. The Republic of Letters as a Communication System, first published under this title in *Media History* (Routledge) 2012, 395–407; Historical Reflections on Urban Violence, first published in *Arv*, 2005, 9–28, Identity, Culture & Communications in the Early Modern World xiv; *Imagining Identity in the Early Modern City,* first published in Christian Emden, Catherine Keen and David Midgley (eds.), *Imagining the City,* Oxford, Peter Lang, 2006, vol.1, 23–38; Urban Sensations: attractive and repulsive, first published in Herman Roodenburg (ed.), *A Cultural History of the Senses in the Renaissance,* London, Bloomsbury, 2014, 23–60; Communication, first published in Ulinka Rublack (ed.), *A Concise Companion to History,* Oxford: Oxford University Press, 2011, 157–79.

INTRODUCTION

This volume brings together some of my essays on on two major interests of mine, the social history of language and the cultural history of cities, most of them united by the theme of communication.

Languages

I cannot remember when I first became interested in languages. As a child during the Second World War, I used to imagine myself as a young officer who knew most of the languages of Europe. When, after Finals at Oxford (in 1960), I decided to specialize, if that is the word, in the history of early modern Europe, my ambition was to learn to read, if not speak, as many European languages as possible – the definition of 'possible' changed over time, especially after struggles with Polish and Hungarian. Eventually I stopped learning new languages on the Forth Bridge principle that keeping the languages I had learned in reasonable repair took all the time I could devote.

It was only a short step to thinking of these languages as themselves interesting objects for a historian to study. Taking this step was encouraged by reading sociolinguists such as Joshua Fishman and Dell Hymes and wondering whether it would be possible to adopt a similar approach to the past. This social history of language would make use of interrogations and plays as evidence in the place of the sociolinguist's interviews but ask similar questions about the ways in which language varied not only according to the speakers but also according to the listeners and even the topic of conversation, using a 'higher' style to speak about religion or national politics, for instance, and a 'lower' style to discuss everyday matters, or adapting one's language to that of the other members of the group.

Adaptation was and is even more central to the enterprise of translation, which I approach here from the point of view of a social or cultural historian. Since many people in early modern Europe spoke more than one language, another short step took me to the social history of translation, asking who translated what, for whom, and according to what rules – since the rules for translation varied not only from one century to another but also according to the material translated. The Bible, for instance, was generally translated in a more literal fashion than other books, but the translation of recently written texts was – by later standards – scandalously free. Early modern translators seem to have regarded themselves as co-authors with the right to make cuts in the text or even add material of their own.

Cities

A second ambition of mine, dating from more or less the same time as the language project, was to visit all the European cities that had been important in the early modern period, from Dublin to Moscow. This is another ambition that has never been completely fulfilled, since I have never reached Vilnius, Kiev or Novgorod. However, the turn from urban tourism to urban history occurred more or less by accident.

As an assistant lecturer at the University of Sussex, arriving when the new campus opened for business in 1962, I was encouraged to offer a course on comparative history. I chose 'Aristocracies and elites', mainly European elites, apart from mandarins and samurai (one of the best students on this course is now the publisher of this collection of essays, John Spiers). Having published a book on the social history of the Italian Renaissance, and looking for a new topic for research, for which I would – for the first time, I must confess – work in archives, I decided to compare and contrast two urban elites, in Venice and Amsterdam in the 17th century (I must also confess that I was already aware of the attractions of both cities).

One result of the research was a slim volume entitled *Venice and Amsterdam,* first published in 1974. Another result was to make contact with full-time urban historians, notably Peter Clark, who works, like me, on the early modern period and Jim Dyos, who studied nineteenth-century London. Jim, a professor of urban history at the University of Leicester, was a great intellectual entrepreneur in his field. The book that I viewed as a comparative history of elites was, in his eyes, a contribution to urban history.

So Jim invited me to take his place at a conference on urban history in Sorrento, to give a paper on recent work on urban history in the Anglophone world. I had never been to Sorrento and accepted the invitation with enthusiasm, despite the need to study, at relatively short notice, contributions to the urban history of the 19th century by scholars such as Asa Briggs (who had offered me my first job at Sussex), Jim Dyos himself and distinguished American historians such as Oscar Handlin, Donald Olsen and Sam Warner.

These scholars asked different kinds of question about cities from the ones to which I was accustomed, about communication systems, for instance, about urban identity or about the city as an artefact, questions that were to influence my later work, as the studies reprinted in this section illustrate. For example, I doubt whether I would have noticed the importance of Boswell's experiences in London or written the piece on 'Imagining Identity in the Early Modern City' if I had not already been familiar with famous essay by the German sociologist Georg Simmel. The essay, 'The Metropolis and Mental Life', focuses on the consequences of anonymity in major cities at the beginning of the 20th century. One moral of this story is that we become able to understand periods as well as places better if we sometimes look outside them, placing them in comparative perspective. Again, the focus on cities and communication – in a double way, since cities are centres of communication with other places but also pose problems of communication for their own inhabitants – would have been almost unthinkable without awareness both of urban sociology and of media studies.

Another moral of the story concerns the importance of conferences. Giving a paper on an international conference on a theme that is not directly concerned with one's own research is often viewed by scholars as an unfortunate – if tempting – distraction from one's own work. The trick is to try to adapt one's research material to the theme of the conference, a kind of cultural translation that sometimes produces new insights. At the same time, presenting one's work to an international audience is likely to provoke different questions from a presentation at home, revealing what had been taken for granted or even left out.

The essays on cities reprinted in the second part of this volume are more diverse than the essays on language, since they include topics such as urban violence, noise and even smells. All the same, most of these pieces share two themes with the essays in the first part. The first and most obvious theme is communication and the second is identity. In cities, where people do not know most of the individuals they pass in the street, outward signs of identity are more important than in villages. These signs include not only clothes but also language. Indeed, there was a proverb in circulation in early modern Europe, 'speak, so that I may see you'. Juxtaposing early modern sources to later sociological theory, I argue that the concern for appearances characteristic in the 'age of the baroque', and more specifically the concern with self-presentation, was a reaction to the anonymity of large cities such as Paris or London.

As for the history of communication, the larger framework of which the history of language is just a part, my interest in it was kindled by the work of three scholars, only one of whom was a historian: Harold Innis came from economic history, Albert Lord from Slavic literatures, and Jack Goody from anthropology. However, I was drawn into writing about the topic, as into the history of cities, by an invitation. The invitation came from an extraordinary Italian, Amleto Lorenzini, a disciple of Marshall McLuhan who was editing a collective study of 'communication in history' and invited me to speak in Rome and then to write a chapter on the Renaissance from this point of view. For a later volume he asked Asa Briggs, who was engaged on a history of the BBC, to write on the 19th century. Later on, Asa and I expanded our contributions into a book, *A Social History of the Media,* first published in 2002. Working with him revived memories of the early days of the University of Sussex, when Asa seemed to be everywhere and engaged simultaneously on a variety of tasks. When we needed to meet and discuss the book, Asa once suggested the railway station at King's Cross, an hour before he caught a train to Scotland, and on another occasion Claridge's, an hour before he was due to receive the Wolfson Prize for History. All the same, we solved whatever problems there were without feeling rushed.

Once again, the story has a moral. Just as giving papers at conferences and hearing them discussed from different points of view is a form of education, so is collaboration with fellow-historians such as Asa Briggs and intellectual entrepreneurs such as Amleto Lorenzini. Thanks to these forms of education, together with reading major studies in neighbouring disciplines, from literature to anthropology, even writing a historical monography alone is part of a collective enterprise!

1: A Civil Tongue: Language and Politeness in Early Modern Europe

One of the domains in which the concept of civility was employed in early modern Europe was that of language. When a naval officer in Conrad's *Lord Jim* complains that 'it was as much as I could do to keep a civil tongue in my head', he was using a term with a long tradition, referring to the refusal to engage in the war of insults discussed elsewhere in this volume. However, this was not the only link between language and civility, as a recent study of the topic shows very clearly.[1] In the seventeenth century, George Wither referred to unseemly jests which 'every civil ear detests', while James Howell claimed that French had 'civiliz'd and smoothed' the English tongue.[2] In the sixteenth century, Sir Philip Sidney described the 'rude style' of traditional ballads as examples of an 'uncivil age', while George Puttenham discussed the language proper to 'men civill and graciously behaboured and bred'.[3]

---

[1] A. Bryson, *From Courtesy to Civility: Changing Codes of Conduct in Early Modern England* (Oxford, 1998), especially 151–92.

[2] ; G. Wither, *Britain Remembered* (1628), 29; J. Howell, *New English Grammar* (1662), 'to the reader'.

[3] P. Sidney, *Miscellaneous Prose*, ed. K. Duncan-Jones and J. van Dorsten (Oxford, 1973), 97; G. Puttenham, *The Arte of English Poesie* (1589: rpr Menston, 1968).

Language, spoken or written, was viewed as one of the most obvious if not the most important ways of demonstrating status, manners or breeding, a point made again and again in the treatises on good behaviour which proliferated in early modern Europe. To discuss the place of politeness in language and of language in politeness is the aim of this essay in what might be called 'historical pragmatics', a field to which Keith Thomas has contributed more than once.[4]

(i)

Two forms of linguistic behaviour will be studied here, 'altruistic' and 'egotistic' politeness. In the first place, consideration for others. In the second place, distinction from others, via 'higher' or 'purer' forms of language. The basic assumption in what follows is that polite language of both types changes over time, just as it varies from place to place, from one social group to another and from individual to individual.

This assumption might appear to have been contradicted, if not completely demolished, by a major study of the subject published some twenty years ago by two British linguists. The central point of Brown and Levinson's lucid and elegant essay is that 'politeness phenomena' can be explained by 'universal strategies of verbal interaction'.[5] Inspired by the work of the sociologist Erving Goffman, the philosopher H. P. Grice and the linguist John Gumperz, the authors analyse expressions of politeness in three unrelated languages (English, Tamil and Tzeltal), centring on the concepts of 'face' and 'face-threatening acts' (FTAs). They distinguish between 'negative face' (the need not to be impeded) and 'positive face' (the need for one's wants to be desired by others).

Politeness, described as a way of minimising these threats, is also divided into positive and negative forms. The authors list and

[4] K. V. Thomas, 'Yours', in C. Ricks and L. Michaels (eds) *The State of the Language* (1990); his paper on accent unfortunately remains unpublished.
[5] P. Brown and S. Levinson, 'Universals in Language Usage: Politeness Phenomena' (1978), revised as *Politeness: Some Universals in Language Usage* (Cambridge, 1987); cf. C. A. Ferguson, "The Structure and Use of Politeness Formulas", *Language in Society* 5 (1976), 137–51.

discuss fifteen strategies of positive politeness ('seek agreement', 'joke', 'promise' and so on), and ten of negative politeness ('give deference', 'apologise', etc). Their emphasis falls heavily on human rationality (sometimes analysed in terms of 'costs' and 'benefits'), and on universality. Criticizing what they call 'the once-fashionable doctrine of cultural relativity', the authors argue that 'superficial diversities can emerge from underlying universal principles and are satisfactorily accounted for only in relation to them'.[6]

What has happened to cultural differences? The authors note that what counts as an FTA varies from one culture to another, and they draw a contrast between 'positive politeness cultures' with low social distance (the USA, for example), and more hierarchical 'negative politeness cultures' such as Britain and Japan.[7] However, they do not take their analysis of difference very far. In the revised version of their essay, they note the relevance of 'folk theories' of face, tact and so on, but they do not develop this point either.[8] In similar fashion, in his classic essay on the subject, Erving Goffman glided from what he called 'the Chinese conception of face' to his own analysis of the USA without discussing differences between the two cultures.[9]

In this essay, on the other hand, the aim is to discuss variations and changes in the rules of civility. I have no intention of denying the existence of universal human strategies, linguistic or otherwise. However, the importance of these strategies cannot be assessed without a study of what is not universal, of what varies between places or changes over time. Rather than assuming that what varies is necessarily 'superficial', as Brown and Levenson put it, the idea will be put to the test. In order to demonstrate the importance of universals, Brown and Levenson adopted the strategy of comparing polite language in three unrelated cultures. To show the importance of variation and change, it may be useful to adopt

---

[6] Brown and Levinson, *Politeness*, 56.
[7] Brown and Levinson, *Politeness*, 13–14, 48.
[8] For criticisms by linguists, see *Politeness in Language*, ed. R. Watts et al. (Berlin and New York, 1992), especially pp. 10, 107.
[9] E. Goffman 'On Face-Work' (1955), rpr in his *Interaction Ritual* (Harmondsworth, 1972), 5–45.

the opposite strategy to theirs and focus on three related cultures, England, France and Italy.

A basic concept in this enterprise of historicization is that of different systems, codes or 'regimes' of civility, which are embedded in larger regimes of everyday life.[10] By a 'regime' is meant a repertoire of practices, consisting of gestures and words (spoken and written), including modes of address such as 'Madam', or 'Your Majesty', formulaic phrases such as 'please' or 'yours sincerely', unspoken rules such as 'don't interrupt', and so on. Each element in the repertoire may have parallels elsewhere, but the regime is distinctive in its combination of items and also in its inflections or emphases, revealing cultural differences and contrasts at the level of tact (or tactics), if not at Brown and Levenson's deeper level of strategy. For these reasons a regime may be regarded as a system. Needless to say (among historians, at least), a linguistic regime is never static, any more than a political regime. In both cases, however, the structures usually have a longer life than individuals.

Regimes of civility are of course related to social structures, even if they are not simply translations of these structures into words. A working hypothesis might take the form of the proposition that the more hierarchical (highly stratified or more sharply stratified) the society, the more formal or elaborate its civility will be. This hypothesis will be discussed, if not tested in the strict sense of that term, in the pages which follow. At this point in the argument what may need emphasis is the distinctiveness of different regimes. The evidence for the distinctiveness comes in particular from the history of encounters between people from different cultures, and the distance (not to mention misunderstandings) which these encounters reveal.

(ii)

Take the case of 'oriental' politeness, for instance, as perceived by westerners. What Brown and Levenson call the 'humiliative mode' of politeness, praising the other and depreciating the self and its

---

[10] Cf. the notion of different 'politeness systems' employed in M. Sifaniou, *Politeness Phenomena in England and Greece: a Cross-Cultural Perspective* (Oxford, 1992). 41.

possessions, has often been described as remarkable, exaggerated and even servile.[11] These descriptions obviously have their place in the occidental construction of Orientalism, especially 'Oriental Despotism'. They also reveal perceptions of cultural distance which tells us something about the perceivers.

For example, the contemporary account of the embassy to the emperor of China sent by the Dutch East India Company in the mid-seventeenth century is full of references to the 'civility' of the Chinese. They treated the Dutch with civility, excused themselves with civility, refused with civility, and so on. The author notes 'the courtly and polite modish way of speaking' in China, in which the speaker refers to himself as 'He, or such a one'.[12] George Macartney, British ambassador to China in 1793–4, was more ambivalent. He commented on 'the most refined politeness and sly good breeding' of the mandarins he met, the slyness referring to 'an immediate acquiescence in words with everything we seemed to propose', combined with 'evasion' in practice. George Staunton, who accompanied the embassy and published a description of it soon afterwards, commented not only on the 'urbanity' of high-status Chinese but also on the 'excess' of Chinese manners, which 'require, in the mention of one's self, that the most abject terms should be employed, and the most exalted towards those who are addressed'. In other words, the British distanced themselves from the 'abject' language of the Chinese, the verbal equivalent of the kowtow to the emperor which the ambassador famously refused to perform.[13]

As for India, even in the seventeenth century, when Englishmen made a considerable use of compliments, they already perceived the polite forms of that country as distant from theirs. The English clergyman Edward Terry noted that 'this people of East India are civil in their speeches', while his successor John Ovington de-

---

[11] Brown and Levinson, *Politeness*, 179, 185.

[12] J. Nieuhoff, *Het Gezantschap der Neerlandsche Oost-Indisch Compagnie aan den Grooten Tartarischen Cham* (Amsterdam, 1665); English translation *An Embassy sent by the East India Company* (1699), 62, 83, 85, 173.

[13] G. Macartney, *An Embassy to China*, ed. J. Cranmer-Byng (1962), 87; G. Staunton, *An Authentic Account of an Embassy* (2 vols, 1797), vol. 2, 29, 35, 240.

scribed 'the Orientals' as 'much more tender and insinuating in their language' than Europeans, so much so that whoever is accustomed to their style of speaking 'can hardly bear the roughness or be brought to digest the rudeness of the others'.[14] By the nineteenth century, attitudes had changed. Francis Day, an English medical officer stationed in Cochin, noted what he called the 'cringing servility' of the low-caste Permauls, while the missionary Samuel Mateer, who worked among the Pulayan of Travancore, described what he called the 'abject' language which the lower castes were compelled to use when speaking to their superiors, including the terms 'your slave' (instead of 'I'), 'dirty gruel' (for 'rice'), 'hut' (for 'house'), and 'monkeys' (for children).[15]

The point is not to assert that Europeans never practise the humiliative mode (which some English people, for example, still do in a mild form), but simply to note that for centuries some of them perceived Chinese and Indian forms and formulae of civility to be different from their own. It is time to investigate whether these forms change over time as well as varying over space and whether they are related to social and political structures such as differences in degrees of liberty or equality.

(iii)

1789 might be considered an appropriate date at which to end an article on 'old regimes' of civility, partly because the best historical evidence for the importance and significance of the rules governing everyday life, including everyday language, comes from breaking them, or more exactly from investigating the moments at which, occasions on which and contexts in which they are broken. Indeed, the traditional regime of French politeness broke down after 1789 precisely because it was associated with and taken to symbolize the ancien régime in general. Reciprocal 'tu' replaced the asymmetrical system of 'tu' and 'vous', the variety and hierarchy

---

[14] E. Terry, *A Voyage to East-India* (1655), 214; J. Ovington, *A Voyage to Surat* (1692), 276.

[15] F. Day, *The Land of the Permauls*, (Madras, 1863), 327, 391; S. Mateer, *The Land of Charity*, (1871), 45.

of modes of address was replaced by 'citoyen' and 'citoyenne', and so on, in order to symbolize equality and fraternity.

In Europe before 1789 there was no such revolution in every-day language, apart from the practice of a few radical religious groups. The sixteenth-century Anabaptists addressed their fellow-believers as 'brother', 'sister', or 'thou'. The seventeenth-century Quakers shocked their contemporaries and anticipated the French revolutionaries by calling everyone 'thee' in what has been called a 'rhetoric of impoliteness' designed to show that 'Christ respects no man's person', in other words that worldly distinctions had no importance for true Christians.[16]

All the same, the European regime of civility was gradually modified in significant ways, especially in the later eighteenth century. Linguistic and other practices changed, and so did the 'folk categories' through which they were discussed in this period. Three at least of these categories may be regarded as central: 'honour', 'civility' itself, and finally 'politeness'. They require consideration here because they offer access to insiders' views of change.

The term 'honour' (*onore, honneur*, etc), as used in England, France and Italy between 1500 and 1800, was a reasonably close equivalent of what Goffman preferred to call 'face'. The concept had a double meaning, but it may be argued that its very ambiguity or circularity was essential to its usefulness. It signified both the outer respect paid to men and women of a certain status, and the qualities which made this respect appropriate, especially courage in the case of men and modesty in that of women. People were honoured because they were honourable, and one knew that they were honourable because they were honoured.[17]

Equally ambiguous was the answer to the question, who possessed honour? According to the treatises on the subject, honour was a prerogative of the nobility. However, judicial records show that ordinary people, at least in towns, often claimed to have hon-

---

[16] C. -P. Clasen, *Anabaptism: a Social History, 1525–1618* (Ithaca, 1972), 146; R. Bauman, *Let Your Words be Few: Symbolism of Speaking and Silence among Seventeenth-Century Quakers* (Cambridge 1983), 43–62.
[17] A. Jouanna, 'Recherches sur la notion de l'honneur au 16e siècle', *Revue d'histoire moderne et contemporaine* 15 (1968), 597–623.

our, and also that the courts took this claim seriously, at least on occasion.[18] The courts were involved because of attacks on the honour of the plaintiffs, in other words insults. The concern they showed reveals the importance attributed to forms of language in the social life of the period.

The second keyword is 'civility' (*civiltà, civilité*). The concept developed first in Italy, where its associations with 'city' were taken very seriously. The countryside was for animals, the city for humans and the *vita civile* (a life which was at once civilized, civilian and civic, and so appropriate for citizens of independent city-republics). Both the term and the idea of civility became increasingly important in western Europe in the sixteenth and seventeenth centuries, partly at the expense of the medieval term 'courtesy' (*courtoisie*).

At the same time civility changed its meaning, referring less and less to political systems and more and more to elegant behaviour, including the practice of collecting statues and other objects. It is tempting to relate this change in the meaning of civility to the decline of city-republics in favour of absolute monarchies, small ones such as the Grand Duchy of Florence as well as large ones such as France.[19] The rise of civility in the new sense was both expressed and encouraged by Erasmus's treatise on good manners for small boys, *De civilitate morum puerilium* (1530), followed by Giovanni Della Casa's *Galateo* (1558), Stefano Guazzo's *La civil conversazione* (1578), Antoine de Courtin's *Nouveau traité de civilité* (1671), and many others. The translation of these texts reveals how far civility or politeness was becoming a European ideal. Della Casa was translated into French, English, Latin and Spanish, and Guazzo into French, English and Latin, while Courtin was adapted into English and German.

A seventeenth-century English writer summed up the new ideal

[18] Y. Castan, *Honneteté et relations sociales en Languedoc* (Paris 1974); cf. P. Burke, *Historical Anthropology of Early Modern Italy* (Cambridge, 1987), 109.
[19] J. Revel, 'Les usages de la civilité', in P. Ariès, (ed) *History of Private Life*, 3 (Cambridge, Mass., 1989), 167–205; R. Chartier, *Lectures et lecteurs dans la France d'ancien régime* (Paris 1987), 45–86; A. Pons, 'Sur la notion de la civilité', in A. Montandon (ed) *Etiquette et Politesse*, (Clermont-Ferrand, 1992).

by declaring civility to consist in three things, two negative and one positive. In the first place, 'not expressing by actions or speeches any injury, disesteem, offence or undervaluing any other'. In the second place, 'in receiving no injuries or offences from others, i. e. in not resenting every word or action which may (perhaps rationally) be interpreted to be disesteem or undervaluing' (this fits the case of Conrad's sailor, quoted at the opening of this paper). On the positive side, 'In being ready to do all good offices and ordinary kindness for another'.[20] The rejection of an earlier honour-based system is particularly clear in this passage, both in the recommendations to refrain from honour-threatening acts and also to show less sensitivity to threats from others. The plural form 'civilities' came into use to refer to compliments and other polite expressions or gestures. As in the case of honours and honour, there was a revealing circularity here. The practice of civilities was a sign that the speaker was civilized.

An alternative term to civility was 'politeness'. La Rochefoucauld associated the two concepts in an epigram: 'La civilité est un désir d'en recevoir et d'être estimé poli'. In similar fashion, in his dictionary, Antoine Furetière defined *civilité* as 'une manière honnête, douce et polie d'agir, de converser ensemble'. *Politesse* became fashionable in seventeenth-century France, where Madame de Scudéry devoted one of her dialogues to the subject, defining it as 'savoir vivre'. According to the duc de Saint-Simon, Louis XIV was a paragon of politeness, 'Jamais homme si naturellement poli', drawing attention to the king's skill in 'measuring' his politeness to fit 'l'âge, le mérite, le rang'. The point made earlier about the influence of social structures on regimes of politeness could hardly be illustrated more clearly. In similar fashion, Bellegarde, the author of model conversations 'pour les personnes polies', distinguished different varieties of *politesse* as suitable for the *homme d'épée*, the *magistrat* and so on.[21]

---

[20] O. Walker, *Of Education* (1673: Menston, 1970), 211.

[21] La Rochefoucauld, *Maximes* (1685: ed. F. C. Green, Cambridge 1946), 67; Saint-Simon, *Mémoires*, vol. 1 (Paris, 1983); J. B. de Bellegarde, *Réfléxions sur la politesse des moeurs*, (Paris, 1703), 46. Cf M. Lacroix, *De la politesse* (Paris 1990); P. France, *Politeness and its Discontents* (Cambridge, 1992).

The terms *politezza* and *polite* had less success in Italian, but in England, so common was the word 'polite' in the early eighteenth century that one scholar has coined the phrase 'the culture of politeness' to refer to this period, while another has entitled a history of England 1727–83 *A Polite and Commercial People*, taking the phrase from the lawyer William Blackstone.[22] Eighteenth-century book titles include *The Polite Philosopher* (1734), *The Polite Student* (1748), *The Polite Lady* (1760), *The Polite Academy* (1762), *The Polite Traveller* (1783), and so on.

Like 'civility', 'politeness' had a political origin – derived from the very terms 'polis' and 'political' – but in the seventeenth and eighteenth centuries it came to refer to elegant or 'polished' as opposed to 'rough' manners. As Lord Chesterfield, considered one of the authorities on manners in eighteenth-century England, wrote to his son, 'Good company, if you make the right use of it, will cut you into shape and give you the true brilliant polish' (6 July 1749). When Chesterfield's views were presented to a wider audience in the form of 'Principles of Politeness', the topics included cleanliness, dress and spitting.[23]

Politeness often took the form of ritualized gestures, of 'making legs' (bowing), making genuflexions, or making curtseys (an expression of 'courtesy', from which the word is derived). However, the verbal genuflexion, what the English were coming to call a 'civil tongue', was considered one of the most important ways of expressing politeness. Thus Courtin devoted specific chapters of his treatise to conversation, compliments and salutations, as well as to posture and gesture. These practices, ranging from competence in the current formulae of respect to the mastery of the art of conversation, showed family resemblances and, so far as language is concerned, might be defined by contrast to the ideal of plain speech, a frankness which in 'civil' circles was considered a breach of good manners.

The number of treatises published on the art of conversation at this time bear witness to the interest in the subject, 'polite conver-

[22] L. E. Klein, *Shaftesbury and the Culture of Politeness* (Cambridge, 1994); P. A. Langford, *A Polite and Commercial People* (Oxford, 1989).
[23] Chesterfield, *Letters* (1774); J. Trussler, *Principles of Politeness* (1775).

sation', as it was often called.[24] In her *Conversations nouvelles*, for instance, Madame de Scudéry included 'savoir toujours parler à propos' in the definition of *politesse*, and advised her readers 'ne vouloir pas être le tyran de la conversation'.[25] Lord Shaftesbury argued that conversation was a means of 'polish'. Lord Chesterfield's frequently-expressed opinions on the subject were soon summarized by his popularizers in the form of thirty-five 'rules for conversation'. It may be worth emphasising that Chesterfield recommended politeness to inferiors. A master was advised to say to his servant that he would be 'much obliged' if the servant would carry out a certain task. In order to avoid misunderstanding, 'Indicate by your language, that the performance is a favour, and by your tone that it is a matter of course'.

How many people or even how many kinds of people followed the rules it is obviously impossible to say with precision. The rules were associated with the upper classes, and they may be analysed in the manner of Pierre Bourdieu as a strategy for distinguishing themselves from those whom they perceived as their social inferiors. Complaining in the 1780s that 'all external evidence of rank' was disappearing, an English gentleman stressed the importance of 'politeness of expression; it is the only external distinction which remains between a gentleman and a valet, a lady and a mantua-maker'.[26]

The rules were codified at the time of the rise of absolute monarchy, so that they may also be analysed in the style of Norbert Elias as one of the means by which rulers tamed their nobilities. The role of aristocratic women, particularly the hostesses of the French salons, in the rise of politeness must not be underestimated. After all, as sociolinguists point out, women in many societies are more

[24] D. A. Berger, *Die Konversationskunst in England 1660–1740* (Munich 1978); C. Strosetzki, *Konversation: ein Kapitel gesellschaftlicher und literarischer Pragmatik im Frankreich des 17. Jhts* (Frankfurt, 1978); E. C. Goldsmith, *Exclusive Conversations: the Art of Interaction in 17th-Century France* (Philadelphia, 1988); P. Burke, *The Art of Conversation* (Cambridge 1993), M. Fumaroli, *Trois institutions littéraires* (Paris, 1994), 111–210.
[25] M. de Scudéry, *Conversations nouvelles* (Paris, 1685), 67.
[26] Quoted in K. Cmiel, *Democratic Eloquence: the Fight over Popular Speech in Nineteenth-Century America* (Berkeley and Los Angeles 1990), 38.

polite than men.[27] Italian and French models were consciously followed in England and elsewhere. As Thomas Sheridan, one of the specialists in the subject, remarked in 1780, 'The Italians, French and Spaniards, in proportion to their progress in civilisation and politeness, have for more than a century been employed, with the utmost industry, in cultivating and regulating their speech'.[28]

That many members of the 'middle classes' (the families of merchants, lawyers and physicians, for example) were participating in this movement by 1700, if not before, is extremely likely. It would be difficult to explain the many editions of the treatises on conversation without such a hypothesis. Politeness in speech as in other forms of behaviour was a way for the middle classes to show that they were close to the upper classes. In England in particular, it has been argued that in the eighteenth century, wealth and politeness were coming to replace (or at least to join) birth as a basis of social status. That certain forms of politeness were practised further down the social scale is likely, but the evidence is sparse. The generalisations about Italy, France and England offered here should therefore be taken as applying to a minority of the population.

(iv)

It is time to be more concrete and to focus more sharply on some of the linguistic forms through which politeness was expressed in the period. Six of these forms will be discussed in turn – the avoidance of contradiction; accent; euphemisms; compliments; forms of address, and finally the humiliative mode of speech to social superiors.

i. Negative civility, sometimes described at the time as 'complaisance', the avoidance of what used to be called 'offence' (in other words, FTAs), is perhaps best illustrated by the advice not to contradict other people, especially one's superiors. Della Casa, for example, recommended his readers to avoid expressions such

---

[27] J. Holmes, *Women, Men and Politeness* (1995).
[28] Quoted in L. Mugglestone, *Talking Proper: the Rise of Accent as Social Symbol* (Oxford 1995), 28.

as 'it wasn't like that' (*Non fu così*) or 'you are wrong (*Voi errate*). In France, Nicole Faret, whose adaptation of Castiglione became one of the most popular manuals of good behaviour in the seventeenth century, also warned his readers not to contradict.[29] Contradiction was considered an offence against 'complaisance', a seventeenth-century term for politeness in the sense of accommodating one's behaviour to the expectations of others. As the anonymous author of *The Art of Complaisance* (1673) put it, 'dissimulation is part of the essence of complaisance'. Similar points might be made about refusal. However, the rise of the ideal of sincerity or 'frankness', especially if not exclusively in England, led to the weakening if not the abandonment of this form of politeness. By the end of the eighteenth century, if not before, it could be perceived (as we have seen) as a peculiarly oriental form of evasiveness.

ii. A second way of expressing politeness was by accent. In the sixteenth and seventeenth centuries, discussions of accent centred on the 'sweet and low'. In France, Nicole Faret, for example, remarked on the need to speak to superiors with what he called a 'sweet' tone of voice or 'un accent plein de soumission'. The critic Jean Chapelain argued that social intercourse between the sexes contribued 'à rendre les langues polies', because in talking to women, 'les hommes apprennent à adoucir la rudesse de la pronunciation, que la mollesse naturelle des organes des femmes ammolit'. This sweetness, or something like it, appears to have been the target of Furetière's satirical *Roman bourgeois* (1666), in which a young abbé 'affectoit de parler un peu gras, pour avoir le langage plus mignard'.[30]

Accent was also a way to distinguish between elites and ordinary people. Chesterfield told his son 'to pronounce properly: that is, according to the usage of the best companies'. When, where and among whom a regional accent came to be stigmatised in different cultures as a vulgar accent remains a problem for historians. An early example of such stigmatisation comes from the rules drawn up for the seminary established in Milan in 1590. The

---

[29] G. Della Casa, *Galateo* (1558: ed. D. Provenzal, Milan 1950), chapter 18; N. Faret, *L'honnête homme*, (1630; Paris, 1925 edition), 54.

[30] Faret, 53; J. Chapelain, *Lettres*, vol. 2 (Paris 1883), 169; A. Adam, ed., *Romanciers du 17e siècle* (Paris 1968), 906.

teachers were instructed to correct 'the mispronunciations which the pupils brought with them from their places of origin' (*vitiosas quasdam inflexiones vocis ... quas a patria secum extulerunt*).[31] As this rule suggests, the English were not unique in their preoccupation with accent. The duc de Saint-Simon condemned the duchesse de Chaulnes because she had 'le ton, et la voix, et des mots du bas peuple'. By the eighteenth century, however, England had probably become the part of Europe in which these matters were taken most seriously. Sheridan, for example, emphasised the need to avoid 'rusticity of accent'. In the 1760s, an English clergyman, confiding to his diary the bad impression made on him by the bishop of Lincoln, declared that prelate's 'humble education and mean extraction' to have been revealed by his 'want of behaviour and manners', including his clumsy way of walking and his 'Yorkshire dialect'. The speech of some prominent people continued to reveal their place of origin – 'Addington still spoke as a Hampshireman, Peel as a Lancastrian, even Gladstone employed a slightly northern brogue' – but these details are recorded precisely because they were breaches of the norm.[32]

iii. Vocabulary, even more than accent, was the way in which high-status, civilized or polite people were distinguished from others in this period. What is often called 'Victorian' language, in the sense of a series of euphemisms for sexual matters in the presence of ladies, is in fact much older than the nineteenth century and was far from a monopoly of the English. The word 'interesting', in the place of 'pregnant', for instance, was in use not only in England but also in nineteenth-century Spain. Or take the well-known example of euphemisms for 'leg'. On occasion, Charles Dickens even describes male trousers as 'unmentionables'. However, in seventeenth-century Portugal, a famous conduct book, modelled on Castiglione's *Courtier*, had already argued that the word *perna* could be used in the presence of ladies only if it referred to a man's

---

[31] A. Prosperi, *Tribunali di Coscienza* (Turin 1996), 314n.

[32] Saint-Simon, *Mémoires*, vol. 1, 589; Sheridan quoted in Mugglestone, *Talking Proper*, 117; W. Cole, *The Blecheley Diary*, (1931), 35; the reference to Addington etc in R. J. W. Evans, *The Language of History and the History of Language* (Oxford, 1998), 15. Cf. Bryson, *Courtesy to Civility*, 189–91.

leg. Ladies were not supposed to have legs.[33] In Italy, Della Casa devoted considerable space to the problem of linguistic 'indecency' (*disonestà*), noting in chapter 22 of the *Galateo* that 'our ladies' speak about 'chestnuts' when they mean 'figs', in order to avoid embarrassing double meanings, and advising female speakers or speakers to women to avoid the word *puttane*, a term which should be replaced by 'women of the world' (*femine del mondo*).

However, the practice of euphemism spread well beyond the 'private parts'. If we are to trust Pietro Aretino, who satirized the practice, ladies, or would-be ladies, in sixteenth-century Rome no longer called a window *finestra* but *balcone*, while a door, formerly *uscio*, became *porta*, presumably because the new terms sounded less vulgar.[34] When Magdelon, in *Les précieuses ridicules* (Act 1, scene 5) called a servant *un nécessaire* and translated 'si vous êtes au logis' into 'si vous êtes en commodité d'être visibles', she was not the first women to distance herself from everyday language. In Spain, Francisco de Quevedo satirised the Spanish equivalent of the *précieuses,* the 'female latinist' (*hembrilatina*), who had coined pretentious new words for 'quarrel', 'fright' and 'stupidities'.[35]

The *précieuses* and their equivalents were mocked only because they went too far. Gentlemen were proceeding more slowly in the same direction. The preface to the first volume of the *Dictionnaire de l'Académie* (1694) declared that it was deliberately limited to 'la langue commune, telle qu'elle est dans le commerce ordinaire des honnêtes gens'. Excommunicated, therefore, were technical terms, 'les termes des arts et des sciences qui entrent rarement dans le discours', together with vulgarities, words which are 'bas et de style familier', associated with low-status people.

The concern with social class and its linguistic signs is sometimes thought to be a peculiarly English preoccupation, not to say malady. Hence it may be of interest to note a French nobleman of this period discussing what he calls 'espèces de classes différentes qu'on reconnait par leurs façons de parler'. Among the 'fa-

---

[33] Galdos, *Fortunato y Jacinta*, (1886–7; Madrid, 1971 edition, 935); F. Rodrigues Lobo, *Corte na Aldeia* (1619; Lisbon, 1972 edition).
[34] P. Aretino, *Sei giornate*, (c. 1530: ed. G. Aquilecchia, Bari, 1975), 82.
[35] F. de Quevedo, *Obras satíricas*, (c. 1650: Madrid 1924), 160.

çons de parler bourgeoises' stigmatised in his dialogue is the use of the phrase 'mon époux', rather than 'mon mari, qui est la bonne manière de se nommer'.[36] Conversely, although no academy came into existence to control the English language, there was a movement to found one. Gentlemen were advised to avoid 'vulgarisms' (a word which is first recorded in English in 1644). 'Vulgar expressions are carefully avoided by those who want to write politely', declared the anonymous *Art of Speaking* in 1676. It was on these grounds that Lord Chesterfield warned his son against using proverbs in his conversation.

iv. The term 'compliments' was used first in Italian and then in French, while from the middle of the seventeenth century it is documented in English, suggesting that the custom, at least in its elaborated forms, followed a similar itinerary (in French, the word *galanteries* occupied some of the same conceptual space). In the narrow sense of the term, compliments were a kind of euphemism used to maintain the face of others by praising them and their possessions. In the wider sense, the term 'compliments' was used to describe formulae of respect, including the term 'respect' itself, as in the seventeenth-century English phrases 'my due respects' or 'my very kind respects'. The practice was known as 'paying' one's respects.

So important were compliments in the seventeenth century – to judge by the treatises on how to use them – that a German scholar has described the period as one of 'the culture of compliments' (*Komplimentierkultur*).[37] In England too treatises with titles such as *The Complete Academy of Compliments* (1705) were published at this time. There was a geography as well as a chronology and a sociology of compliments. The cultural distance between Italy and England in this respect is apparent from reactions of English travellers. In Siena, the English gentleman Fynes Moryson remarked that the term 'Palaces' was used in Italy to refer to houses of 'small magnificence' as a form of civility to their owners, while his visit

---

[36] F. de Callières, *Des mots à la mode*, (Paris 1692), 43, 65.
[37] M. Beetz, 'Negative Kontinuität: Vorbehalte gegenüber barocker Komplimentierkultur', in K. Garber (ed) *Europäische Barock-Rezeption* (Wiesbaden 1991), 281–302.

to Verona prompted the observation that 'The Italian epitaphs are often more extravagant than those of other countries, as the nation is more given to compliment and hyperbole'.[38]

v. Forms of address, like other compliments, appear to have been more elaborate on the Continent than in Britain, as travellers sometimes noted. Thus Thomas Palmer noted what he called (like Brown and Levenson) the 'humilious phrases and kind compliments of kissing their hands' in both Italy and France, while Sir John Lauder commented with admiration on the manners of the French peasants. 'A man might have seen more civility in their expressions ... than may be found in the first compliments on a rencontre between two Scots gentlemen tolerably well bred'.[39] Modes of address also made explicit the employment of different forms of language to different kinds of people, when speaking to one's superiors, equals or inferiors.

There is apparently the least to say about England in this respect. However, even here a shift in modes of address between fathers and children among the English gentry has been noted by Lawrence Stone. 'In the first half of the seventeenth century a son, even when grown up, would commonly address his father in a letter as "Sir", and sign himself "your humble obedient son", "your son in continuance of all obedience", or "your most obedient and loving son"'. By the 1720s, however, a shift from what Stone calls 'deference' to what he calls 'respect' was already noticeable, and by the 1770s it was at its 'height'. 'Sir', for example, was replaced by 'Dear Papa'. Stone discusses this change as evidence for changing relationships within the family, but it should also be placed in the context of the history of forms of address.[40]

In France, Saint-Simon was, as might have been expected, much concerned with forms of address, especially among the nobility. Again and again he returns to the uses of 'Monseigneur' and 'Altesse', with occasional observations on 'Monsieur', 'Mademoiselle'

---

[38] F. Moryson, *An Itinerary*, (4 vols, Glasgow, 1907–8), vol. 1, 307, 378.

[39] T. Palmer, *An Essay of the means how to make our travel into foreign countries more profitable and honourable* (1606), 68; J. Lauder, *Journals 1665–76* (ed. Donald Crawford, Edinburgh, 1900), 82.

[40] L. Stone, *The Family, Sex and Marriage in England 1500–1800* (1977), 171, 412–4.

and 'Madame'.[41] The impression he gives of an old 'formalist' who is shocked by the increasing informality of the younger generation is consistent with the English evidence. However, the richest vein of evidence for changing forms of address comes from Italy.[42] It suggests two phases, an increase in formality in the sixteenth century countered by a movement towards informality in the eighteenth. Going still further than Stone's young noblemen, Cosimo de' Medici, future Grand Duke of Tuscany, wrote to his father as 'Illustrissimo signore mio padre', and to his mother as 'Magnifica et dilectissima madre'. From the middle of the sixteenth century onwards, honorific titles proliferated; *La Vostra Signoria, Excellenza, Magnificenza,* or even *Sublimità*, together with adjectives such as *illustrissimo*. The hyperbolic mode already discussed had spread to forms of address.

This inflation of titles did not take place without protest. Most complaints emphasised the debasement of the linguistic currency, but a few were more political in thrust. Andrea Spinola 'the philosopher', for example, a Genoese patrician who defended the tradition of civic equality when it was going into decline at the beginning of the seventeenth century, denounced the use of *illustrissimo*. His was a self-consciously republican civility.[43] All the same, the trend towards titles continued. Only in the mid-eighteenth century did it go into reverse, when men of letters such as Gasparo Gozzi and Pietro Verri argued for a more informal mode of address. Gozzi pleaded in the *Gazzetta Veneta* (2 April 1760) for a simplification of both language and ceremonies, while Verri denounced *le formalità* in the journal *Il Caffé* and praised the English Quakers for their simplicity of language.

vi. The humiliative mode. In the sixteenth and seventeenth centuries, in Spain and Italy in particular, expressions such as 'I kiss your hand' or even 'I kiss your foot' were in use in speech and writing, not to mention gesture. It was not unknown for nobles to describe

---

[41] Saint-Simon, *Mémoires*, vol. 1, pp. 64, 188, 597, 661, etc.

[42] B. Croce, *La Spagna nella vita italiana durante la rinascenza* (Bari, 1917); J. Brunet, 'Un "langage colakeitiquement profane", ou l'influence de l'Espagne sur la troisième personne de politesse italienne', in *Presence et influence de l'Espagne dans la culture italienne de la Renaissance* (Paris, 1978), 251–315.

[43] A. Spinola, *Scritti scelti*, ed. C. Bitossi (Genoa, 1981), 247.

themselves in a letter to their sovereign, the emperor Charles V for instance, as 'your slave and servant (*vostre esclave et serviteur*)'. In his famous conduct book Giovanni Della Casa cites the example of 'your slave in chains' (*Vostro schiavo in catena*). Letters to the pope might be signed by 'quello che sta sotto i piedi di V. Beatudine'.[44]

The English did not normally go so far in this direction, and the Cambridge rhetorician Gabriel Harvey, writing to his friend the poet Edmund Spenser, associated Della Casa's *Galateo* with what he called 'cringing'. All the same, traces of this mode can be found, leading Keith Thomas to write, in a rare lapse from his normal detachment, of an Elizabethan 'tendency to undue obsequiousness'.[45] It has been argued that it was the court environment in the period 1500–1800 which produced 'phrases of submission and devotion', such as offering 'humble thanks' for 'favours' and describing oneself as 'your humble (or obedient) servant'.[46] Even more important, in my opinion, was the prevalence of patron-client relationships in English society at this time. Formulae of a kind which would later be denounced as oriental can be found in the letters of noblemen in the Tudor and early Stuart period, as in the following three examples. In a letter to Lord Lisle in 1534 about the plans for a marriage alliance between the two families, Sir Francis Lovell contrasted 'your noble blood' with 'my poor stock', although a baron was only one degree above a knight in the social hierarchy. When Sir Christopher Hatton wrote to William Cecil about the house he was having built, magnificent even by Elizabethan noble standards, he called it his 'rude building'. When the Earl of Arundel wrote to Sir Dudley Carleton in 1619 about their common interest in collecting pictures, he thanked him for his care 'to satisfy my foolish curiosity in enquiring for the pieces of Holbein'.[47]

In the eighteenth century we see a strong reaction against this humiliative style. Already by 1673 the author of one English con-

---

[44] Della Casa, *Galateo*, ch. 16; M. Pensa, *La Biblioteca Vaticana* (Rome, 1590), 42.
[45] Thomas, 'Yours', 453.
[46] C. McIntosh, *Common and Courtly Language* (Philadelphia, 1986), 69ff, 82ff, 137ff.
[47] *The Lisle Letters*, ed, M. St Clare Byrne (1983), no. 61; Hatton quoted in C. Read, *Mr Secretary Cecil* (1925), 216; Arundel quoted in J. Brown, *Kings and Connoisseurs: Collecting Art in Seventeenth-Century Europe* (New Haven, 1995), 19.

duct book was associating compliments with 'duplicity and deceit'. 'They consist in praising immoderately and pretending greater love and friendship than either is deserved by or intended to him to whom they are offered'. They are examples of 'an abusing of language', for example offering 'imaginary services' or engaging in imaginary 'humiliations'.[48] A few years later, a sermon by arch-bishop Tillotson denounced the conversation of his day as 'swelled with vanity and compliment' and 'surfeited' with 'expressions of kindness and respect'. The *Spectator* made similar points, and was praised by Samuel Johnson for its campaign against what he called 'the impertinence of civility'. In France, *Les règles de la bienséance* (1781), discussing compliments, warned its readers against what it called 'hyperboles démesurées'.[49]

The positive aspect of this shift was the rise of sincerity. Montaigne was a pioneering critic of the inflation of what he described in his essays as the 'abjecte et servile prostitution de presentations; la vie, l'ame, devotion, adoration, serf, esclave, tous ces mots y courent si vulgairement que, quand ils veulent fair sentir une plus expresse volonté et plus respectueuse, ils n'ont plus de manière pour l'exprimer' (Book 1, ch. 40). The cult of sincerity reached its apogee at the end of our period, when Rousseau and Herder, among others, attacked the culture of civility on these grounds. The permeation of everyday life by the new values was symbolised by such epistolary forms as 'yours sincerely' and 'yours truly'.[50] The reaction against hyperbole would eventually lead to such a deflation of the language of politeness that by the nineteenth century, Englishmen in India would be astonished, as we have seen, by the 'servility' of the humiliative mode.

(v)

Cultural difference, notably the difference between the hyperbolic Italians and the less demonstrative English, has been the minor

---

[48] Walker, *Of Education*, 212–3; cf Beetz, 'Negative Kontinuität'.
[49] Berger, *Konversationskunst*, 179, 225; *Règles*, 320.
[50] Thomas, 'Yours', 452. On the early modern period, L. Trilling, *Sincerity and Authenticity*, (1972); J. Martin, 'Inventing Sincerity, refashioning Prudence', *American Historical Review* 102 (1997), 1309–42.

theme of this article, but the major emphasis has fallen on the direction and significance of linguistic change. In the case of Italy, some at least of the hyperbole developed in course of the sixteenth century, rather than forming part of an unchanging 'national character'. The essential point, most clearly illustrated by the decline of elaborate forms of address and the humiliative mode of politeness, is the decline of formality in the eighteenth century. The old regime of politeness was undermined generations before the French Revolution.

Why did these changes take place? The 'folk theories' on the subject make an excellent point of departure for analysis, though they may be in need of development or qualification. Andrea Spinola, as we have seen, linked the rise of *Illustrissimo* to the decline of republican values. According to him, civic modesty and equality was giving way to display and hierarchy. In similar fashion Pietro Verri denounced the people who wanted to be addressed as *Vostra Signoria* as despotic 'sultans'. The rise of titles may be viewed as an outward sign of the process of social and political change in Italy which historians often describe as 'refeudalisation', in other words a shift of wealth and power away from merchants and cities and back to aristocratic landowners.[51]

In the eighteenth century, what has to be explained is the shift from the 'honour system' (aggressive, masculine, and sharply hierarchical), to the 'politeness system' (gentler, oriented towards the opposite sex, and more egalitarian, at least in appearance). Shaftesbury gave a political explanation of the new politeness, which he defined by contrast to the flattery of courts, linking it to the rise of liberty and the Whig party. Some historians of eighteenth-century Britain have recently put forward a less partisan version of the same thesis, to the effect that the 'language of manners' was incorporated into political controversy and used as a means of moderating its violence.[52]

If the shift had been confined to Britain, the point would be persuasive. However, as we have seen, the Italians and the French

---

[51] R. Villari, *Ribelli e riformatori* (Rome, 1979), 95–6.

[52] Klein, *Shaftesbury*; N. Phillipson, 'Politics and Politeness in the Reign of Anne and the Early Hanoverians', in J. G. A. Pocock (ed), *The Varieties of British Political Thought 1500–1800*, (Cambridge, 1993), 211–45.

were moving in the same direction without the aid of the Whigs or even of increasing liberty. Indeed, the same treatises on polite language were current in all three countries. Bellegarde, for instance, was translated into Engish and Italian. There must therefore have been other forces at work to civilise tongues besides the political one.

In the history of European rituals, a parallel shift towards informality has been noted more than once.[53] The painted portrait is another cultural domain where a shift towards the informal presentation of self has been dated to the eighteenth century. Famous examples include van Loo's Diderot, with dishevelled hair, and Reynolds' Baretti, peering short-sightedly at a book. These clues point in the direction of a major cultural shift which affected more than one region and more than one domain of behaviour. If we wish to explain the shift, we might reasonably invoke the parallel rise of commercial society, most obvious in eighteenth-century England, but also visible in France at this time and to a lesser extent in northern Italy, in the Venice of Gozzi or the Milan of Verri.

To explore the connection further, we might once again take a folk theory as a point of departure, for example the idea of Philip Withers, quoted above, that the rise of polite language was a reaction to the decline of 'external evidence of rank'. It was a new way for upper-class people to distinguish themselves from others at a time when mass-production was making it possible for the first time for ordinary people to imitate the dress of their social superiors. Polite language could of course be imitated in its turn and the proliferation of treatises on the subject suggests that this was precisely what happened. All the same, at least as an explanation of the rise of the English preoccupation with accent at this time, Withers' explanation has much to be said for it.

There is much more to be said on this subject than is possible in a short article. All the same, even a limited number of examples from early modern English, French and Italian may be sufficient to suggest that even if the same strategies of politeness can be found

---

[53] Burke, *Historical Anthropology of Early Modern Italy*, 223–38; E. Muir, *Ritual in Early Modern Europe* (Cambridge, 1997), 269–75.

in many cultures, as Brown and Levinson argue, these strategies have not been used to an equal extent everywhere. Hence the surprised or even contemptuous reactions of Englishmen in Italy or westerners in China to forms of politeness which they found excessive or even servile.

As in the case of clothes, so in that of language, the apparently 'superficial' deserves to be studied as a system of signs expressing what lies underneath. However, the language of 'surface', of 'expression', or 'reflection', or even 'refraction', may not do justice to the power of everyday actions, including linguistic actions. Trivial in themselves, a multitude of such acts – acts of deference, acts of identity, and so on – are capable of reinforcing or even reconstructing a regime.

2: Diglossia in Early Modern Europe

'Diglossia' is a contested concept among linguists. The term was coined in the 1880s to refer to two major varieties of modern Greek, *katharevousa* and *dhimotikí*, one of them with a high status and the other with a low one (the situation in Greece today is of course rather different, thanks to the political events of the last half-century, notably the rise and fall of a military regime).[1]

In a much-cited article that was originally published over half a century ago, a specialist on Arabic, Charles Ferguson, used the term 'diglossia' to refer to two varieties of the same language that differed in vocabulary, grammar and pronunciation and that were used, often by the same speakers, in different social situations or speech domains. There was a 'high' variety (H), otherwise known as classical Arabic, used for sermons, speeches and lectures, and a 'low' or colloquial variety (L) used in ordinary conversation or for employers to give orders to their employees. 'The speakers', wrote Ferguson, 'regard H as superior to L'.[2] Refining the model, it has also been pointed out that individuals may switch between High and Low according to the topic they are speaking about. In nineteenth-century France, for instance, peasants spoke about local politics in *patois* but about national

---

[1] Mackridge, Peter, *Language and National Identity in Greece, 1766–1976* (Oxford: Oxford University Press, 2009), 27–31.
[2] Ferguson, Charles, 'Diglossia', *Word* 15 (1959), 325–40.

politics in French, the language of the newspapers.[3]

A few years later another distinguished linguist, Joshua Fishman, extended the idea of diglossia to include the use of two different languages by the same speakers in similar conditions to the ones described by Ferguson. These speakers would employ a language regarded as High in formal situations and a language regarded as Low in informal situations or to speak to people of lower social status (for whom the 'Low' form may be their only language).[4]

Much has been written about diglossia (a bibliography lists nearly 3,000 items published in the thirty years 1960–1990), but the definition of the term remains contested.[5] Some linguists limit it, like Ferguson, to varieties of the same language, while others, following Fishman, are more inclusive. The application of the term is also contested, since some linguists are unwilling to use it in the cases of Greek and Arabic, the original examples of diglossia, on the grounds that some speakers mix H and L forms, while other linguists treat some degree of mixing as inevitable. It might be added that Ferguson's assertion that 'The speakers regard H as superior to L' does not apply everywhere. In Britain today, some working-class people mock the H variety as 'BBC English', because to them it sounds artificial.[6]

I shall be following Fishman's wide definition of diglossia because what most concerns a social historian is the use of language to mark differences in social statuses or social situations. In the spirit of scholars concerned with the 'politics of diglossia', there will also be much to say about the role of the state in this process.[7]

---

[3] Weber, Eugen, *Peasants into Frenchmen: the modernization of rural France, 1870–1914* (Stanford: Stanford University Press, 1976).

[4] Fishman, Joshua, 'Bilingualism with and without Diglossia', *Journal of Social Issues* 32 (1967), 29–38. On concepts of diglossia, Perikles Daltas, 'The Concept of Diglossia from Ferguson to Fishman to Fasold', in Irene Philippaki-Warburton et al. (eds.) *Themes in Greek Linguistics* (Amsterdam and Philadelphia: Benjamins, 1994) 341–8.

[5] Fernandez, Mauro, *Diglossia: a comprehensive bibliography* (Amsterdam and Philadelphia: Benjamins, 1993).

[6] For a French parallel, Gardy, Philippe, and Robert Lafont, 'La diglossie comme conflit: l'exemple occitan', *Langages* 15 (1981), 75–91.

[7] Grillo, Ralph D., *Dominant Languages: Language and Hierarchy in Britain and France* (Cambridge: Cambridge University Press, 1989), 4.

Using the term 'diglossia' in a broad sense, it is not difficult to find examples from many places and periods. In ancient Indian drama, for example, men are represented as speaking to their wives in Sanskrit while the wives reply in Prakrit, the Low form of the same language.[8] In similar fashion, in the eighteenth century, in the plays of Goldoni, the masters and mistresses speak Italian while the servants speak Venetian. In the case of early modern Europe, there are so many examples of this kind of practice that the topic of this chapter will have to be limited to the use of different languages, ignoring dialects and other varieties of the same language. From now on, therefore, the term diglossia will be employed in the sense of bilingualism.

What follows is divided into two parts. The first part is descriptive, a kind of map of the main uses of foreign languages as High forms in early modern Europe, between the sixteenth and the eighteenth centuries. Diglossia can of course be found in Europe in the Middle Ages (French as a High language in England, for instance), just as it can be found in the nineteenth and twentieth centuries. All the same, it seems plausible to speak of a golden age of diglossia between the rise of printing, which helped to standardize vernacular languages and so make them more suitable for High functions, and the rise of nationalism, which discouraged the use of foreign languages at home.

The second part will consider the different meanings of diglossia for both speakers and listeners and attempt to explain its geography, its sociology and its chronology. This second part is necessarily more speculative, but even the mapping is far from certain. Written sources, from plays to interrogations, do not tell historians all that they would like to know about informal practices in general and ways of speaking in particular. They have to rely more than they would like on the comments of travellers and even on anecdotal evidence. Hence historians can only envy the sociolinguists who are able to listen to and record informal usage in the 'field'. On the other hand, the sociolinguists depend on historians

---

[8] Lee, Gina M., 'Diglossia in Ancient India', in Brian D. Joseph (ed.) *Studies on Language Change* (Columbus OH, Ohio State University, 1986), 151–64.

for observations about change in these informal practices over the long term.

II

In the first place, when, where and among whom could diglossia be found? Huge questions. In order to limit them it will be necessary to exclude the frequent use of a foreign language, usually but not always Latin, to write a poem, a letter or a book. For example, the Frenchman Joachim Du Bellay and the Englishman John Milton sometimes wrote poems in Italian, Mozart wrote letters in Italian, while the Germans Gottfried Leibniz and King Frederick the Great both published books in French. Given this limitation to speech, the principal languages that will need to be discussed, in approximate chronological order, are Latin, German, Italian, Spanish and French.

Early modern Latin is best known as a written language and as a lingua franca in multilingual environments, but spoken Latin was in use in the Church and in universities. Latin presents a good example of a high form since it was no one's first language at this time, or virtually no one's (Michel de Montaigne famously claimed that he learned Latin before he learned French or Gascon).[9] Latin also fits Ferguson's criteria quite well in the sense that it was commonly employed in formal situations, including three that he specifically mentioned: sermons, speeches and lectures. It was also the language of the Church.[10]

Whether Latin was much used in conversation between scholars or priests who shared a mother tongue is a more difficult question to answer. The only surviving evidence of Erasmus speaking Dutch, his mother tongue, was on his deathbed. I suspect that Erasmus did speak Latin most of the time, but it is impossible to

[9] Montaigne, Michel de, *Essais*, Book 1, ch. 25.
[10] Kühlmann, Wilhelm, 'National-literatur und Latinität', in Klaus Garber, (ed.) *Nation und Literatur im Europa der Frühen Neuzeit* (Tübingen: Niemeyer, 1989), 165–206, discusses the situation in terms of diglossia. Cf Burke, Peter, '*Heu Domine adsunt Turcae*: a Sketch for a Social History of Post-medieval Latin', in Peter Burke and Roy Porter, eds., *Language, Self and Society* (Cambridge: Polity Press, 1991), 23–50.

be sure. On the other hand, it is known that Martin Luther regularly spoke both Latin and German. His so-called 'Table-Talk', recorded by students who lived in his house in Wittenberg, catch him in the act of mixing or more exactly as switching between the two languages, according to a logic that is clear (although it may not have been conscious). Luther used Latin to discuss philosophy and theology, for instance, but German for more everyday topics.[11]

Let us turn to Italian, or more exactly, to Tuscan, which spread to other regions of Italy as a High form from the fifteenth century onwards before spreading beyond the boundaries of the peninsula. Among the South Slavs, for instance, especially in two cities, Ragusa (now known as Dubrovnik) in Dalmatia and Ljubljana (the capital of Carniola, now known as Slovenia). In Hungary, Italian was used at court in the time of Matthias Corvinus and his successor Vladislaus II (who were married successively to Beatrice of Naples, who lived in Hungary 1476–1501), and later in the sixteenth century, according to the historian Szamoskozy, at the court of Transylvania.[12] In Poland, Italian was spoken at court in the time of Zygmunt Stary, whose wife Bona Sforza arrived from Milan in 1519 with a group of Italians in her suite. Bona appears to have begun a tradition. As late as 1575, the Venetian ambassador Girolamo Lippomano commented on the continuing use of Italian at court.[13] However, the best-known example of the use of Italian at a foreign court is France in the age of Catherine de' Medici, from 1547, when she married Henri II, till her death in 1589. Italian was also in use at the court of Vienna under the emperor Joseph I (who ruled from 1705 to 1711).

Spanish, or Castilian, was another language used for High purposes in early modern Europe – leaving aside the obvious examples from the New World. In the Iberian peninsula, Castilian was in use as a High form in the regions where Spanish was not the mother tongue: in Catalonia, in the Basque country, in Galicia and

---

[11] Stolt, Birgit, *Die Sprachmischung in Luthers Tischreden* (Stockholm: Almqvist and Wiksell, 1964).

[12] My thanks to Professor Gábor Klaniczay for this information.

[13] Klemensiewicz, Zenon, *Historia języka polskiego* (Warsaw: PWN, 1974), 151–2.

in Portugal.[14] As a sixteenth-century Swiss traveller, Thomas Platter, acutely observed, the Catalans understood Castilian but the Castilians did not understand Catalan.[15]

Castilian was also used as a High form at least on occasion in some regions of early modern Italy, especially the parts that were under Spanish rule from the later sixteenth century onwards: Milan, Naples and Sicily.[16] In similar fashion and for similar reasons, Spanish was spoken in the Southern Netherlands after 1567 in the higher ranks of the army and in the administration.[17] At the imperial court in Prague, Rudolph II (reigned 1576–1612) was 'happy to converse in Spanish', the language of his mother Maria, the daughter of the Emperor Charles V.[18] After a considerable gap, Spanish returned to the imperial court, now in Vienna, under Charles VI (who ruled from 1711 to 1740). Charles had claimed the Spanish throne and lived in Spain for five years before becoming Emperor, and he insisted on Spanish etiquette and Spanish fashions at his court.

German was another language used as a High form in parts of Europe where it was not the first language of the majority of inhabitants. In the late Middle Ages, Low German (more exactly *Mittelniederdeutsch*) was the language of the Hanseatic League of trading cities. In this way, it spread to Scandinavia and the Baltic countries, where it came to be used for non-commercial, High purposes.[19] In Denmark, German became the language of the court from the Middle Ages to the late eighteenth century, especially in the time of two kings, Frederick IV (1699–1730), whose mother (Charlotte

---

[14] The idea of diglossia is central to Marfany, Joan-Lluís, *La lengua maltractada; El castellà i el català a Catalunya del segle xvi al segle xix* (Barcelona: Empúries, 2001).

[15] Marfany, *La lengua maltractada*, 117.

[16] There is a brief reference to this in Beccaria, Gian Luigi, *Spagnolo e spagnoli in Italia* (Torino: Giappichelli, 1968), 6–7.

[17] Verdonk, Robert A., *La lengua española en Flandes en el siglo xvii* (Madrid: Ínsula, 1980, 24–5.

[18] Béranger, Jean, *History of the Habsburg Empire, 1273–1700* (English translation, London: Longman, 1994), 244.

[19] Glück, Helmut, *Deutsch als Fremdsprache in Europa vom Mittelalter bis zur Barockzeit* (Berlin: W. de Gruyter, 2002) 263–93. He calls German 'eine H-Varietät' in Scandinavia (298, his only reference to Ferguson in the volume).

Amalie of Hesse-Kassel) and first wife (Louise of Mecklenburg-Güstrow) were both German, and his son Christian VI (reigned 1730–46), whose mother (Louise) and wife (Sophia Magdalena of Brandenburg-Kulmbach) were also German. German was spoken not only at court but also in the army and in the Church, which was Lutheran.[20]

In Bohemia, German was already in use in some noble circles in the fifteenth century but its domain increased after 1526, when the Habsburg Ferdinand I began to rule the lands of the Bohemian crown, and still more after 1620, under Ferdinand II, when a process of germanization accompanied the recatholicization of the country after the defeat of the Protestants at the battle of the White Mountain. In Russia in the reign of Peter the Great (1682–1725) and also in that of his niece Tsarina Anna (1730–40), German was spoken not only at court but also in the administration, in the army (as in Denmark), not to mention the lectures given by expatriate scholars, the majority of whom had German as their mother tongue.[21]

French, however, is the most famous instance of the use of a foreign language as a High form in early modern Europe, especially in the second half of the period, 1650–1800. It was already in use in this way in some regions in the late Middle Ages, in England and the Netherlands, for instance, but its golden age in this respect ran from Louis XIV to Napoleon.

The best-known example of the use of French as a high form of language, the language of the aristocracy, comes from eighteenth- and early nineteenth-century Russia. Opening a copy of *War and Peace*, the frequent French words and phrases jump out of a sea of Cyrillic. Tolstoy was writing about the world of his parents, so his testimony deserves to be taken seriously. This Russian practice went back to the reign of the Empress Catherine the Great (who reigned from 1762 to 1796). Reporting what Diderot had told him, Voltaire wrote to Madame du Deffand that people speak a more pure French at the court of the Empress than they do at Versailles:

---

[20] Winge, Vibeke, *Dänische Deutsche – deutsche Dänen. Geschichte der deutschen Sprache in Dänemark 1300–1800* (Heidelberg : Winter, 1992), who refers to 'Diglossie' (19).
[21] Koch, Kristine, *Deutsch als Fremdsprache im Russland des 18 Jhts* (Berlin: W. de Gruyter, 2002), 49, 52, 56, 61, 70.

'On parle français à la cour de l'Impératrice plus purement qu'à Versailles'.[22]

The Russian aristocracy were far from alone in their use of this language. French played a similar role in other parts of Europe, notably in the German-speaking world. Catherine was of course German herself and at the court in which she grew up, at Zerbst, to speak French was the norm.[23] The same was true of the court of Brunswick in the late seventeenth century, thanks to the presence of Eléonore d'Olbreuse, first as mistress and then as the wife of the Duke, and of the Frenchmen and women she brought with her.[24] As for Prussia in the age of Frederick the Great, Voltaire was pleasantly surprised to discover the widespread use of French on a visit to Berlin, writing that 'Je me trouve ici en France. On ne parle que notre langue'. Being Voltaire, he could not resist commenting that 'L'allemand est pour les soldats et pour les chevaux'.[25] French was also spoken at the court of Vienna in the reign of Maria Theresia (1740–80) and that of her co-rulers, her husband Franz Stephan (1745–1765), whose father was the duke of Lorraine, and their son Joseph II (1765–1790).[26]

In Spain, French was spoken at court under the Bourbon dynasty from Philip V (who came to the throne in 1700) onwards.[27] In Italy, French was spoken at the court of Parma after Philippe, the son of Philip V of Spain, became Duke in 1748. The adventurer Casanova recorded his surprise when walking the streets of the city and hearing only French and Spanish spoken. He noted in his memoirs (themselves written in French) that 'Il me sembla que je n'étais plus en Italie'.[28] It was virtually the same story in Tuscany, which was 'invaded' by Lorrainers after the succession of the Lorraine dynasty in 1737.[29]

---

[22] Fumaroli, Marc, *Quand l'Europe parlait français* (Paris: Fallois, 2001), 239.

[23] Koch, *Deutsch als Fremdsprache*, 54.

[24] Brunot, Ferdinand, *Histoire de la langue française* (12 vols., Paris: A. Colin, 1905–53), vol.8, 325–7.

[25] Voltaire to the marquis de Thibouville, 24 October 1750, in Voltaire, *Complete Works*, vol. 95 (Oxford: Voltaire Foundation, 1970), 375–6.

[26] Brunot, *Langue française*, vol.8, 548–51.

[27] Brunot, *Langue française*, vol.8, 49ff.

[28] Brunot, *Langue française*, vol. 5, 101.

[29] Brunot, *Langue française*, vol.5, 115.

In the North of Europe, we find the same trend. In England, if elites did not speak French, at least they peppered their English with French terms such as *grande monde, risque, épuisée* or *à la mode* itself (as in Italian), according to William Congreve's *Marriage à la Mode* (1673). In Sweden, French was in use at the court of Gustav III (who reigned from 1771 to 1792). A French diplomat wrote home that the king pronounced French well.[30] In the United Provinces, French was spoken alongside Dutch at the court of Prince Fredrik Hendrik (in office 1625–47), while in the eighteenth century, French was the language of high society in The Hague. By 1805, according to a French newspaper, French was spoken by 'la plupart des Hollandais distingués par leur fortune et leur éducation', even 'dans l'intérieur de leurs familles'.[31] French was also spoken in Brussels at this time.[32] Mixing the mother tongue with French phrases appears to have been common practice. From this point of view the Dutch equivalent of *War and Peace* is the epistolary novel *Sara Burgerhart* (1782) by Betje Wolff and Aagje Deken, in which the letters are full of phrase such as *petits maîtres, charmant, ma chère, je suis enragée* and so on.

It is a similar story in East-Central Europe, where French replaced Italian as the High language. In Hungary, French was in use among the upper classes in the eighteenth century.[33] In Poland, French was the court language in the seventeenth century, especially in the reign of Władisław IV (1632–1648) and his French queen, Marie-Louise de Gonzague, who is said to have spoken nothing but her mother tongue to her husband, and that of Jan Sobieski (1674–1696), who always spoke and wrote to his wife Marie Casimire in French; and also in the age of Augustus of Saxony, who was twice

---

[30] Brunot, *Langue française,* vol.8, 440; Fumaroli, *L'Europe,* 353.

[31] *Gazette nationale,* quoted in Frijhoff, Willem, *Meertaligheid in de Gouden Eeuw* (Amsterdam: KNAW, 2010), 8n.

[32] Brunot, *Langue française,* vol.5, 223, vol. 8, 191, 340; Deneckere, Marcel, *Histoire de la langue française dans les Flandres* (Ghent: Romanica Gandensia, 1954); Frijhoff, *Meertaligheid.*

[33] Evans, Robert J. W., 'The Politics of Language and the Languages of Politics: Latin and the Vernaculars in eighteenth-century Hungary', in Hamish Scott and Brendan Simms, eds., *Cultures of Power in Europe during the long eighteenth century* (Cambridge: Cambridge University Press, 2007), 200–224, at 207.

King of Poland between 1697 and 1733.[34] In other words, in the case of French, the Russian court was following the example of its Polish neighbour, as it had done in other cultural domains in the seventeenth century, although the initiative in the Russian case came from a German empress. In Moldavia and Wallachia, Greek was the High language in the seventeenth and eighteenth centuries, used in education, for instance, before it was displaced by French. Its use was doubtless encouraged by the political dominance of some Greek merchants, the Phanariots, in the eighteenth century.[35]

Maps are useful simplifications but they are usually less reliable than they look. As was remarked earlier, reconstructing the history of speech from the evidence of texts is a hazardous enterprise. We should not take the testimonies of travellers and diplomats too literally and assume that many people spoke a foreign language either correctly or all the time. Arguing by analogy with later situations studied by sociolinguists, it might be more plausible to suggest that people often spoke foreign languages incorrectly and that they did not speak them all the time, even in the High domains. In the case of the Dutch, for instance, as the example of *Sara Burgerhart* suggests, Willem Frijhoff is surely correct to compare what he calls the 'Franderlands' spoken in the seventeenth and eighteenth centuries with today's 'Dunglish'.[36] Returning to Ferguson, it is worth noting that he has been criticized for exaggerating the separation between High and Low Arabic and ignoring mixtures of the two.

All the same, the spread of French was so rapid that by the late eighteenth century, some European writers, notably Antoine de Rivarol, were describing it as a 'universal' language.[37]

---

[34] Brunot, *Langue française*, vol. 8, 453–6; Klemensiewicz, *Historia języka polskiego*, 153; Birn, Jozef, 'Język francuski w Polsce w epoce saskiej', in Henryk Barycz and J. Hulewicz, eds., *Studia z dziejów kultury polskiej* (Warsaw: PWN, 1949), 379–90.

[35] Camariano-Cioran, Ariadna, *Les academies princières de Bucharest et de Jassy et leurs professeurs* (Salonika: Institute for Balkan Studies, 1974); cf. Lia Brad Chisacof, 'Modern Greek in the Romanian Principalities: the eighteenth century', in Philippaki-Warburton, *Themes*, 463–9.

[36] Frijhoff, *Meertaligheid*, 45.

[37] Storost, Jürgen, *Langue française, langue universelle? die Diskussion über die Universalität des Französischen an der Berliner Akademie der Wissenschaften: zum Geltungsanspruch des Deutschen und Französischen im 18. Jahrhundert* (Bonn: Romanistischer Verlag, 1994).

III

It is time to move from description to explanation, following the precedent of Rivarol's German contemporary Johann Christoph Schwab in a dissertation on 'the reasons for the universality of French', first published in German in 1784.[38] Comparing the spread of Italian, Spanish, German, French and English in the past, present and future, Schwab offered both internal and external explanations. After claiming that some languages, notably French, are superior to others (or more exactly, become superior to others) as instruments of communication, Schwab turned to external explanations of what he called the 'propagation' of languages,, in terms of both politics (the preponderance of particular nations, first Spain and then France) and culture (the association between the French language and French civilization). What follows may be described as a series of footnotes to Schwab, developing and expanding his suggestions.

In the first place, internal explanations. The early modern period was the time of the so-called rise of the vernaculars, in other words the increasing use of some of these vernaculars, at the expense of Latin, especially for High purposes such as writing philosophy or epic poems, making speeches or delivering lectures. However, different vernaculars emerged as rivals of Latin at different times. Until this happened it would be difficult to have a conversation about philosophy, for instance, without switching into Latin or into a language in which people had already borrowed the relevant terms from Latin or created equivalents of their own. Girolamo Lippomano, Venetian ambassador, in Poland 1574, noted that 'everyone' spoke Latin as a result of the poverty of Polish ('tutti universalmente studiano nella lingua latina ... quasi tutti parlano comodamente' because Polish is 'molto ristretto e povero di parole').[39] These considerations are more relevant to writing than speaking and to scholars than nobles, but they should not be forgotten.

---

[38] Schwab, Johann Christoph, *Dissertation sur les causes de l'universalité de la langue françoise* (1784; French translation 1803; new edn, Amsterdam: Rodopi, 2005).

[39] Albèri, Eugenio, ed., *Relazioni degli ambasciatori veneti*, first series, vol.6 (Florence: a spese dell'editore, 1862), 273–316, at 284.

There is much more to say about external explanations, where politics dominates. Indeed, some linguists refer to the 'geopolitics' of language, and others to dominant and dominated languages.[40] Languages of conquest, for instance, like Spanish in Mexico and Peru, French in Brittany and Occitania or English in Wales or Ireland.[41] The terms 'dominant' and 'dominated' are particularly appropriate in cases in which the use of the language of the conquerors is enforced, at least in some domains. For example, in 1768, Charles III of Spain made Castillian the obligatory language of education in Catalonia. More often, though, the use of a foreign language as a High form reveals cultural hegemony rather than naked power relations. In the south of France in the nineteenth century, for instance, where Gascon or Provençal was still the everyday language, French was used as a mark of respect, by a boy inviting a girl to dance, for example. French might also be expected by the audience in the case of sermons preached on special occasions, even if the language was not understood by everyone.[42]

The use of a foreign language as a High form implies a view of one's own language as inferior or barbarous, either because of its perceived 'poverty' or by association with a view of the country as culturally backward. It is part of a more general phenomenon that might be described as 'xenophilia', the complementary opposite of xenophobia. The famous Russian debate between Westernizers and Slavophils should be viewed not only as a unique event but also as an extreme case of a common phenomenon.

Xenophilia seems to have been widespread among the upper classes in many parts of early modern Europe, although it was sometimes challenged. The critique of the invasion of German by French words, especially in the domain of good behaviour (*com-*

---

[40] Simone, Raffaella, 'Geopolitica delle lingue tra Cesarotti e Leopardi', in Harro Stammerjohann, ed., *Italiano: lingua di cultura europea* (Tübingen: Narr, 1997), 37–48; Grillo, *Dominant Languages.*

[41] Jenkins, Geraint, ed., *The Welsh Language before the Industrial Revolution* (Cardiff: University of Wales Press, 1997), 63–4, 80–1; Palmer, Patricia, *Language and Conquest in Early Modern Ireland* (Cambridge: Cambridge University Press, 2001).

[42] Weber, *Peasants into Frenchmen*, 87–88.

pliment, galant, mode, etc), was particularly intense in the middle decades of the seventeenth century.[43] This linguistic campaign was part of a more general reaction against foreign and especially French cultural models, from clothes to cuisine, the 'imitation of the French' (*Nachahmung der Franzosen*) denounced by the philosopher Christian Thomasius.[44]

In the case of Spanish from the age of Philip II to that of Philip IV, like French in the age of Louis XIV, this linguistic hegemony was in part the result of the association between the language and the political power of the state where it was spoken as a mother tongue. On the other hand, the hegemony of German was mainly associated with trade, while that of Italian (Tuscan) was almost purely cultural (even if Grand Duke Cosimo de'Medici supported the spread of Tuscan for political reasons), since its status depended on the poems written by Petrarch and his many followers, and later on Italian opera.[45] Latin was a possible High language, and in Russia, Church Slavonic, but the upper classes did not adopt either, probably to distinguish themselves from the clergy and from scholars, whom they often regarded as 'pedants'.

As for French, especially in the eighteenth century, it came to be seen by the upper and middle classes in many parts of Europe as the language of politeness, civilization, enlightenment and universalism. By the end of the period we can add the idea of modernity. Early in the 19th century the Italian poet Leopardi called France 'the thermometer of all that is modern'.[46] One might compare the spread of the French language with that of French fashions, which replaced Spanish fashions in Italy and elsewhere from the middle

---

[43] Hans Wolff, *Der Purismus in der deutschen Literatur des siebzehnten Jahrhunderts* (1888: rpr Leipzig: Zentralantiquariat der Deutschen Demokratischen Republik, 1975).

[44] Christian Thomasius, *Von Nachahmung der Franzosen* (1687: rpr Stuttgart: Göschen, 1894).

[45] Bertelli, Sergio, 'Egemonia linguistica come egemonia culturale', *Bibliothèque d'Humanisme et Renaissance* 38 (1976), 249–81; Folena, Gianfranco, *L'italiano in Europa: esperienze linguistiche del Settecento* (Torino, Einaudi, 1983) and Stammerjohann, Harro (ed.) *Italiano: lingua di cultura europea* (Tübingen, Narr, 1997).

[46] Brunot, *Langue française,* vol.5, 303; Leopardi quoted in Simone, 'Geopolitica', 46 (my translation).

of the seventeenth century onwards. In the case of Russia, as Juri Lotman puts it, French was 'the bridge for the movement of ideas and cultural values'. The English writer and politician Thomas Macaulay, arguing in 1835 favour of the use of English in India, took this example as a precedent, claiming that 'the languages of Western Europe civilized Russia'.[47]

The work of Pierre Bourdieu reminds us that diglossia may also be used as a weapon in conflicts within a given society. His famous study of *La distinction* (1979) discussed the many ways in which one social class, especially one considered to be high, distinguishes itself from another class that it considers to be lower, in food, clothes, the furnishing of rooms and so on. In this book Bourdieu had little to say about language (oddly enough, since he was himself a Gascon speaker from Béarn) but he made up for this omission in a later book, *Ce que parler veut dire* (1982).[48] In a way the use of foreign languages by the upper and middle classes in the early modern period resembles the use of slang by teenagers or thieves. In all these cases, language acts as a symbol or marker of an in-group. In similar fashion, Richard Wortman has argued that by 'displaying themselves as foreigners, or like foreigners, Russian monarchs and their servitors affirmed the permanence and inevitability of their separation from the population they ruled'.[49]

In the case of early modern Europe the importance of a single institution, the court, in spreading the use of High forms deserves to be emphasized, especially when the court was full of foreigners who had arrived in the train of the queen. The example of the court was often followed by nobles elsewhere, the nobles by the middle class and so on. In his famous study of the civilizing process, the sociologist Norbert Elias had little to say about language as either a means of civilizing or as an object of the process. All, the same

---

[47] Etkind, Alexander, *Internal Colonization: Russia's Imperial Experience* (Cambridge: Polity Press, 2011), 15.
[48] Bourdieu, Pierre, *La distinction* (Paris: Minuit, 1979). Cf Bourdieu, Pierre, *Ce que parler veut dire* (Paris: Fayard, 1982).
[49] Wortman, Richard, *Scenarios of Power: myth and ceremony in Russian monarchy*, vol.1 (Princeton: Princeton University Press, 1995), 5.

the history of language illustrates his arguments rather well.[50] It should be added that what we see in this case are High forms defined by location rather than (as in Ferguson's formulation), by topic.

Another conclusion that emerges from this brief comparative survey may be summed up in the phrase, 'Cherchez la femme'. The role of queens in the process of diglossia deserves to be noted: rulers in their own right such as Catherine de'Medici and Catherine the Great, but also wives and mothers. In the case of Italian, there was Beatrice of Naples and Bona Sforza, and in that of Greek, Theodora Kantakouzene, the mother of Michael the Brave (Mihai Viteazu, 1558–1601), the ruler of Wallachia, Transylvania and Moldavia. For Spanish, there was Maria of Spain. For German, Louise of Mecklenburg-Güstrow (the wife of Frederik IV of Denmark and the mother of his successor Christian VI). In the case of French, Marie-Louise de Gonzague, Marie Casimire and Eléonore d'Olbreuse all played significant roles.

In short, in a more literal sense than one might have expected, a number of European rulers spoke their 'mother tongue', or more exactly their 'mother's tongue', even if it differed from the language of the majority of their subjects. These examples illustrate the power of women, whether directly as rulers in their own right or indirectly, behind the scenes – even if this is soft power, cultural power. Catherine the Great was unusual among these women only in not promoting her native language.

There were of course many counter-examples in this period of foreign queens who did not launch a fashion for their language. In the case of England, Catherine of Aragon, Henrietta Maria and Catherine of Braganza respectively failed to launch Spanish, French and Portuguese. Foreign kings, such as the Dutchman William III and the German George I, also failed to set a fashion for their languages at the English court. Lest it be thought that the English were unusual in this respect, we should remember that neither Louis XIII's Anne of Austria nor Louis XIV's Maria Theresa

---

[50] Elias, Norbert, *The Civilizing Process* (1939; English translation, revised edn, Oxford: Blackwell, 2000). Cf.Burke, Peter, 'Language in the Civilizing Process', *Figurations* 23 (June 2005), 2–3.

persuaded the French court to speak Spanish. Queens played an important role in the history of diglossia, but only when circumstances were favourable.

What were the consequences of this widespread phenomenon of diglossia? In a brilliant essay, the Russian polymath Juri Lotman argued that for Russian nobles in the age of compulsory westernization from Peter the Great onwards, everyday behaviour became 'a sphere in which teaching was needed', making the nobleman 'a foreigner in his own country'. Learning how to behave was like learning a foreign language, and as a result life was perceived as a kind of play.[51] Lotman did not mention diglossia in this essay, but the practice of Russians speaking French to other Russians makes one of the most vivid illustrations of his argument.

This argument leads to an important question. Was there a psychological price to be paid for this practice? Were these eighteenth-century Russians divided selves? Did they feel linguistic or cultural self-hatred? If such a price did have to be paid, then one might view the decline of the use of foreign languages as High forms in Europe in the age of nationalism as an inevitable reaction to an intolerable situation.

In any case, however, in the industrial societies of nineteenth-century Europe, national identity was coming to prevail over social identity, while the internationalist and universalist mode of thought characteristic of the Enlightenment declined. In these respects industrial societies may be contrasted with earlier agrarian societies in which the nobility, the group that most practiced diglossia, were part of an international network while the peasants were tied to their regions.[52] Diglossia did not disappear in the nine-

---

[51] Lotman, Juri, 'The Poetics of Everyday Behaviour in Russian Eighteenth-Century Culture' (1977): English translation in Alexander D. Nakhimovsky and Alice S. Nakhimovsky, eds., *The Semiotics of Russian Cultural History* (Ithaca: Cornell University Press, 1985), 67–94, at 68–72.

[52] This argument is central to Ernest Gellner, *Nations and Nationalism* (Oxford: Blackwell, 1983). On the conflict between the French universalist and the German regionalist and historicist modes of thought, see Karl Mannheim, *Conservatism: a contribution to the sociology of knowledge* (1927: English translation London: Routledge, 1986).

teenth century, but it was increasingly confined to agrarian societies, from Ireland to Russia and beyond Europe to colonial societies. French was a High language in the Middle East for instance, and English in India, while both languages were used for High purposes in Africa south of the Sahara.

3: THE RENAISSANCE TRANSLATOR AS GO-BETWEEN

One important characteristic of the Renaissance, according to Mikhail Bakhtin, was what he called – in English translation, of course – the 'interanimation' of languages, in other words a sharper consciousness of the differences between languages, linked to increasing linguistic inventiveness and playfulness. Whether or not Bakhtin was right to single out the Renaissance in this respect at the expense of the later Middle Ages, say, or the seventeenth century, there can be little doubt that there was plenty of such linguistic interanimation at this time.[1]

One of Bakhtin's favourite examples was that of Rabelais, whose fascination with language is apparent in his romance, notably in the episode in which Panurge first meets Pantagruel and speaks to him in two invented languages and ten real ones – German, Italian, English, Basque, Dutch, Spanish, Danish, Hebrew, Greek and Latin – before finally admitting to being francophone.

In sixteenth-century Munich there lived a local equivalent of Panurge, a master of macaronics, the musician and composer Roland de Lassus or Orlando Lasso. Lassus moved between four lan-

---

[1] Mikhail Bakhtin, 'From the Prehistory of Novelistic Discourse', English trans in his *The Dialogic Imagination* (Austin 1981), 41–83; cf his *Rabelais and his World* (English trans Cambridge, MA, 1971).

guages with ease. Born in Mons in the Netherlands, he was fran-cophone. He studied in Italy before coming to the court of Herzog Wilhelm of Bavaria. Lassus wrote hymns in church Latin, *chansons* in French, madrigals in Italian and *Lieder* in German.

In addition to his musical duties, Lassus seems to have per-formed the role of a court fool (describing himself as a *poltrone*). When he was away from his young master, he used to amuse Wil-helm with letters that were regularly written in a mixture of four languages, French, German, Italian (with a slightly Venetian fla-vour) and Latin (and occasionally in Spanish as well). Two brief quotations may give some idea of his linguistic inventiveness and the rapidity with which he switched codes. 'Je me retrouve avec la gracieuse letterine qu'il placuit a vostre Excellence mihi scribere ... surtout, questo mi piace tregrandissamente de son retour sano et gagliardo'. Or again: 'Affin que votre Excellence voie que je veux accomplir sa bonne volonté, qui est que je donne neu Zeitung ... io lasso saber a vuestra Excellentia si come per la gratias de dios todas las compagnias ... se portent mediocrement asses fort bien'.[2] Lassus was certainly a Renaissance go-between.

Translators as a Social Group

The idea of a go-between is exciting but slippery. There is a dan-ger of the concept expanding to include virtually everyone, as the participants discovered in the course of a conference on *médiateurs culturels* organized in Aix-en-Provence in the 1970s.[3]

However, even a fairly strict definition of 'go-between' should include translators, 'those in the middle', as André Lefevere called them, 'who do not write literature but rewrite it'.[4] They 'transfer' texts from one language to another, cross borders and in the pro-cess sometimes develop multiple identities. Translators also facili-tate contacts and encourage interests. In the sixteenth century, for example, translators such as Richard Eden encouraged the English

---

[2] Horst Leuchtmann (ed.) Orlando di Lasso, *Briefe* (Wiesbaden, 1977).
[3] Michel Vovelle (ed.) *Les intermédiaires culturels*, (Paris, 1981).
[4] André Lefevere (ed.) *Translation/History/Culture: a Sourcebook* (London, 1992), 1.

interest in the Americas through his versions of the work of Peter Martyr, Oviedo and Lopez de Gomara.[5] Translators spread the ideas and ideals of the Renaissance from one European country to another.

The activity of translation was becoming increasingly important in the Renaissance, as Greek texts were translated into Latin, Latin texts into the vernacular, and some European vernaculars into others or into Latin, a practice that is probably underestimated today: over 1000 texts were translated into Latin between 1500 and 1800, with the practice reaching its peak between 1600 and 1650.[6]

This lecture is a part of a more ambitious study of what might be called the 'culture of translation' in early modern Europe, or better, perhaps, 'cultures' of translation in the plural, a study that will attempt to grapple not only with the question, who translates? but also with what, with what intentions, how, for whom, and with what consequences.[7] In what follows, however, I shall concentrate on Renaissance translators as a social group or groups, while venturing some generalizations about the methods they employed. There were two main groups involved in translation.

In the first place, a relatively small number of Renaissance translators were professional in the sense of devoting a considerable amount of their life to this task, usually for money. The sixteenth-century record, so far as I know, is held by the Frenchman Gabriel Chappuys, who translated some eighty texts, followed by another Frenchman, François de Belleforest, who made nearly forty. The Spaniard Alfonso de Ulloa, who worked for Giolito in Venice, the Englishman Arthur Golding, the Dutchman Aegidius Albertinus and the Flemish Jesuit Frans de Smidt made about thirty apiece. Another prolific translator, the French lawyer Jacques Gohorry (c1520–76), deserves a mention here because his choice of texts –

---

[5] John Parker, *Books to Build an Empire* (Amsterdam, 1965).

[6] Peter Burke, "Translations into Latin in Early Modern Europe", in Cultural Translation in Early Modern Europe, ed. Peter Burke and Ronnie Po-chia Hsia (Cambridge, 2007), 65–80.

[7] After writing these lines I discovered a similar formula in Anthony Pym, *Method in Translation History* (Manchester, 1998), 5. We both owe a debt to the communication theory of Harold Lasswell.

Machiavelli, Oviedo, Paracelsus, the *Polifilo* – reveals a number of different facets of the Renaissance.

It might be better to call these people 'semi-professional' because it was common to combine the career of translator with a career in the Church, like Smidt, or with teaching languages, interpreting, acting as a secretary compiling dictionaries or writing for money.

However, the vast majority of translators were amateurs, most of whom only engaged in this activity once or twice in their lives. Some translators were noble or princely amateurs such as Ludwig Prince of Anhalt, who translated Gelli and Petrarch into German; Lord Berners, who translated Froissart, Guevara, and the *Carcel de Amor* into English in the reign of Henry VIII; or Jacobus Geuder von Heroltzberg, a Nuremberg patrician, who was especially interested in the history of the Ottoman Empire.

Devotional writers translated other devotional writers (Luis de Granada and Emmanuel Nieremberg both translated Thomas Kempis). Medical men translated herbals, artists and connoisseurs translated treatises on art and architecture. For example, the painter Patrizio Caxès, Italian in origin but living in Spain, translated Vignola's book on architecture into Spanish, while Jehan Martin, a former secretary to the French ambassador in Rome who was also one of the designers of the decorations for King Henri II's state entry into Paris, translated the architectural works of Alberti, Serlio and Vitruvius.[8]

Among these amateurs were women. Although women accounted for only a low percentage of the translators whose names we know, a high percentage of female writers were active in this domain. A famous example is that of Mary Sidney, who translated the French playwright Antoine Garnier and the religious writer Philippe de Mornay. Other English examples from this period include Lady Margaret Beaufort, Thomas More's daughter Margaret Roper (who translated Erasmus), Queen Elizabeth (who in her youth translated Marguerite de Navarre), Anna Cook wife of

---

[8] Jean-Claude Arnould, 'Jean Martin dans ses prefaces', in Charles Brucker (ed) *Traduction et adaptation en France* (Paris, 1997), 335–44.

Nicholas Bacon (who translated Jewel and Ochino), Ann Lok (who translated Calvin), Jane Lumley (who translated Euripides), and Margaret Tyler (who translated a Spanish romance).

It has sometimes been suggested that translation was considered more compatible with female modesty (often defined to include silence), than engaging in original writing, and one feminist scholar has castigated 'the misogyny that drove women to use translation as a way of justifying their education and character'.[9] However, it is also worth noting that Margaret Tyler viewed her enterprise as a blow struck for women, since her preface denounces the claim that men are the 'sole possessors of knowledge'.[10]

I should like now to reflect on the importance among translators of people who might be described as go-betweens in other respects as well, driving the concept hard in order to see how far it will go and distinguishing six groups: merchants, diplomats, teachers, missionaries, inhabitants of border regions and displaced persons.

In the first place, merchants, economic go-betweens such as the Englishmen John Frampton, who translated Marco Polo, and Thomas Nicholas, who translated the letters of Hernan Cortés and other works dealing with the Spaniards in the New World.[11] Certain printers, who may be regarded as a kind of merchant, played an important role as entrepreneurs of translation; Theodor de Bry and his son Johann Theodor, for instance, who commissioned German and Latin translations of travel books; the Antwerp printer Martin de Keyser or L'Empereur, (d. 1537), his double name suggesting a double identity, who published Tyndale's New Testament; and Nicholas Hill (otherwise known as Nicolaes van den Berghe), who was active in the border city of Emden.[12] In France there was Abel L'Angelier of Paris, who employed Chappuys, and

---

[9] Mary Ellen Lamb, 'The Cooke Sisters', in Margaret Hannay, ed., *Silent but for the Word: Tudor Women as Patrons, Translators and Writers of Religious Works* (Kent, Ohio, 1985), 115.

[10] On Tyler, Tina Krontiris, *Oppositional Voices: Women as Writers and Translators of Literature in the English Renaissance* (London, 1992), 44–62; on Mary Sidney, ibid., 64–78.

[11] Jonathan Hart, *Representing the New World: The English and French Uses of the Example of Spain* (New York, 2000), 107–8, 156, 158.

[12] Andrew Pettegree, *Emden and the Dutch Revolt* (Oxford, 1992).

Longis and Sertenas, also of Paris, who employed Gruget.[13]

In England, William Caxton was both a translator and a patron of translators. In France, the printer Etienne Dolet translated Cicero and Plato as well as writing a guide to good translation. Gabriel Giolito of Venice was also a translator himself as well as employing translators such as Ulloa and Ludovico Dolce.[14] Another Venetian printer, Barezzo Barezzi, translated some famous Spanish picaresque novels into Italian. Jean de Tournes, son of the famous printer of Lyon, translated Bandello's stories and the conduct book *Galateo* into French.

A second group of go-betweens were diplomats, who were playing an increasingly important role at this time, the age of the rise of the resident ambassador.[15] Bernardo de Mendoza, Spanish ambassador to France, translated Lipsius. Krzysztof Warszewicki, a Polish diplomat, translated the Spanish political writer Fadrique Furio Ceriol into Latin. Spies too (often employed by diplomats) were active in this way, including Sir Geoffrey Fenton, an English agent in Ireland as well as the translator of Bandello, Guevara and Guicciardini, and Richard Percyvall, official Spanish translator to Queen Elizabeth (the equivalent, one might say, of being a Russian interpreter during the Cold War).

In the third place, teachers, in other words mediators between the generations. Jacques Amyot, tutor to the French royal children, is a famous example, although he is better known as a bishop. Philemon Holland, headmaster of Coventry school, was nicknamed the 'translator-general', his works including English versions of Ammianus, Livy, Pliny, Plutarch, Suetonius and Xenophon as well as Latin versions of Bauderon and Speed.

An important fourth group of go-betweens is that of missionaries, as illustrated by the collective example of the Society of Jesus. When Ignatius, following St Paul, advised his own followers to be

---

[13] Jean Balsamo (1988) 'Les traducteurs français d'ouvrages italiens et leurs mécènes, 1574–89', in Pierre Aquilon and H. -J. Martin (eds) *Le Livre dans l'Europe de la Renaissance* (Paris, 1988), 122–32.

[14] Antonio Rumeu de Armas, *Alfonso de Ulloa: introductor de la cultura española en Italia* (Madrid, 1973).

[15] Garrett Mattingly, *Renaissance Diplomacy* (London, 1955).

'all things to all people', *omnia omnibus,* he was recommending a policy of what we might call the 'cultural translation' of the Christian message. The Jesuits were active on all the four known continents. They learned Chinese and Japanese, Tamil and Tagalog, Quechua and Tupí in order to further their missionary endeavours, producing grammars and dictionaries of exotic languages as well as many translations.

This part of the story is well known. What is less well known is that in Europe too the Jesuits were deeply involved in the collective enterprise of translation, especially but not exclusively from the vernacular into Latin. Jesuits specialized in translating texts by other Jesuits, including many texts concerned with the activities of the order and its members. They appear to have developed a translation policy. A few Jesuits specialized in this activity, including Frans de Smidt, whose thirty translations have already been mentioned; the Pole Simon Wysocki (twenty-three texts), or the German Conrad Vetter (nineteen). Jesuits appear to have been particularly important as translators into the languages of East-Central Europe, mainly into Polish, Czech and Hungarian.[16]

A fifth group of go-betweens is made up of the inhabitants of linguistic borderlands.[17] Alsace and Lorraine, for instance. Claude Chansonette, or Claudius Cantinuncula, was a humanist from Metz who faced in both directions, translating Erasmus into French and More's *Utopia* into German. A more famous case is that of Johann Fischart of Strassburg, the translator not only of Rabelais but also of Calvin and also, from Dutch, of Philip Marnix's satire on the Catholic Church, *The Beehive.* Other Alsatian translators include Johannes Sleidan, who turned Froissart and Commynes into Latin; Jerome Boner, who turned Greek and Roman historians into German, and Walter Ryff, who produced a German version of Vitruvius.

The frontier city of Emden has already been mentioned (above, p. 47). The German-Dutch border was also the home of two translators into Latin and German who were well known in their day even if they are more or less forgotten now. Aegidius Albertinus

---

[16] Peter Burke, 'The Jesuits and the Art of Translation in Early Modern Europe', reprinted below, 63–73.

[17] A point made and illustrated from other periods by Pym, *Method,* 105.

was born in Deventer and emigrated to Bavaria for religious reasons. Appointed *Hofbibliothekar* in Munich, he published twenty-six translations from Spanish (including Antonio de Guevara), and others from French and Italian.[18] Caspar Ens, who was also born in the Dutch Republic, was a Lutheran who lived for twenty-five years in Cologne. He too translated Guevara and also the picaresque novel *Guzman de Alfarache* and one of the exemplary novels of Cervantes, as well as Dutch and Italian texts.

Extending the concept a little, the whole of the Netherlands may be regarded as a border area between France and Germany in which an unusually large number of translators were active.

People out of Place

As the last two examples suggest, translators are often displaced people, who have been 'translated' from one region to another themselves. Interpreters, for instance, form a distinctive group in which members of marginal communities were important. Relations between the Ottoman Empire and Western Europe, for instance, depended on the services of Jews and Greeks as linguistic intermediaries.[19] Deserters were important, people who changed sides, like Doña Marina, 'La Malinche', who went over to Cortés, or the so-called 'renegades' who converted from Christianity to Islam, or the 'new Christians' (converted Jews) who interpreted for the Portuguese in South Asia.[20]

In Europe too Renaissance translators were often émigrés, exiles or refugees, taking advantage of their liminal position and making a career of mediating between the two countries to which they owed a kind of allegiance. It is likely that these people had a 'double consciousness', to use the famous phrase of W. Du Bois about North

---

[18] Richard Newald, *Die Deutsche Literatur vom Späthumanismus zur Empfindsamkeit* (Munich, 1951), 121–31.

[19] Bernard Lewis, 'From Babel to Dragomans', *Proceedings of the British Academy* 101(1999), 37–54.

[20] Frances Karttunen, *Between Worlds: Interpreters, Guides and Survivors* (New Brunswick, 1994), 1–22, 114–35.

American blacks, and that this double consciousness assisted them in the task of translation. These European amphibians, like the professional interpreters and the European Jesuits, have been studied less intensively than their equivalents in the Americas and in Asia.

For example, Greek refugees to Italy before and after the fall of Constantinople were responsible for some influential translations from ancient Greek into Latin. Manuel Chrysoloras, for instance, translated Plato, Theodore Gaza translated Aristotle, and George of Trebizond (encouraged by Nicholas V), translated both philosophers and Demosthenes as well. They offer an obvious example of the way in which immigrants can make a contribution to the culture of the community in which they settle.

Italian Protestant refugees played an important role in the reception of the Renaissance in northern Europe. John Florio, whose hybrid name expresses a hybrid identity, grew up in England, where he translated Montaigne.[21] Lodowick Bryskett, alias Lodovico Bruschetto, the translator of Giambattista Giraldi into English, was born in London of Italian parents.

Protestants were also prominent in the group of Italian translators into Latin. They included the lawyer Scipione Gentile, who lived in Germany and translated Tasso; the scholar Celio Secundo Curione, who lived in Basel and translated Guicciardini; and the physician Giovanni Niccolò Stoppani, who also settled in Basel and translated Machiavelli and other Italian writers. It is worth noting that in all three cases these Protestants chose to translate secular, 'Renaissance' texts. Indeed, it may be and has been argued that Italian Protestants played an important role as go-betweens in the spread of the Italian Renaissance outside Italy.[22]

Some French and Flemish Protestant exiles were also active as translators. Adrian Damman, from Ghent, migrated to Scotland and translated the work of the French Protestant Du Bartas into Latin. Charles de l'Ecluse was a French Protestant émigré who became a professor of botany at Leiden and translated from French and Spanish into Latin.

---

[21] Frances Yates, *John Florio* (London, 1934).

[22] John Tedeschi, 'Italian Reformers and the Diffusion of Renaissance Culture', *Sixteenth-Century Journal* 5 (1974), 79–94.

Catholic refugees appear to have played a less important role as translators. However, Mateo Martinez van Waucquier (d. 1643), who came from Middelburg but lived in Antwerp, translated many texts into Latin including works by St Teresa of Avila, François de Sales and Alfonso Rodriguez. It is a pity that little is known about this intriguing figure whose very name, like that of John Florio, suggests his cultural hybridity.

An important figure in mediating between Italian and Spanish culture was a displaced person: Alfonso de Ulloa, a Spanish noble and soldier who lived in Venice and worked for Giolito and other printers as an original writer and an editor as well as a translator. His thirty published translations include four from Italian into Spanish as well as twenty-four from Spanish into Italian (the remaining two translations were made from Portuguese).[23]

The Translation Process

What kind of translations did these people produce? The subject is of course a vast one and the practice of translation at this time has been relatively little studied so far, at least from the cultural history viewpoint adopted in this chapter.[24] Hence the suggestions that follow should be understood as provisional formulations, little more than a public sharing of problems.

A first point, a personal impression that may not be shared by others, is that of a serious discrepancy between the Renaissance theory of translation – which has been studied relatively thoroughly – and its practice.[25] There was considerable interest in what contemporaries called the rules or 'laws' of translation. A

---

[23] Rumeu, *Alfonso*, 50.

[24] There is an eloquent plea for a historical approach in Pym, Method. The planned five-volume *Oxford History of Translation into English*, edited by Peter France, will also adopt this approach.

[25] Glyn P. Norton, *The Ideology and Language of Translation in Renaissance France* (Geneva, 1984), 58–61; cf. Valerie Worth, *Practising Translation in Renaissance France: the Example of Etienne Dolet* (Oxford, 1988); Anne-Marie Chabrolle (1997) 'L'idée d'une spécificité linguistique et culturelle aux 16e siècle', in Charles Brucker (ed) *Traduction et adaptation en France* (Paris, 1997), 319–24.

phrase from Horace about the 'faithful translator, *fidus interpres,* the equivalent for translation theory of his phrase *ut pictura poesis* in Renaissance art criticism, was discussed again and again.[26] Many debates revolved around the distinction between translating word-for-word and translating the sense of a given text, and also between translation in the strict sense and paraphrase or imitation.

The theory often sounds quite familiar, indeed obvious, since many writers note the need to follow the sense rather the words, for example, or to respect the special qualities of the two languages involved. The not infrequent descriptions of literal translation as 'slavery', 'servility' or 'superstition' may strike us as a little over-dramatic, but we too generally reject literalism. The recurrent metaphor of a language as clothing for ideas may not be one that we would use, but on first reading at least it does not seem to be unacceptable.

By contrast, the practice of translation during the Renaissance seems frequently to have been extremely or even scandalously free by modern standards, a practice that reveals considerable cultural distance between Europe in 1500 and Europe in 2000. Looking back at the theory after examining the practice, the metaphors 'slavery' and 'superstition' take on a different significance. As for 'clothing', it suggests the assumption that meaning can be conveyed independently of words, that the medium does not affect the message.[27]

One aspect of the freedom of Renaissance translations is that they were often made at second hand.[28] The English translated Italian and Spanish texts from French, the French and the Germans translated Spanish texts from Italian, and so on. On occasion the translation was even more distant from the original. An extreme case is that of the fables of Bidpai: Sir Thomas North produced what has been described as 'the English version of an Italian adaptation of a Spanish translation of a Latin version of a Hebrew

---

[26] Glyn Norton, *Ideology.*

[27] On the metaphors of the period, Theo Hermans, 'Images of Translation', in Hermans (ed) *The Manipulation of Literature* (New York, 1985), 103–35.

[28] Jürgen von Stackelberg, *Übersetzungen aus zweiten Hand* (Berlin, 1984).

translation of an Arabic adaptation of the Pahlevi version of the Indian original'.[29]

In other words, go-betweens made use of other go-betweens. To quote a somewhat unusual case, Claude Seyssel translated Xenophon without knowing Greek, working with the Greek scholar Janos Lascaris who may not have known French (presumably the two men communicated in Latin).[30] As far as I know, the practice of translating modern texts at second hand was never criticized in the sixteenth century, despite the concern of humanists to study the Bible in the original languages. Today, by contrast, it is generally viewed as unprofessional, at least as far as the major European languages are concerned (as I write, a translation into English of Sándor Marai's *Embers* has reached the bookshops, made not from the original Hungarian but from German).

Distinctions are in order here. Some translators of the period favoured relatively literal renderings, as Alonso de Cartagena and George of Trebizond did where Aristotle was concerned. In similar fashion, the Valencian humanist Juan Luis Vives argued in favour of leaving certain passages in their original obscurity rather than running the risk of a speculative interpretation. However, others, such as Leonardo Bruni and Johannes Argyropulos, allowed themselves more liberty in rendering the sense rather than the words of the text they were translating. Hence we may speak of 'cultures' or perhaps of 'subcultures' of Renaissance translation.

Fidelity, or what might be called respect for the text, also varied with the kind of author translated. The Bible was most respected, following the advice of St Jerome to translate it 'word for word' (*pro verbo verbum*). Next came the classics, especially philosophical classics such as Aristotle and Plato. The modern texts that are the focus of attention here were treated with most freedom of all, the prose as well as the poetry. Modern texts were not infrequently considered capable of improvement by their translators. Thus Jean Martin, the translator into French of the Italian romance *Polifilo*,

---

[29] J. Jacobs, *The Earliest English Version of the Fables of Bidpai* (London, 1888), quoted in Francis Matthiessen, *Translation: an Elizabethan Art* (Cambridge, MA, 1931), 63n.
[30] The collaboration is described in a letter prefixed to Seyssel's translation of Xenophon's *Anabasis* (1529).

boasted – with some justification, it is true – that 'd'une prolixité plus que Asiatique il l'a reduict à une brieveté françoise', while Pierre Boiastuau called his version of Bandello's stories 'mieux poly' in French than in the original language.

The freedom of Renaissance translators also included contraction, amplification, adaptation and what might be called 'transposition'.

Contraction, the freedom to subtract, took different forms. Long texts might be abridged in translation, reduced to as little as half of their original length. Passages might be omitted – without warning to readers – for religious, moral or political reasons. For example, the Dominican friar Francesco Pipino's translation of Marco Polo's travels omits a passage in praise of Buddha as well as eliminating some of the rhetoric of chivalry.[31] Fischart, better known for amplification, omitted some passages in Rabelais discussing religion. The German translation of *Lazarillo de Tormes* omitted some anticlerical remarks.[32] The Italian translation of Bacon's *Essays* left out one essay altogether, the one about religion and superstition. The French version – made from the Italian, not from the original English – also removed some of Bacon's references to recent French history.[33]

The liberty of Renaissance translations also included the freedom to add material, or as the rhetoricians put it, amplification. It was common to add words and phrases, generally to reinforce the message but sometimes to introduce a new one. Pipino's translation of Marco Polo, for instance, inserted condemnations of Islam. The translation of Erasmus's *Enchiridion* by Alonso Fernández has become notorious for its amplification of the original text (as well as for its omissions).[34] I would suggest, however, that it is best seen not as an aberration but rather as an extreme example of a general

---

[31] John Larner, *Marco Polo and the Discovery of the World* (New Haven and London, 1999). 76, 104, 107, 113.

[32] Charlotte L. Brancaforte, *Fridericius Berghius's Partial Latin Translation of Lazarillo* (Madison, 1983), xv.

[33] Enrico De Mas, *Sovranità politica e unità Christiana nel seicento anglo-veneto* (Ravenna, 1975), 160; Harold W. Lawton, 'Notes sur Jean Baudouin', *Revue de Littérature Comparée* 6 (1926), 673–81.

[34] Peter Russell, *Traducciones y traductores en la península ibérica (1400–1550)* (Barcelona, 1985), 52.

tendency in the Renaissance culture of translation. Barezzi's Italian translation of a Spanish picaresque novel was about three times the length of the original.[35]

Again, the linguistic exuberance of Rabelais, especially his penchant for lists, encouraged two of his translators, Fischart and Urquhart, to go still further in the same direction, emulating rather than simply translating the original text and producing in the process something much longer (in the case of Fischart, even longer in the editions of 1582 and 1590 than in the first edition of 1572). The extra material was sometimes derived from other texts that the 'translator' assembled in a kind of collage, a practice that Albertinus described as *Colligiren*.[36]

At this point it may be useful to step back from the examples for a moment in order to consider the significance of these changes and to make two points in particular. The first is to compare the practices of translators with those of copyists of manuscripts in this period, at least the manuscripts of contemporary writers (scribes had more respect for the Bible and the classics). It was not uncommon for copyists of poems, for instance those of John Donne, which circulated in manuscript at the beginning of the seventeenth century, to leave out stanzas or even to insert new ones. Manuscript was what we might call an 'interactive' medium.[37] We might therefore say that in the Middle Ages the sense of authorship was relatively weak (it would be misleading to say that it did not exist at all). With the rise of printing came the rise of a stronger sense of individual authorship, sometimes misleadingly described as the 'birth' or the 'invention' of the author.[38]

A second point concerns emulation. It is a commonplace to say that in the Renaissance what we call 'original' works were viewed as 'imitations' which competed with the models they followed,

---

[35] José Luis Colomer, '*Il picariglio castigliano* de Barezzo Barezzi', in J. C. Santoyo et al. (eds) *Fidus Interpres*, 2 vols, León 1989, vol. 1, 255–9.

[36] Newald, Literatur, 124.

[37] Harold Love, *Scribal Publication in Seventeenth-Century England* (Oxford 1993); Arthur M. Marotti, *Manuscript, Print and the English Renaissance Lyric* (Ithaca, 1995); Henry Woudhuysen, *Sir Philip Sidney and the Circulation of Manuscripts* (Oxford 1996).

[38] Michel Foucault: Alain Viala, *Naissance de l'écrivain* (Paris, 1985).

as Ariosto (say) competed with Virgil, and Spenser with Ariosto, whose *Orlando Furioso* he attempted to 'overgo'. I should like to suggest that in similar fashion, as the extreme cases of Fischart and Urquhart suggest, translators viewed themselves as competing with the authors they were rendering into other languages.

In this context, some of the conscious modifications of originals by translators become more intelligible. Translators are generally concerned to adapt texts to a new cultural environment, but they may have stronger or weaker inhibitions about 'interfering' with the text. In the Renaissance, such inhibitions were relatively weak, as a few out of the many possible examples may suggest.

In Niclas Ulenhart's German version of the *Novelas ejemplares* of Cervantes, for instance, Rinconete and Cortadillo become Isaak Winckfelder and Jobst von der Schneidt, taking up the original metaphors of the corner and the knife and elaborating them. Where Stefano Guazzo, discussing the art of conversation, wrote of the low voices of the Huguenots (*ugonotti*), his English translator Young wrote 'holy Ankers', thus replacing a gibe at Protestants by a critique of Catholics. 'Equivalent effect', one might say. Again, Diego de Salazar turned Machiavelli's *Arte della Guerra* into a dialogue between two Spaniards, the Great Captain Gonzalo Fernandez de Cordoba and the Duke of Najara. Abraham Fraunce went still further in a translation of Tasso into which he inserted a new character, 'Pembrokiana', in honour of his patroness Mary Sidney. The English translator of St François de Sales turned a female participant in a dialogue, Philothée, into a man, Philotheus.

Still more creative was a not uncommon kind of adaptation that I should like, following the musicians, to call 'transposition'. Translated plays, for instance, are placed in new settings, more familiar to the new audiences. Péter Bornemisza's Hungarian version of *Electra* set the play in Hungary, while a Polish translation of Plautus's play *Trinummus* relocated the action in Lwów.[39]

This tradition survived into the twentieth century, as Hugo von Hofmannsthal's famous adaptations and transpositions of Calderón may remind us. Some directors still follow this convention,

---

[39] Cieklinski's *Protrójny* (1597).

just as they sometimes stage Shakespeare in modern dress. In the Renaissance, on the other hand, non-dramatic examples of transposition are also easy to find. In the middle of the fifteenth century, for instance, the Spanish humanist Juan de Lucena adapted a text by Bartolomeo Fazio on the happy life, moving the dialogue from Ferrara to the court of Castille. Fischart moved the settings of chapters of Rabelais from France to Strassburg or Basel. The Polish version of Castiglione's *Cortegiano,* the *Dworzanin Polski* by Łukas Górnicki, transferred the setting from Urbino to the archbishop's court in Cracow.

Again, Bryskett transposed the dialogue on civil life by Gianbattista Giraldi to Ireland, 'to my little cottage which I had newly built near to Dublin', and transformed the characters into his own friends or acquaintances such as the archbishop of Armagh, Sir Robert Dillon and Edmund Spenser. Actually, the book is not presented as a translation either on the title-page (1606), or in its dedication, and only at the conclusion does the reader learn that Bryskett had 'Englished' the work, 'for my exercise in both languages' and that he had omitted passages and added others (he makes no comment on the transposition). 'I would not tie myself to the strict laws of an interpreter', he comments.[40]

Given the freedom of so many translations, it is natural to wonder what these laws were and who observed them. However, Bryskett was not the only translator to refer to rules of this kind. The French poet Jacques Peletier, for instance, wrote about the 'laws' of translation. The Spanish version of Garzoni's *Piazza* was described on its title-page as 'parte traduzida del toscano y parte compuesta'. When the Jesuit Polanco's *Directorium* was translated into Slovene by Sime Budinic, the title-page carried the warning, 'paraphrastice non verbatim Illyrico idiomata conscripsit'.

The variety of sixteenth-century practice may be illustrated from a passage from the famous conduct book *Il Galateo,* where the subject is language itself. It is argued that Lombards, for example, should speak their own dialect because they speak it better than Tuscan. The English and French translations of the text keep the

---

[40] Ludovic Bryskett, *Of Civill Life* (1606; reprinted, Amsterdam 1971), 278.

Italian example, but the German translator replaced it with a reference to High German and Saxon.

The obvious question for a cultural historian to raise at this point is one about change over time. I should like to suggest that there was a gradual change in the conventions of translation in the course of the sixteenth century. The change was in the direction of greater fidelity. Another way of making this point, and one that suggests a historical explanation of the change, is to say that a minority of translators came to show an increasing sense of the cultural distance between themselves and their texts, often far from them in time and space.

A few examples may illustrate the direction of change. The first is that of the Bible. Protestant translators in particular were concerned to emphasize the cultural distance between the 'primitive' church and the Catholic Church. Faced with the Greek term *episkopos* in the New Testament, for instance, they sometimes refused to translate it as 'bishop', since this would legitimate the Catholic claim to continuity of institutions. Instead, they prefer a more literal translation of the term, for instance 'overseer', the word chosen by Sir John Cheke, professor of Greek at Cambridge and a supporter of the Protestant Reformation. The foreword to the Authorized Version of the English Bible (1611) criticized the 'scrupulosity of 'the Puritans' who 'put washing for Baptism'.[41]

In the case of the Old Testament, Szymon Budny coined the word *ofiarnik*, 'sacrificer', to replace the traditional rendering, *kaplan*, 'chaplain', 'because', as he put it, 'some simple uneducated people may understand that such saintly men as Samuel and Zacharias … were equal to our contemporary Roman priests, yet the two kinds are different as day differs from night'.[42]

Translations of classical texts posed similar problems. The medieval custom of rendering *miles* as 'knight' or *dux* as 'duke' reduced or abolished the cultural distance between past and present. On the other hand, Renaissance humanists from Valla onwards

---

[41] Quoted in Görlach 1978, 269.
[42] Quoted in Andrzej Borowski, 'General Theory of Translation in Old Polish Literary Culture', in G. Brogi Bercoff et al., eds, *Traduzione e rielaborazione nelle letterature di Polonia, Ucraina e Russia* (Alessandria, 1999), 23–38, at 29.

showed themselves increasingly sensitive to the changing meaning of technical terms such as these.

The great problem for humanists was that of translation into Latin, the difficulty of writing about phenomena unknown to the ancient Romans in a Latin which was classicizing if not classical. Translating Guicciardini into Latin, Celio Secundo Curio explained in his preface that 'in hac historia … locorum, officiorum, armorum et machinarum nova vocabula retinuerimus', the reason being 'tanta … veterum à novis dissimilitudo', making it necessary to write about *Ammiralii, Cardinales,* and so on.[43]

Writing about the Ottoman Empire raised similar problems in a still more acute form. When the German humanist Johannes Leunclavius translated the Ottoman annals into Latin, he had to decide what to do with technical terms. He decided to be useful rather than elegant, and so to employ terms like *Bassa, Genizari, Sangiacus, Vezir.*[44] A similar solution was adopted by Johannes Geuder when he translated Minadoi's history of the war between the Turks and the Persians. After hesitating over place-names such as 'Babilonia (quae hodie Bagadat dicitur)', he opted for keeping technical terms like *Caddi, Calif, Deftadar* and so on.[45]

In other words, the style or mode of translation, what contemporaries called the 'laws', what Anthony Pym describes as the 'regime' and what I am calling the 'culture' of translation was changing at this time.[46] By the middle of the seventeenth century, the conflict between elegance and accuracy had become a matter of vigorous debate, at least in France. In the discussion of 'les belles infidèles', the translator Nicolas d'Ablancourt was criticized by some people for a freedom which had been virtually taken for granted in the previous century. He was accused of anachronism, of putting the ancient Romans into modern clothes.[47] Going still

---

[43] F. Guicciardini, *Historiae*, trans C. S. Curio (Basel, 1566).

[44] Johannes Leunclavius, *Annales Sultanorum* (Frankfurt, 1588).

[45] J. Minadoi, *Bellum Turco-Persicum*, tr Geuder (Frankfurt, 1601).

[46] Pym, *Method*, 125–42.

[47] Georges Mounin, *Les belles infidèles* (Paris, 1955); Roger Zuber, *Les belles infidèles* (Paris, 1968); Luce Guillerm, 'Les belles infidèles, ou l'auteur respecté', in M. Ballard and L. d'Hulst (eds) *La traduction en France à l'âge classique* (Paris, 1996), 28–42.

further in the direction of 'foreignizing', as Lawrence Venuti has called it, in Britain in the nineteenth-century, the age of historicism, it was not uncommon to translate an old text into archaic English in order to preserve its 'period flavour', as in the case of William Morris's version of the *Aeneid*.[48]

This narrative of change may be emplotted in two opposite ways. It may be viewed as a story of progress towards greater fidelity or as a story of decline, the loss of freedom or creativity. It seems a pity that the two approaches to translation could not coexist and that they cannot coexist today. It is true that many directors of plays still allow themselves the freedom of transposition from one place or time to another (for example, from ancient Greece to colonial India), while translators are becoming more visible and more conscious of their creativity than they were a generation ago.[49] All the same, the current law of intellectual property means that people who engage in creative transposition now run the risk of finding themselves in court on a charge of plagiarism.

Looking back, then, we may view a certain free style of translation as especially characteristic of the culture of the Renaissance, of a period in which 'original' works were often imitations, while 'translations' were frequently creative.

---

[48] Susan Basnett, *Translation Studies* (3rd ed., London 2002), 19, 70.
[49] Lawrence Venuti, *The Translator's Invisibility* (London, 1995). On the transposition of Racine's *Phèdre* to colonial India, see Basnett, *Translation Studies*, 125–6.

4: The Jesuits and the Art of Translation in Early Modern Europe

The concept of 'cultural translation', which once circulated in the relatively narrow circle of the British anthropologist Edward Evans-Pritchard and his pupils, has now become common currency to describe the process of adaptation through which items from one culture are domesticated in another. In the early modern period this process was often described as 'accommodation', a concept well known to the Jesuits and their historians. When Ignatius, following St Paul, advised his own followers to be 'all things to all people', *omnia omnibus,* he was recommending a policy of what we call the cultural translation of the Christian message.

The career of Matteo Ricci neatly exemplifies what Ignatius meant. One might describe Ricci's change of clothing on his arrival in China as an attempt to translate Christianity in the sense of dissociating it from its western cultural baggage and searching for an 'equivalent effect' in the local culture. We might even describe Ricci's famous exchange of the robes of a bonze for those of a mandarin as a sign of his awareness that a cultural mistranslation had occurred and needed to be corrected.

In this chapter, however, the focus will be on translation in a more literal sense, translation between languages. Here too the contribution of the Jesuits, or part of their contribution, is well known.

One thinks for example of the many grammars and vocabularies of non-European languages compiled by Jesuit missionaries. In the New World, famous examples include the Portuguese José de Anchieta's grammar of Tupí, for instance, published in 1595, the Italian Luigi Bertonio's grammar of Aymara (1603), and the dictionary of Guarani compiled by the Peruvian missionary Antonio Ruiz de Montoya (1639). In the case of Asia, one thinks of João Rodriguez and his Japanese grammar, or of Florian Bahr (1706–71), a missionary in China, who helped compile a dictionary of Chinese, Latin, French, Italian, Portuguese and German.

The contribution of Jesuit translators concerned with non-European languages is also relatively well known, as in the case of the seventeenth-century volume *Confucius Sinarum Philosophus*, translated by Philippe Couplet, Prospero Intorcetta and other members of the Society or Martino Martini's translation into Chinese of Lessius on the soul. The acute problems faced by missionaries of translating theological concepts into the language of the mission field have often been discussed, whether the people they were attempting to convert was the Chinese, the Japanese or the Iroquois.[1]

There is still work to be done in this area, especially if one leaves the relatively well-cultivated fields of China, Japan and the Americas for other countries to study the context in which Pierre Fromage, for instance, a missionary in Egypt and Syria, translated Emmanuel Nieremberg, Paolo Segneri and other Jesuit writers into Arabic, while the Portuguese Luis de Azevedo, a missionary in Ethiopia, translated Jerónimo Nadal 'in sermonem Chaldaeum'; and the Bohemian Paul Clain, who worked in the Philippines, translated Dominique Bouhours into Tagalog.[2]

Roberto Bellarmino's famous *Catechism* was translated into no fewer than seventeen non-European languages, including Ara-

---

[1] See Zhang Longxi, *Mighty Opposites: from Dichotomies to Differences in the Comparative Study of China* (Stanford 1999), 366; George Elison, *Deus Destroyed: the Image of Christianity in Early Modern Japan* (Cambridge MA 1988).

[2] On translation into Tagalog, see Vicente Rafael, *Contracting Colonialism: Translation and Christian Conversion in Tagalog Society under Spanish Rule* (Ithaca 1988), a reference for which I should like to thank Luce Giard. Rafael does not mention Clain.

bic, Bikol (a language of the Philippines), Bisaya (spoken in Borneo), 'Chaldean', 'Congolese', Coptic, 'Ethiopian' (now known as Ge'ez), Georgian, Hebrew, Malagasi, Maratha, Quechua, Tagalog, Tamil, and Tinigua (an Amerindian language). These translations are themselves evidence of the policy of accommodation, although they need to be studied in depth to see how much interpretative freedom this policy permitted.

Here, however, emphasis will fall on a part of the story that is paradoxically both less-known and more familiar: the European part. The Jesuits were extremely active as translators from one European language into another throughout the early modern period, but this aspect of their activities has attracted relatively little attention. A few general remarks on the history of translation in early modern Europe may be useful at this point in order to place the work of the Jesuits in a broader context.

From the sixteenth century onwards a rapid rise of published translations becomes visible in Europe. These publications include translations from Greek into Latin, from Latin into the vernaculars, from one vernacular into another (notably from Italian, Spanish and French into other languages). They also include translations from the European vernaculars into Latin. Over a thousand translations from the vernaculars into Latin were produced between 1500 and 1800, of which some 40% were religious books.[3] It was in the course of my research on this topic that the role of the Jesuits became apparent, and it then turned out that this role was not confined to translation into Latin. In the early modern period, the Society produced more than six hundred printed translations into European languages.

The observations that follow are confined to translations into Latin and European vernaculars made by Jesuits between 1540 and 1773. It may be illuminating to approach these translations with six questions in mind. In the first place, Who was doing the translating? Then, from What language into What? In the third place, What kind of text? Fourthly, for Whom, what kind of read-

---

[3] Peter Burke, "Translations into Latin in Early Modern Europe", in Cultural Translation in Early Modern Europe, ed. Peter Burke and Ronnie Po-chia Hsia (Cambridge, 2007), 65–80.

ership? Fifth, with What intentions? And sixth, with What consequences?

It will be noticed that an extremely important question has been omitted: In what manner or style were the translations carried out? Fascinating as it would be to see whether or not the concept of 'modus noster' works in the context of translation, it would be premature to venture generalizations at this point. Too little is known about different cultures of translation in early modern Europe to place the Jesuits with any accuracy. In this respect the history of translation lags behind the history of architecture, for instance, the history of science or the history of the theatre.

Who translates? It would be good to know how many Jesuit translators were active in this period. The problem is that even an exhaustive analysis of Sommervogel's invaluable – if not always completely accurate – volumes would not be sufficient to answer this question.[4] A major difficulty is the number of anonymous translations, described on title-pages (the main source which Sommervogel used), as 'a quodam sacerdote Societatis Jesu', 'ab alio eiusdem societatis sacerdote', 'por otro de la misma compañia', etc. There are even references to what appears to be collective translation, as in the case of the *Litterae Japonicae et chinesenses* (Antwerp, 1611), where the title-page claims that the book was translated 'by the rhetoricans of the college' (*a rhetoribus collegii*).

So far, I have identified 260 individual Jesuit translators. There were probably many more, but this group may be a reasonable sample on which to base some provisional conclusions.

In the case of early modern translators in general, it is useful to distinguish two groups. On one side there is a large group who produced only one or two texts in the course of a life devoted to other things. Let us call them the 'amateurs'. On the other side, there was a small group who might produce as many as forty texts apiece. We might speak of them as 'professionals', or better, as 'semi-professionals', since they gained their living by combining the tasks of writer, interpreter, secretary and so on.

---

[4] Carlos Sommervogel et al., *Bibliothèque de la Compagnie de Jésus*, 12 vols (Brussels, Paris, Toulouse, 1890–1932).

In the case of the Jesuits, even though translating was not a way of making a living, we find a similar distinction between two groups. A small number of translators produced a relatively large number of texts in the course of a life that might also include preaching, teaching, or writing their own books. Ten individuals produced at least 172 translations, nearly 30% of the total. The highest number of texts translated by a single individual is thirty (in the case of the Fleming Frans de Smidt), followed by twenty-three (the Pole Simon Wysocki), nineteen (the German Conrad Vetter), eighteen (the northern Netherlander, Jan Buys), seventeen (both the Frenchman Jean Brignon and the Czech Jiři Ferus), fifteen (the Italian Luigi Flori) twelve (the Dutchman Gerard Zoes), eleven (the Spaniard Joseph Echaburu), and ten (the Czech Jiři Constanz). Most of the remaining translators may reasonably be described as amateurs.

These 260 individuals are distributed unevenly over time. It is no surprise to discover that seventeen were born before 1550. What is more worthy of note is the fact that ninety-one were born between 1550–99, the largest group in any fifty-year period. Thereafter, although the Society as a whole was growing, the number of translators steadily diminished, from sixty-eight born in the period 1600–49 to forty-five born 1650–99 and twenty-one between 1700 and 1749 (total 242, the birth dates of the remaining eighteen translators being unknown). It would seem that the order's strategies or priorities were changing.

From what into what? The main language into which translation was made was Latin, with 77 individuals involved in the process. I have so far discovered 518 translators from the vernacular into Latin during the whole early modern period, so that the Jesuit contribution was substantial in this domain, about 15%.

Next, but a long way behind, came French, with 32 translators, followed by German, with 25; Spanish, with 22; and Polish, with 20. Behind this group come translators from Italian (14); Dutch (11); Czech (11), and Hungarian (9). There were only four translators into English, four more into modern Greek, four into different South Slav languages or dialects (Croat, Slovene, 'Illyrian'), three into Portuguese (together with a number of anonymous translations), two into Breton and one each into Basque, Irish, Lithuanian, Maltese, Romanian and Welsh (omitting the translations of Bellarmine into Furlano and Torinese on the grounds that these 'languages' are usually classified as dialects). The importance of the Slav languages and Hungarian is worth noting, and I shall return to this topic later.

What was translated? Pending a complete quantitative study, my strategy here is to begin with the texts that had the greatest international success in the sense of being translated into many languages. It is difficult to be sure into quite how many languages and it might be wise to treat the figures which follow, derived from Sommervogel, as minima which research in Portuguese or East-Central European libraries in particular might well amplify.

Sixteen authors were translated by Jesuits into eight or more languages. The record is held by Bellarmino, whose *Catechism* was translated into twenty European languages (as well as seventeen non-European ones, as I remarked earlier). A long way behind come three texts each of which was translated into eleven languages: the Catechism of Peter Canisius, and the *Exercicio de perfeción* of Alfonso Rodrigues, and, less predictably, the *Pensées* of Dominique Bouhours (translated not only into Tagalog, as we have seen, but also, by a German Jesuit, into Greek).

Four texts were translated into nine languages apiece. One was Ignatius's *Spiritual Exercises,* which one might have expected to find at the head of the list. The remaining three works are little known today, but for this very reason worth mentioning now, the *Massime* of Gian-Battista Manni, the *Meditaciones* of Luis de la Puente, and the *Purgatorio* of Martin de Roa.

Seven texts were translated into eight languages each: a Latin grammar by Emmanuel Alvarez, the famous *Ten Reasons* by Edmund Campion, the biographies of Luigi Gonzaga by Virgilio Cepari and of Ignatius by Pedro Ribadeneira, the devotional work *Pia Desideria* by Herman Hugo, a description of Loreto by Orazio Torsellini and the sermons of Antonio Vieira.

It should be noted that these references are to texts rather than authors and to numbers of languages, not numbers of editions. I am not denying Carlos Eire's claim that Emmanuel Nieremberg was a best-seller – and his works were indeed translated into at least eight languages – but no one text by him, so far as I know, was translated into more than seven.

In some of these cases of multiple translation it might be prudent to avoid the term 'best-seller', reserving it for cases of multiple editions in a given language as evidence of continuing demand. The evidence is at its best when the printer remains the same since he would presumably have sold his stock before reprinting. A different printer in another city may pirate the book because he believes that it will sell, rather than because he knows that it has sold well.

On this criterion some works of Jesuit devotion qualify as bestsellers but others do not. The prolific translator Jan Buys was also the author of original works of devotion of which the *Meditationes* was translated into Polish (Wysocki) 1608; French 1611; Dutch (Thielmans) 1628; second French translation (Portail) 1644; third French translation (Binet) 1669; fourth French translation, 1669; Italian (Coll'Amato) 1684; fifth French translation (Macé), 1689; sixth French translation (Brignon) 1691; Portuguese 1751. Five languages but ten translations, suggesting the appeal of Buys in France, confirmed by the analysis of the editions of the 1644 version, at least nine by 1697 (though the sixth known edition, 1665, calls itself the 'tenth').

It is worth noting that on occasion, Jesuit texts were translated by non-Jesuits, secular works like the *Historia natural y moral* by José de Acosta, for instance, the *Uomo di lettere* by Daniele Bartoli, the *Oráculo* of Baltasar Gracián, or Martino Martino's *De bello tartarico*, a history of the overthrow of the Ming dynasty by the Manchus.

In complementary fashion, a few Jesuits translated writers who were not members of their order, including Thomas Kempis (four times), St François de Sales (twice), Luis de Granada (twice) and Lorenzo Scupoli. The Bible was translated by a Polish Jesuit, Jakob Wujek and again by a South Slav Jesuit, Bartul Kašić. Jesuits also translated a few lay writers, including Guicciardini (the maxims not the history), Richelieu's *Testament Politique,* a military treatise by Montecuccoli, and the philosophy of Leibniz (like

Confucius, beyond the limits of this study).[5]

All the same, to list Jesuit translations is to be impressed by the overwhelming concern of the translators with diffusing books written by their colleagues within the Society. The Jesuit Famiano Strada's well-known history of the Revolt of the Netherlands, for instance, was translated into Italian by two of his colleagues, Carlo Paini and Paolo Segneri.

It is possible to go still further in this direction. A substantial number of the works translated were concerned with the activities of the Jesuits themselves. Letters from the missions, for instance, were translated by Balinghem, Busaeus, Coyssard, Oranus, Simon and others. Again, we not infrequently find that a biography of a Jesuit written by another Jesuit might be translated by a third, as in the case of biographies of Loyola, Xavier, Francisco Borja, Aloysius Gonzaga, Emond Auger, Roberto Bellarmino, Peter Canisius, Pierre Coton, Antonio Possevino, François Régis and Pedro Ribadeneira.

Fourthly, For whom were these translations made? One of the target audiences was of course the Jesuits themselves. After all, they were a large enough group in the seventeenth century – by 1640, over 16,000 – to consume all this literature. The fact that they would not have bought copies does not matter, since the translations did not cost anything and printing was sometimes done in house, especially in Central and Eastern Europe, where Jesuits virtually controlled higher education; in Braunsberg, for instance, Prague, Trnava, Vilnius and so on.[6]

There was also a ready-made distribution network available through these colleges (revealed by Stephen Harris's studies of information coming the other way, from the periphery to the centre).[7] The students in the colleges may also be regarded as virtu-

---

[5] Kempis was translated by Brignon, Fabricy, Kasic and Pazmany; St François by Constanz and Lamormaini; Luis of Granada by Cuvelier and Schott; Guicciardini by Bourghesius; Leibniz by Bosses.

[6] Prague 1652, 1721 (translations by Constanz and Rogacci); Trnava 1693 (translation by Rogacci), Vilnius 1705 (translation of Lancicius).

[7] Stephen J. Harris, "Mapping Jesuit Science," in *The Jesuits: Cultures, Sciences and the Arts, 1540–1773*, ed. John O'Malley et al. (Toronto 1999), 212–40.

ally captive readers, and title-pages sometimes make it clear that a given text was directed towards them in particular. Some editions of the catechism of Canisius are described as 'in usum juventutis scholasticae', and the Würzburg 1736 Latin translation of the *Pensées* of Bouhours.as 'in gratiam juventutis studiosae'.

All the same, I do not believe that all these texts were produced for internal circulation alone. Some commercial publishers were involved. It is possible that they were subsidized on occasion, but unlikely that this happened all the time. It is obviously difficult to assess the importance of the circulation of books by Jesuits outside the order, and more research on library inventories is needed, but it is clear enough that the Jesuit 'loud-speaker' was a powerful instrument. The example of Emmanuel College Cambridge in the seventeenth century, a strongly anti-Catholic college yet one with books by Caussin and Kircher in the library, has many parallels in the Protestant world at this time.

Fifthly, With what intentions were translations made? Given the concern of Jesuits to translate works by Jesuits about Jesuits, it is only a mild exaggeration to speak of a 'conspiracy' to translate. At the very least we might speak of a 'policy' or what has been called a 'corporate strategy.'[8] Whether this strategy was devised at headquarters in Rome or whether it was originally a local initiative that was imitated elsewhere I am afraid that I am unable to say.

To put this policy in perspective one might compare the Jesuit initiative with Christian missions in general (Wulfila and the Goths, Cyril and the Slavs, and so on), or, thinking of early modern Europe, of the translation campaigns of the Protestants, the Lutherans in particular. The first books printed in a number of European languages were Lutheran texts, as in the case of Latvian (1525), Estonian (1535, a catechism), Romanian (1542, another catechism), Lithuanian (1547, a translation of Luther's small catechism), and Slovene (1550, yet another catechism).

All the same, the focus by the Jesuits on the Jesuits remains distinctive. Indeed, it is my impression that other religious orders

---

[8] Gauvin A. Bailey, "Jesuit Corporate Culture and the Visual Arts," in *The Jesuits*, 38–89, at p. 73.

engaged in the enterprise of translation to a much smaller extent than the Jesuits did (in the case of translation into Latin, this point is easy to demonstrate). There would appear to be a link between this translation activity and what John O'Malley has called the 'official promotion' of the history of the Jesuits.[9]

In other words, the Society, or at least some leading figures in it, had a concern for collective self-representation, an acute sense of their 'image' relatively unusual in this period. This image-consciousness is revealed with particular clarity in the Jesuit celebration of their centenary in 1640 including the publication of the famous *Imago primi saeculi*.[10] This enterprise was all the more remarkable because a concern for centenaries was still relatively unusual in the seventeenth century. The best-known example is that of the celebration of the centenary of Luther's 95 theses in Protestant Germany in 1617, and it may not be too fanciful to view 1640 as a Catholic reply to 1617.

The role of printers and publishers in the enterprise of translation deserves a few words, although the subject is a large one as well as little studied. Most of the texts discussed here were produced by so-called commercial printers. Certain publishers were associated quite closely with the order in certain cities: Christophe Plantin and his successors in Antwerp, for instance, or Kink or Mylius in Cologne, all three of whom produced a good deal of Catholic devotional literature. Other names which recur include Albinus of Mainz (for Buys), Bogard of Douai (Balinghem), Rictius of Vienna (Bucelleni).

Finally, what were the effects of this collective enterprise? It is not difficult to imagine what these effects may have been, but measuring them is rather more difficult. In certain limited fields it is possible to say something relatively precise, so this chapter ends not with a general conclusion but with a partial one, concerning East-Central Europe.

The so-called 'rise of the vernaculars' in early modern Europe is well known, including the proliferation of printed books in more

---

[9] John W. O'Malley, "The Historiography of the Society of Jesus," in *The Jesuits*, 3–37, at p. 6.

[10] Marc Fumaroli, *L'école du silence* (Paris 1998), 445–76.

or less standard forms of certain vernaculars at the expense of both Latin and local dialects. The importance of translation for the development of these vernaculars is also well known, especially in the case of languages where the published literature was not extensive, in Scandinavia for example, or in East-Central Europe. So far I have discovered the names of 112 early modern translators into the languages of East-Central Europe, mainly into Polish, Czech and Hungarian. Of these 112, 51, or nearly half, were Jesuits.

One of the great defenders of the Czech language in the difficult times which followed the battle of the White Mountain was the Jesuit Bohuslav Balbín, while two more Czech Jesuits, Jiři Constanz and Jiři Ferus, published grammars of the language). 'Jesuit Slovak' (*jezúitska slovencina*) is a term still in use to refer to a kind of koine that the Jesuits adopted to reach both the Czechs and the Slovaks.[11] It might be compared to the *lingua geral,* based on Tupí, which Jesuits such as José de Anchieta employed in the missions in Brazil, or the *lengua general* employed in Mexico and Peru.

It is fair to say that the Jesuit contribution to the cultural history of East-Central and indeed to that of Eastern Europe was much more important than it was in the West. This contribution is highly visible in the architecture of their churches and colleges. It was crucial in education. It is also clearly discernible in Jesuit translations.

---

[11] L'ubomir Durovic, "Slovak," in *The Slavic Literary Languages: Formation and Development*, ed. Alexander M. Schenker and Edward Stankiewicz (New Haven 1980), 211–28, at p. 212.

5: EARLY MODERN VENICE AS A CENTRE OF INFORMATION AND COMMUNICATION[1]

⁓

This topic stands at the cross-roads of the history of Venice and the history of information. The chapter will attempt to keep a balance between a concern with the uniqueness of Venice and with problem-oriented history, notably the rise of what might be called a new regime of information and communication following the invention of printing with movable type. The essential claim made and I hope justified in the pages which follow is that Venice was, in the fifteenth and sixteenth centuries in particular, the leading centre of information and communication in Europe, its closest rivals being Genoa and Antwerp for economic information, and Rome for political news. Even in the seventeenth century, when Amsterdam became a great information centre, Venice still had a role to play.

What made all these cities into centres was the regular arrival of information on many subjects (trade, war, politics, religion, and

[1] My thanks to the conference participants for their questions and comments, and especially to John Martin, Juergen Schulz and Jonathan Walker. I should also like to thank Brendan Dooley for his constructive criticisms of an earlier draft of this paper.

so on) from so many different places, both inside and outside Europe. Given the relative cheapness of water transport, ports had an advantage over inland cities like Florence or Paris. Success bred success, because some foreign traders and diplomats went to Venice to acquire information and in the process passed on some of their own. The great problem is to decide how long the centrality of Venice lasted, how and why and in what domains it was undermined, and by what city or cities it was replaced.

Historiography

The fundamental idea of Venice as a communication centre is not new. It was fifty years ago that Pierre Sardella, in a study of news based on Sanudo's diary, described Venice as 'l'agence d'information la plus important du monde moderne naissant'.[2] Braudel drew on Sardella's work in his famous study of the Mediterranean world (published only a year later), noting that Venice was almost exactly halfway between Madrid and Istanbul.[3] Since Sardella's day, especially since the Hale volume on Renaissance Venice, intensive research on certain aspects of the topic has been carried out by economic historians, political historians, historians of religion, art historians, historians of literature, geographers, and bibliographers. Indeed, it sometimes looks as if all roads lead to Venice.

The later 1970s, for example, saw studies of the Venetian press by Gerulaitis, Grendler, Lowry and Quondam, and a substantial collection of essays on Venice as centre of mediation between east and west, a topic also discussed by William McNeill in an essay describing Venice as 'a cultural metropolis', although 'a marginal

---

[2] Pierre Sardella, *Nouvelles et Spéculations à Venise au début du xvie siècle* (Paris: Armand Colin, 1948), 10, 14. Cf the analysis of Sanudo in Elisabeth Crouzet-Pavan, 'Les mots de Venise', in *La circulation* (Rome, 1994), 205–18.

[3] Fernand Braudel, *La Méditerranée et le monde méditerranéen à l'époque de Philippe II* (Paris: Armand Colin, 1949), 317; cf Federico Melis, 'La diffusione dell'informazione economica nel Mediterraneo', *Mélanges Braudel* (2 vols, Toulouse: Privat, 1973), vol. 1, 389–424.

polity', between 1481 and 1669.[4] In the 1980s, contributions included Federica Ambrosini's book on the impact of the discovery of America on Venice, Claudia Bareggi's study of the activities of the *poligrafi*, Julian Raby on Venetian 'orientalism', and a number of contributions to the multivolume *Storia della cultura veneta*.[5] In the 1990s, one thinks of Paolo Preto's monumental work on the Venetian secret service, John Martin on heresy, and a collection of essays on the impact of America on Venetian culture.[6]

After so many monographs, some of which have undermined traditional ideas and assumptions, there is obviously a need for synthesis, for arranging the material in other ways to order to reveal connexions and to engage with the general themes of continuity and discontinuity in Venetian history. It is obviously important to discuss the relation between the shape of Venetian society and the kinds of information circulating or failing to circulate in the city. Hans Kissling was surely right to place an emphasis on Venice as a 'mercantile state', but it is equally important to discuss the effects on the diffusion of information of the Venetian political system.[7]

In attempting the twin tasks of synthesis and reconsideration, this paper will focus on two general problems and trends. In the

---

[4] Leonardas V. Gerulaitis, *Printing and Publishing in Fifteenth-Century Venice* (Chicago and London: Chicago University Press, 1976); Paul Grendler, *The Roman Inquisition and the Venetian Press* (Princeton: Princeton University Press, 1977); Martin Lowry, *The World of Aldus Manutius* (Oxford: Blackwell, 1979); Hans-Georg Beck et al., eds, *Venezia Centro di mediazione tra Oriente e Occidente (secoli xv-xvi) Aspetti e problemi* (2 vols, Florence: Olschki,1977); William McNeill, *Venice the Hinge of Europe* (Chicago: Chicago University Press, 1974).

[5] Federica Ambrosini, *Paesi e mari ignoti: America e colonialismo europeo nella cultura veneziana (secoli xvi-xvii)* (Venice: Deputazione editrice, 1982); Claudia di Filippo Bareggi, *Il mestiere di scrivere: lavoro intellettuale e mercato librario a Venezia nel '500*, Rome: Bulzoni, 1988); Julian Raby, *Venice, Dürer and the Oriental Mode* (London: Islamic Art Publications, 1982); Girolamo Arnaldi and Manlio Pastore Stocchi (eds) *Storia della cultura veneta*, vols 3, 4, (Vicenza: Neri Pozzo, 1980-3).

[6] Paolo Preto, *I servizi secreti di Venezia* (Milan: Il Saggiatore, 1994); John Martin, *Venice's Hidden Enemies: Italian Heretics in a Renaissance City* (Berkeley and LA: University of California Press, 1993); Angela Caracciolo Aricò, ed., *L'impatto della scoperta dell'America nella cultura Veneziana* (Rome: Bulzoni, 1990).

[7] Hans J. Kissling, 'Venezia come centro di informazione sui Turchi', in Beck, *Venezia Centro*, 97-109.

first place, on the relation, or better the tension, between private and public information, secrecy and publicity, political pressures and economic ones. The second major theme will be the decline of Venice as a provider of information, or more exactly, its 'intellectual involution', in other words its shift from a centre of information about the world (especially the East) to being a centre of information about itself.

Private information

Some scholarly debates were conducted more or less in private in the academies, on some occasions at least in order to restrict the flow of information.[8] Venice was also an important centre for studies of 'occult philosophy' (as Heinrich Cornelius Agrippa called it), on the edge between what we call 'religion' and 'science'. The rise of interest in Cabbala is obviously linked to the growing importance of the Jewish community in the sixteenth century, but the adepts also included christians, from the local friar Francesco Zorzi to the French scholar Guillaume Postel. Postel probably visited Venice in the first place because it was on the way to the Holy Land, but it was there he discovered the cabbalist text *Zohar* and he went back several times to learn from people as diverse as the Jewish printer Daniel Bomberg and the living saint Madre Giovanna.[9]

However, it was not esoteric knowledge so much as practical everyday information for which Venice was most famous in this period. The following sections will concentrate on the place of news in economic and political life.

Economic information.

The letters home written by merchants stationed abroad were an important source of information for the Venetians, a kind of 'data

---

[8] William Eamon, *Science and the Secrets of Nature: Books of Secrets in Medieval and Early Modern Culture* (Princeton: Princeton University Press, 1994).

[9] Marion L. Kuntz, *Guillaume Postel* (The Hague, Nijhoff, 1981), 73–83.

bank' as a historian of Genoa has put it.[10] So it is not surprising to find that the Venetians were pioneers in the organization of a postal system. It was in the fourteenth century that the government founded the *Compagnia dei corrieri*. In the mid-sixteenth century, when the Tasso family of Bergamo set up their *corrieri ordinari*, departing at fixed times, one of their main routes was Milan-Venice. Even more important was the route from Rome to Venice.[11]

The latest 'news on the Rialto' was of obvious economic importance, with serious consequences for the corn market and the spice market in particular.[12] No wonder that four Venetian nobles once removed part of the roof of the Doge's Palace in order to listen to a confidential report from Istanbul.[13] When rumours about spices from India arriving in Lisbon reached Venice in 1501, the reaction of the government was to send an agent, Lunardo Masser, to Portugal to discover what was happening and report back to them. His report still survives.[14] When Antonio Pigafetta of Vicenza returned from his voyage round the world with Magellan, he visited Venice, where the Collegio heard his account of India 'con gran atention'.[15]

Given the presence of a colony of Venetian merchants in Istanbul and their permanent representative, the *bailo*, Venice was a natural centre for economic information about the East, especially about the Ottoman Empire. The role of the *bailo* in the collection and transmission of information about the Turks and some of his main sources, from the official translators or dragomans to the sultan's physicians, have been investigated.[16]

Information arrived from Aleppo and Alexandria, where other Venetian merchants were established, and occasionally from more

[10] Giorgio Doria, 'Conoscenza del mercato e sistema informativo: il know-how dei mercanti-finanzieri genovesi nei secoli xvi e xvii', in *La repubblica internazionale del danaro*, ed. Aldo Da Maddalena and Hermann Kellenbenz (Bologna: 1986), 57–115.

[11] Bruno Caizzi, *Dalla posta dei re alla posta di tutti* (Milan: Angeli, 1993), 211–62.

[12] Sardella (1948), 19–37.

[13] Donald E. Queller, *The Venetian Patriciate: Reality versus Myth* (Urbana and Chicago: University of Illinois Press, 1986), 214.

[14] Preto (1994), 218.

[15] Marin Sanudo, *I Diarii* (58 vols, Venice : Visentini, 1879–1903), vol. 35, 173.

[16] E. g. Kissling (1977), 106; Mantran (1977) 113–4.

remote parts of the East. Nicolo Conti, for instance, spent nearly a quarter of a century in India and Burma between 1419 and 1444. Cesare Federici spent some twenty years in Baghdad, Hormuz, Ceylon, Sumatra and Burma, returning to Venice in 1581. Gasparo Balbi went first to Syria in 1576, then to India and Burma, returning in 1589.[17]

Given these economic interests, it is scarcely surprising to discover that Venice was an important centre of map-making in this period. In the fifteenth century, a Venetian map-maker, Andrea Bianco, worked for the brother of the Portuguese prince Henry the Navigator. The Portuguese crown also bought a map from Fra Mauro of Murano. One of the earliest and one of the most famous city maps of the Renaissance was the map of Venice by Jacopo de'Barbari.[18] In the sixteenth century, the Venetian Giovanni Andrea Vavassore was a major publisher of maps (of Spain, France, Greece and Britain as well as of Italian provinces), while the Piedmontese Giacomo Gastaldi, an engineer in Venetian service, produced a series of detailed maps of Italy.[19] At the end of the seventeenth century, this tradition was revived by Vincenzo Coronelli (discussed below).

Political information

By the late fourteenth century, Italian diplomats were collecting information on behalf of their governments and sending it home in their dispatches. At first there seems to have been little interest in preserving these documents – the earliest collection of dispatches in the Venetian archives dates from 1477 – but practice changed in the sixteenth century, with the Venetians among the pioneers.

---

[17] Luca Campigotto, 'Veneziani in India nel xvi secolo', *Studi Veneziani* 22 (1991), 75–116; Alessandro Grossato, *Navigatori e viaggiatori veneti sulla rotta per l'India* (Florence: Olschki, 1994).

[18] Jürgen Schulz, 'Jacopo de'Barbari's View of Venice', *Art Bulletin* 60 (1978), 425–74.

[19] Numa Broc, *La géographie de la Renaissance* (1980: second ed., Paris: Editions du Comité des Travaux historiques et scientifiques, 1986), 51, 126; Luisa d'Arienzo, 'La presenza veneziana in Portogallo', in Aricò (1990), 57–69, at 65.

It has often been noted that the Venetians were among the first European powers to adopt the system of resident ambassadors, as much to gather information about other countries as to negotiate with them. The government expected to receive from its representatives abroad not only regular dispatches but also formal reports at the end of the mission, the famous *relazioni*, describing the political military and economic strengths and weaknesses of the state to which the ambassador had been accredited.[20] These were read aloud in the Senate before being filed in the archives (as a decree of the Senate in 1524 required). However, these *relazioni* were better known abroad than the government would have wished. Indeed, they were used as models, not least for reports on Venice itself which ranged from the objective to the satirical. A favourable example is Giovanni Botero's report, published in Venice itself in 1595 with a dedication to doge Grimani and the Senate.[22]

The unfavourable, naturally anonymous, are perhaps most easily distinguished by their incipits. They include one addressed to Philip II, c. 1567 ('Se ad alcuno ambasciatore, cattolico re ...'); another, c. 1584 ('Tutto il governo della Repubblica di Venezia, si puo dire...'); a third of 1620 ('Venetia sola tra tutte le città d'Italia'); and the report of around 1621 ascribed to the Spanish diplomat Alonso de la Cueva, marquis of Bedmar, beginning 'Laboriosa impresa per certo è questo alla quale mi avingo', copies of which are still to be found in many European libraries.[21] This is not the place to discuss the genre further, although it surely deserves a monograph.

The Venetian government had other ways of acquiring information about foreign powers. The Council of Ten's cipher secretary

---

[20] Armand Baschet, *Les archives de Venise* (Paris: Payot, 1870), 331–61; Donald E. Queller, 'How to succeed as an ambassador', *Studia Gratiana* 15 (1972), 665–71, especially 670–1; *id.*, 'The development of ambassadorial *relazioni*', in *Renaissance Venice*, ed. John R. Hale (London: Faber and Faber, 1973); 174–96; Angelo Ventura, *Nobiltà e popolo nella società veneta del '400 e '500* (Bari: Laterza, 1964); J. Kenneth Hyde, 'The Role of Diplomatic Correspondence and Reporting', in his *Literacy and its Uses: Studies on Late Medieval Italy*, ed. Daniel P. Waley (Manchester: Manchester University Press, 1993), 217–59.

[21] British Library, Dept of Mss, Sloan 697, ff. 35–62; Sloan 697, ff. 1–32; Add. 18, 660, ff. 137–46; Sloan 1834.

[22] Giovanni Botero, *Relatione della repubblica venetiana* (Venice: Varisco, 1595).

Soro (active 1506–44), for example, was an expert in breaking the codes used by other states. The government also maintained a network of agents or 'spies'. The inverted commas are used here not to suggest that the motives of the Venetians were idealistic but rather that the later division of labour between professional activities had not taken place: there was spying rather than spies.[23] Venetian interest in the Ottoman Empire was at least as much political as economic. The *bailo* was expelled in 1491, accused of spying.[24] In 1511, the consul at Damascus was accused of the same offence. In 1507, the *rettore* of Cyprus sent agents to Persia.

More informally, Venetian merchants in Damascus and elsewhere in the Middle East sent political information to the government.[25] It seems appropriate that one of the ways to code information in this period was to describe political events in the language of merchants. At the time of Lepanto, for example, secret dispatches to Venice described the Turks as 'drugs', the army as a 'caravan', artillery as 'mirrors' and so on.[26] Economic espionage was also practised.[27]

The information was of course confidential, more or less. Considerable effort was expended in keeping it secret, but equal effort was expended in uncovering it. One duty of sixteenth-century Spanish ambassadors to Venice was to discover what the government knew about the Turks. Rome tried to do the same.[28] The government was extremely sensitive on the subject of secrecy, even for the early modern period, a time when, as recent research shows, material which we might expect to be public was commonly regarded as confidential.[29] In the fifteenth century, a considerable number of individuals were put on trial on a charge of revealing secrets of state.

---

[23] Cf. Ugo Tucci's intervention in the discussion in Beck (1977), 137.
[24] Kissling (1977), 101.
[25] Preto (1994), 248–9.
[26] Preto (1994), 269; cf. Hyde (1993), 244.
[27] Preto (1994), 381–96.
[28] Hassiotis (1977), 127; Peri in the discussion in Beck (1977), 137.
[29] Geoffrey Parker, 'Maps and Ministers', in David Buisseret, ed., *Monarchs, Ministers and Maps: the Emergence of Cartography as a Tool of Government in Early Modern Europe* (Chicago: Chicago University Press, 1992), 124–52, at 125.

In the sixteenth century, the topic was a major preoccupation of the Council of Ten and of a new institution, the *inquisitori di stato* (given this name in the 1590s but active earlier).[30] For example, in 1501 the Council of Ten forebade gossip about the ballots cast in the Maggiore Consiglio.[31] In 1515 the Council gave permission to two patricians, Andrea Mocenigo and Marin Sanudo, to use the archives for their histories of recent events, but on condition that these histories were submitted for approval before publication.[32] The secret archives were guarded with such care – at least in theory – that even the doge was forbidden to enter the room in which they were kept unless he was accompanied, while the keeper was supposed to be unable to read and write.[33] As is well known, Venetian nobles were forbidden to have contacts with foreign ambassadors, for fear that they would reveal what was being discussed in the Senate and other places.

Some scholars have spoken of the government's 'obsession' with secrecy. Their concern was not pathological, but simply a reaction to a political system in which an unusually large number of people had access to *arcana imperii* which in monarchies were the preserve of the few. As Paolo Giovio suggested, the leaking of confidential information may also be linked to conflicts between factions.[34] Despite official discouragement, secrets continued to be revealed. Among the more notorious cases were the accusation against Angelo Badoer in 1612 and the execution of Antonio Foscarini in 1622, part of the 'witch-hunt' following the recall in 1618 of the Spanish ambassador, Bedmar, who had a large network of agents in his service and was believed to have plotted to overthrow the Venetian government.[35]

Three examples of the sensitivity of the Venetian government (especially the Council of Ten) in this area are worth quoting here.

---

[30] Preto (1994), 55–7.
[31] Queller (1986), 75.
[32] Gerulaitis (1976), 55.
[33] Baschet (1870), 175–6.
[34] T. C. Price Zimmermann, *Paolo Giovio: the Historian and the Crisis of Renaissance Italy* (Princeton: Princeton University Press, 1995), 171.
[35] Preto (1994), 66, 79, 123–8.

One might not have thought that Daniele Barbaro's famous commentary on Vitruvius (1556) was a politically dangerous work, but objections were made to its publication on the grounds that designs of fortifications might help Venice's enemies. In the second place, the arrest of Lazzaro Soranzo by the Council of Ten in 1598, following his publication (in Ferrara) of an anti-Turkish treatise which the government considered to have divulged confidential information about the Ottoman regime.[36]

In the third place, the request by the heirs of doge Niccolò Contarini for permission to publish his history of Venice. The reply of the consultants in 1638 was that the history should not be published, on the grounds that it contained confidential political maxims which they thought better not to divulge (*massime molto intime del governo che per verità non sappiamo se stia bene divulgarle*). The manuscript was therefore to be kept 'in a secret place' in the archives.[37]

Information about Venetian territory was also collected. For example, 'the earliest state-sponsored maps' in Europe appear to be those commissioned by the Council of Ten in 1460.[38] Needless to say, they were highly confidential documents. The famous 'Golden Book' (begun in 1506), recording the births of patricians is another early example of the state's concern with recording information for practical purposes. Censuses of the population were carried out more frequently in Venice than elsewhere, at least from the sixteenth century onwards, and the eighteenth-century census in particular is a model of precise and detailed information.

Like the Inquisition, the Venetian government encouraged ordinary people to denounce law-breakers. Written denunciations used to be left in churches or on the stairs or at the doors of public buildings, until the notorious *bocche di leone* (which fascinated foreign visitors such as Skippon, Saint-Didier and Veryard) were constructed around the beginning of the seventeenth century, allow-

---

[36] Preto (1994), 433.

[37] Emmanuele Cicogna, *Delle iscrizioni veneziane* (6 vols, Venice, Orlandelli, 1824–53) vol.3, 287–90.

[38] John Marino, 'Administrative Mapping in the Italian States', in Buisseret (1992), 5–25, at 6.

ing delators to post their information to particular departments of government.[39]

Venice also has a special place in the history of archives. It was in 1586 that an order was made to make a subject index of documents concerning the Senate, and in 1601 that the first patrician was appointed to the new post of *sopraintendente*. The first holder of the office, Andrea Morosini, collaborated with grand chancellor Antelmi to make a catalogue, while a still more elaborate catalogue was compiled in 1669 under the supervision of *soprainten-dente* Battista Nani and grand chancellor Ballarin.[40] One of the first books ever published about archives, *De archivis*, by Balthasar Bonifacio, was published in Venice by Pinelli in 1632. It was indeed appropriate that Ranke, 'the real originator of the heroic study of records' (as Lord Acton called him) should have paid so much attention to Venice, but he was fortunate enough to arrive after 1797.

Religious information

Venice was a centre of information about heresy, whether intended for the heretics themselves or for those who wished to persecute them. The city was the principal gateway through which the ideas of the German reformation reached Italy. A clandestine synod of Anabaptists was held in Venice in 1550. Clandestine publication also flourished. Italian translations of Luther (without Luther's name on the titlepage) could be found in the city. Sanudo notes that copies of a treatise by Luther were found in a Venice bookshop in 1520.[41] Heretical books were sometimes published in Venice, as in the famous case of the *Beneficio di Cristo*, published by Bindoni in 1543 (the only surviving copy, out of reach of censors and inquisitors, is still to be found in the library of St John's College Cambridge). In the 1540s, the smuggling of heretical books was well organized, with Pietro Perna in Basel as the chief supplier and a

---

[39] Preto (1994), 168–77.
[40] Baschet (1870), 167–78, 194.
[41] Martin (1993), 26.

number of Venetian booksellers involved (Andrea Arrivabene, the Valgrisi, the Ziletti).[42]

In the first years after the Inquisition was established, it was the clergy, parish priests and friars, who drew the attention of the Holy Office to heretics. From the 1560s on, denunciations came from the laity.[43] Some printers, Valgrisi for example, were brought before the Inquisition on charges of owning or publishing heretical books.

The commercialisation of information

Private information had its ways of becoming public. A remarkable example is the text of an interrogation by the inquisition of a certain fra Baldo Lupetino on a heresy charge, published in 1547 as *Articoli proposti a fra Baldo*.[44]

One famous institution for divulging confidential information, as well as criticizing individuals was the so-called 'Gobbo di Rialto'. The Rialto was of course a place where official decrees were 'published'. Sanudo records an irreverent message attached to a column there in 1532. From the late sixteenth century onwards, a statue which had been placed there in 1541 and nicknamed 'the hunchback' became the equivalent of the Roman Pasquino, a site for outspoken anonymous political comment.[45]

The crucial point of contact and tension between public and private was the news. Oral information about political events had its own geography. When the Florentine humanist Giannozzo Manetti was on a mission to Venice in 1448, he went to the Doge's Palace on Mondays and Saturdays to visit the Signoria, attend sessions of the Maggior Consiglio and learn the news from Lombardy, Tuscany and elsewhere.[46] The Doge's Palace was

---

[42] Grendler (1977), 102–15; Martin (1993), 80–1.

[43] Martin (1993), 67, 185–6.

[44] Adriano Prosperi, *Tribunali di Coscienza* (Turin, 1996), 162.

[45] Andrea Moschetti, 'Il Gobbo di Rialto', *Nuovo Archivio Veneto* 5 (1893), 1–85.

[46] Nadia Lerz (ed.) 'Il diario di Griso di Giovanni', *Archivio Storico Italiano* 422 (1959), 247–78, at 265; Hyde (1993), 242; Francesca Trivellato, 'La missione diplomatica a Venezia del fiorentino Giannozzo Manetti', *Studi Veneziani* 28 (1994), 202–35, at 213.

also the main source for Sanudo's famous diary, which has been called a 'news chronicle' because the entries so often begin with the formula 'news came'. However, as we have seen, private or even top secret information had a way of becoming public property. In 1567, a German called Venice the metropolis of news.[47] By this time weekly manuscript *avvisi* were in circulation.[48] The Council of Ten outlawed the activities of the *novellisti*, as they were often called, in 1571, describing them as those 'che fanno publica professione di scriver nove, per il che sono salariati di diversi'.[49] All the same the writing of manuscript newsletters by 'reporters' (*reportiste*) continued to flourish in the eighteenth century.[50]

Patricians needed information about one another, about offices and about ballots in order to plan their careers, and by the early seventeenth century they were able to buy such information from clerks and *ballottini* in the form of manuscript pocket-books such as the *zuccheta* and the *consegi* or *brogietti*, to the shock of the Council of Ten, who complained about this practice in 1618.[51] Manuscript copies were made of the official *relazioni* – by whom we do not know. Francesco Sansovino's biography of Charles V, for example, made use of *relazioni* by Bernardo Navagero and Marino Cavalli, ambassadors to the imperial court.[52]

By the seventeenth century at the latest, these *relazioni* were on sale in certain European cities, notably Rome (to the shock of Venetian ambassadors to Rome such as Leonardo Donà, in 1600 and Lorenzo Tiepolo in 1713), and some copies still survive in public

---

[47] Biagio Brugi, *Gli scolari dello studio di Padova* (Padua, 1905), 27.

[48] Castronovo (1976), 9–10.

[49] Preto (1994), 89.

[50] Mario Infelise, 'Professione reportista. Copisti e gazzettieri nella Venezia del '600', in *Venezia: Itinerari per la storia della città*, ed. Stefano Gasparri, Giovanni Levi and Pierandrea Moro (Bologna: Il Mulino, 1997), 193–219; id, 'Le marché des informations à Venise au 17e siècle', in H. Duranton and Pierre Rétat (eds) *Gazettes et information politique sous l'ancien régime* (St-Estienne: Publications de l'Université, 1999), 117–28.

[51] Dorit Raines, 'Office Seeking, Broglio and the Pocket Political Guidebooks in '500 and '600 Venice', *Studi Veneziani* 22 (1991), 137–94.

[52] Alfred Morel-Fatio, *Historiographie de Charles-Quint* (Paris: Champion, 1913), 152.

and private libraries.[53] The ex-secretary to the French ambassador to Venice, Amelot de Houssaie was able to use letters, memoirs and *relazioni* of ambassadors for a history of Venice which made public what he called 'les mystères de la domination'.[54]

It was only to be expected that sooner or later someone would be enterprising and bold enough to print some *relazioni*. This step was taken by a printer of Bergamo, Comin Ventura, who edited an anthology of texts under the name of *Tesoro Politico*, published (according to the titlepage) in Cologne in 1593. Later editions appeared in Milan and Vicenza, but not, prudently enough, either in Bergamo or in Venice. Three more *relazioni* by Venetian ambassadors to Rome were published in 1672 under the title *Li Tesori della corte romana*. The place of publication was given as 'Brussels' and there was no printer's name on the titlepage.

Given this flourishing trade in political information, one might have expected Venice to become an early centre of newspapers. However, in comparison with other Italian cities, such as Genoa, Rome, Bologna, Milan or Turin, Venice was slow to develop printed *gazzette* dealing with current events.[55] Presumably the authorities, concerned as usual with secrecy, discouraged these activities. What was printed was relatively anodyne. Albrizzi, for example, published a list of office-holders in 1673 under the title *Protogiornale Veneto*, and Coronelli published a similar *Giornale* for four consecutive years, 1713–16. Albrizzi also published flysheets about the wars with the Turks, for example the *Giornale del Campo Cesareo sotto Buda* (1686).

All the same, when early modern Venice is described as a centre of information and communication, it is above all on account of print. It was appropriate for Venice to become a printing centre

---

[53] Baschet (1870), 348–52; Ugo Tucci, 'Ranke and the Venetian Document Market', in Georg G. Iggers and James M. Powell (eds) *Leopold von Ranke and the Shaping of the Historical Discipline* (Syracuse: Syracuse University Press, 1990), 99–107, at 100; Preto (1994), 66.

[54] Amelot de Houssaie, *Gouvernement de Venise*, (Paris: 1685), preface.

[55] Valerio Castronovo, 'I primi sviluppi della stampa periodica fra cinque e seicento', in Castronuovo et al., *La stampa italiana dal '500 al '800* (Rome and Bari: Laterza, 1976), 1–65, at 20.

because it was already a centre for other kinds of communication, as an international port, as the capital of what was still in part a maritime empire, and as an unusually large city for this period.

In the course of the fifteenth century, more books were printed in Venice than in any other city in Europe (4,500 titles, in other words around 150 a year, and two and a half million copies seems a reasonable estimate).[56] In the sixteenth century, when the city began to lose this relative lead over other centres, Paris for example, book-production remained stable or even continued to increase. It has been estimated that about five hundred printers and publishers produced from 15,000 to 17,500 titles (150 to 175 a year) and possibly eighteen million copies in the course of the century.[57] The work of Aldus was continued by such printers as Gabriel Giolito, who printed about 850 books at Venice before his death in 1578, and owned shops in Bologna, Ferrara, and Naples.[58]

Scholars have emphasised the oligarchic structure of the printing industry in the fifteenth century, the small group in control. Jenson, for example, was supported by two merchants from Frankfurt. His press, with thirty employees, has been described as 'possibly the largest private industrial establishment in Venice'.[59] By the sixteenth century, on the other hand, the large number of rival printing houses was one of the attractions of Venice for Aretino and other professional writers of the time, like Ludovico Dolce, Ludovico Domenichi, Girolamo Ruscelli and Francesco Sansovino. These were the famous *poligrafi*, men who made a living without depending on patrons by producing what publishers such as Marcolini, Giolito, or Valgrisi thought would sell – prose and verse, fact and fiction, translations, adaptations and plagiarisms from other authors.[60]

Domenichi, for example, translated Alberti, Polybius and Xenophon. Dolce (who is supposed to have published no fewer than 358 works), wrote comedies, translated Euripides, edited Aretino,

---

[56] Gerulaitis (1976).
[57] Grendler (1977), 5–6; Martin (1993), 77.
[58] Salvatore Bongi, *Annali di Gabriel Giolito* (2 vols, Rome: Ministero della pubblica istruzione,1890).
[59] Lowry (1979), 18.
[60] Bareggi (1988).

Boccaccio, Castiglione and Petrarch and plagiarised a treatise on the art of memory. Ruscelli edited a rival version of Boccaccio's *Decameron*. Sansovino in particular specialized in providing practical information including a manual of letter-writing and a guide to Venice for visitors (to be discussed below). In other words, there was by the middle of the sixteenth century a 'Venetian Grub Street' which would probably not be parallelled until the seventeenth century in the Dutch Republic and the eighteenth century in London and Paris.[61]

Given the importance of rival information centres in early modern Europe, it is important to distinguish the domains in which Venice was strong from those in which it was relatively weak. One of these weak points was mathematics and natural philosophy (with exceptions such as Euclid, Archimedes and Tartaglia on mathematics, Vesalius and Colombo on anatomy, Fracastoro and Falloppio on medicine).[62] The reason may have been a division of labour between printers in Venice and in Padua, since a university town was an obvious place from which to publish this kind of book. On the other hand, in the military field, Venice played a dominant role. No fewer than 145 military books were printed there between 1492 and 1570.[63]

For books on the arts, Venice probably fell behind Florence, with the exception of illustrated treatises on architecture by Vitruvius, Alberti, Serlio, Palladio, Scamozzi, and so on, of which at least sixty editions appeared in two centuries, 1495–1694 (Appendix 1). Like Florence, Venice was a major centre for the publication of classics of vernacular literature. Castiglione's *Courtier*, for instance, the first edition published by Aldus in 1528, followed by at least forty-three more editions by 1606.[64] Like the works of Petrarch and Ariosto, the *Courtier* was provided by the *poligrafi* with an editorial apparatus to help the reader – tables of contents, marginal glosses,

---

[61] Martin (1993) 78n.

[62] Ezio Riondato et al., *Trattati scientifici nel Veneto fra il xv e il xvi secolo* (Vicenza: 1985), is less useful than the title suggests.

[63] John R. Hale, 'Printing and the Military Culture of Renaissance Venice' (1977: rpr in his *Renaissance War Studies*, London: Hambledon Press, 1983, 429–70).

[64] Peter Burke, *The Fortunes of the Courtier* (Cambridge: Polity Press, 1995), 158–62.

summaries, indexes and so on.[65] Venice was an early centre of music publication, associated in particular with Ottaviano dei Petrucci, who had a monopoly in this field from 1498 to 1520, and later with the Gardano family, active in this field for more than sixty years (1538–1600).

In history and geography, Venetian publishers was strong. Looking only at general books or reference books, we find at least eight editions of Ptolemy's geography (translated from the Greek by Ruscelli) published in the sixteenth century by Pedrezano and others. Botero's *Relazioni Universali* went through nine editions in Venice between 1599 and 1671. Venetian printed maps of the sixteenth century have an important place in the history of cartography. The Venetians published more than one edition of Guicciardini's classic history of Italy, and at least three of Giovio's history of his own time (translated into Italian by Domenichi and edited by Ruscelli). They published Gonzalez de Mendoza on China and the Jesuit letters on Japan. They published chronologies such as Sansovino's world chronology (1580) and its rival, Bardi's universal chronology (1581), as well as Marco Guazzo's history of the world. The most important works of contemporary history published in Venice in the seventeenth century are listed in Appendix four.

Cosmopolitan publishing

One reason for the importance of Venice as a communication centre was that the presence of many foreigners, temporarily or permanently. Venice was a point of 'confluence of divergent traditions', Greek, Jewish, German, 'Slavonian', and so on.[66] It was via a diaspora of German printers that the process of printing with moveable type spread through Europe, one of many examples of the importance of diaspora in European cultural history. In Venice, the first printer was Johan von Speyer, who arrived in the city in 1469. By 1500 about twenty-five German printing firms had opened in

---

[65] Brian Richardson, *Print Culture in Renaissance Italy* (Cambridge: Cambridge University Press, 1994); Burke (1995), 42–3.
[66] McNeill (1974), 157.

the city.[67] Printers also included Frenchmen (Nicolas Jenson, who arrived c1471, and Vincent Vaugris, who arrived from Lyon in 1530s, and became known as Valgrisi). Aldus Manutius, whose family came from Bassiano near Rome, was also an immigrant.

The existence of sub-cultures within Venice made it possible for local printers to play the role of cultural middlemen more fully than elsewhere. Venice was not unique in this respect in the sixteenth and seventeenth centuries. Rome, Istanbul, Lyon, Antwerp, Seville and Amsterdam were all cosmopolitan cities with ethnic sub-cultures. All the same, a distinctive feature of Venice as an information centre was a polyglossia linked to the importance of its minorities.[68] For example, it was obviously easier to publish Greek books in Venice than in many other cities because Greek refugees from the Turks came to Venice, especially after the fall of the Byzantine empire in 1453. The role of Greek scholars, such as Musurus in editing classical Greek texts is well known, but a thought should also be spared for the compositors, who were presumably Greeks as well.[69]

Publishing in ancient Greek in Venice has been studied in detail.[70] The first Greek text printed in Venice was in 1471 (Pertusi's correction of the traditional date of 1486), while Aldus entered this field in 1494.[71] The best-known of Greek printers was probably Zacharias Callergi (Kalliergis), together with his partner the merchant Nicholas Vlastos, both originally from Crete. Janos Grigoropoulos corrected proofs for him and for Aldus.[72] Other Greek

---

[67] F. Geldner, *Die deutsche Inkunabeldrucker* (2 vols, Stuttgart: Hiersemann, 1968–70), vol. 2, 61–97.

[68] Lucien Romier, 'Lyon et le cosmopolitanisme', *Bibliothèque d'Humanisme et Renaissance* 11 (1949), 28–42; Peter Burke, *Antwerp: a Metropolis in Comparative Perspective* (Antwerp: Martial and Snoeck, 1993); Guido Marnef, *Antwerp in the Age of Reformation* (English translation, Baltimore: Johns Hopkins University Press, 1996).

[69] Burke (1993).

[70] Enrica Follieri, 'Il libro greco per i greci nelle imprese editoriali romane e veneziane della prima metà del Cinquecento', in Beck (1977), 483–508; Léandre Vranoussis, 'Les imprimeries vénitiennes et les premiers livres grecs', ibid. 509–20.

[71] Alessandro Pertusi, 'Per la storia e le fonti delle prime grammatiche greche a stampa', *Italia medievale e umanistica* 5 (1962), 323–4.

[72] *Dizionario Biografico degli Italiani* (henceforward DBI: 46 vols, in progress, Rome: Instituto della Enciclopedia Italiana, 1960–) 16, 750–3.

printers included Demetrios Zenos, active in the 1520s; Dominikos Hetepolonios, who was printing in 1602; and Nikolaos Saros, active 1689–95.[73] These enterprises seem to have been small ones, but large firms like Sessa and Zanetti published in Greek occasionally, sometimes the classics, sometimes the liturgy. From 1509 onwards, Venetians also printed books in demotic Greek for export throughout the Greek-speaking world, beginning with the *Apokopos* of Bergadhis, reprinted more than once in Venice before the end of the century.[74]

From the beginning of the sixteenth century, when the Jews began to arrive from Spain, the Hebrew press in Venice was 'the most important in Europe'.[75] This aspect of Venetian publishing has also been studied in detail. Among the printers were Daniel Bomberg, originally from Antwerp, active 1515–48, and producing some 200 titles, notably the Talmud (one assumes that the compositors too were Jewish). It is somewhat more surprising to find two Venetian patricians in the business; Marco Antonio Giustiniani, active 1545–51, who squeezed Bomberg out but was ruined when the Council of Ten forbade printing in Hebrew; and Alvise Bragadin, who accused Giustinian of trying to ruin him but was active 1550–74 (the family continued the business). Jewish printers included the Parenzo family, Asher and Meir, who helped Bragadin, active 1545–96; and Giovanni di Gara, active 1563–1600.[76]

Venice was also a centre of production of translations of Arabic books, thanks perhaps to the tradition of trade in the Middle East, but this aspect of Venetian publishing has attracted less attention. Arab works translated into Latin were already being published in the late fifteenth century. Avicenna, for instance, was published in

---

[73] *Catalogue of Seventeenth-Century Italian Books in the British Library* (3 vols, London: British Library, 1986).
[74] Linos Politis, 'Venezia come centro della stampa e della diffusione della prima letteratura neoellenica', in Beck (1977), 443–82; David Holton, ed., *Literature and Society in Renaissance Crete* (Cambridge: Cambridge University Press, 1991), 4–6, 71–3.
[75] Grendler (1977), 90.
[76] Alfredo Cioni, 'Bomberg', DBI 11, 382–7; Grendler (1977), 90–3, 255; Avraham Rosenthal, 'Daniel Bomberg and his Talmud editions', *Gli Ebrei e Venezia*, ed. Gaetano Cozzi (Milan, 1987), 375–416; Fausto Parente, 'La chiesa e il Talmud', *Storia d'Italia, Annali* 11 (Turin: Einaudi, 1996), 524–643, esp. 580–9.

Venice in 1486, and at least thirteen more times by 1595. Averroes did not do so well, though there were editions of works of his on 1542 and 1553, not to mention the commentaries. The astrologer Abd Al-Aziz was printed in 1482, 1491, 1512, 1521, etc.[77] It was in 1538 that a Venetian printer, Paganino de Paganinis, produced a Koran in Arabic, presumably to sell in the Ottoman Empire (despite the prohibition).[78] Another, Arrivabene, published a Koran in Italian in 1547. Books about the Muslim world will be discussed below.

The role of Venice (like its rival Tübingen) in the publication of books in Old Church Slavonic and Croat also deserves to be emphasised (Appendix 2). A few 'Slavonian' printers established there printed books in their own language: Jakov iz Kamene Reke, for instance, Jeronim Zagurovic, Frano Ratkov and above all the Vukovic family, active 1519–80. Other Venetian firms also catered for this market, including Andrea Torresano, the father-in-law of Aldus: Marcolini; Bindoni; and Rampazetto. The majority of these books, sixty in all, were liturgical texts in Cyrillic or Glagolitic, in other words (as in the case of music publication) information for performance. However, there were also a few vernacular literary texts, now considered the early classics of Croat literature, by authors such as Marko Marulic, Marin Drzic, Hanibal Lucic, Petar Hektorovic, Petar Zoranic, Dinko Zlataric, and Ivan Gundulic. These were printed in the Latin alphabet. There was one translation from Italian into Croat, Tasso's *Aminta*, as well as translations from Croat into Italian.[79]

Finally, the Spanish connection deserves to be emphasised. A considerable number of Spanish books were published in Venice. For example, the famous romance of chivalry *Amadis de Gaula* was published in Venice in Spanish by Pedrezano (a printer who seems to have specialized in Spanish books), in 1533. Giolito published the works of the Spanish poets Juan Boscán and Garcilaso

---

[77] Alfred F. Johnson, Victor Scholderer and D. A. Clarke, *Short-Title Catalogue of Books Printed in Italy from 1465 to 1600 now in the British Museum* (London: British Museum, 1958).

[78] A. Nuovo, *Alessandro Paganino* (Padua:, 1990).

[79] Josip Badalic, *Jugoslavia usque ad annum 1600* (Baden-Baden: 1959); cf W. Schmitz. *Südslavische Buchdruck in Venedig* (Giessen:, 1977).

de la Vega and even Spanish translations of Ariosto and Giovio, presumably for export either to Spain or to Milan. Medina's *Arte del navegar* was published in Spanish by Pedrezano, while Jorge de Montemayor's pastoral novel *Diana* was published by Comin de Trino (Appendix 3). Books translated from Spanish were much more numerous, and some of them will be discussed in the section dealing with the world beyond Europe. An important figure in mediating between Venice and Spanish culture was Alfonso de Ulloa, a Spanish gentleman who became a leading *poligrafo* in Venice.

As in the cases of Greek, Hebrew and Slavonic books, the presence in Venice of writers from the culture facilitated the task of the printers. The texts of the *Celestina*, *Amadís*, and Primaleón (another romance of chivalry), were all revised by the writer Francisco Delicado, who seems to have worked regularly for the publisher Pedrezano. The Spanish nobleman Alfonso de Ulloa spent over twenty years in Venice (1548–70), beginning his career there as secretary to Hurtado and later turning *poligrafo* and working for Giolito and others not only as an original writer (the author of a biography of Charles V), but also as a translator and as an editor (Montemayor's *Diana* appeared 'corregida y revista por Alfonso Ulloa').[80]

Venice was also a centre for the publication of translations from Spanish into Italian, whether of moral works like those of Guevara (a sixteenth-century best-seller whose letters became a school textbook in Italy), works of piety such as those by Luis de Granada, or works of history (especially the history of the New World, to be discussed below). Ulloa translated Columbus, Covarrubias, Mexía, Urrea, and Zárate into Italian. Works of Spanish fiction published in Italian in Venice included not only romances of chivalry such as *Amadís* and *Tirant lo Blanc* but also *Don Quixote* and the picaresque novels *Lazarillo*, *Guzmán* and *Justina*, thanks in large part to the efforts of a single printer, Barezzo Barezzi, who translated most of them himself.[81]

---

[80] Antonio Rumeu de Armas, *Alfonso de Ulloa: introductor de la cultura española in Italia* (Madrid: Gredos, 1973); Bareggi(1988).

[81] DBI, s.v. 'Barezzi'.

The world beyond Europe

News of the discovery of America reached Venice later than Rome, Paris and Florence).[82] All the same, thanks perhaps to the Spanish connection, Venice was second only to Paris in terms of the amount of Americana published in the sixteenth century. It included accounts by Columbus, Vespucci, Cortés, and Oviedo (whose *Summario* was published in 1534), as well as a plagiarism of Pietro Martire d'Anghiera (the anonymous *Libretto de tutte le navigationi del Re di Spagna* of 1504), and the later histories of Mexico, Peru and so on by López de Gómara, Cieza, Zarate, Benzoni and others. For example, twelve editions of the Italian translation of López de Gómara were published in Venice between 1557 and 1599, and at least six editions of the translation of Cieza between 1555 and 1576.[83]

Some accounts of the discoveries were either written or compiled in Venice, like the collection of *Navigationi e viaggi* (3 vols, 1550–9) edited by the Venetian civil servant Giovanni Battista Ramusio.[84] Ramusio, who had already edited Oviedo's *Summario*, was a member of a group of intellectuals interested in the New World: Bembo, for instance, Fracastoro, and Andrea Navagero, who used his time in Spain as a diplomat not only to study the peninsula but also to make friends with Pietro Martire and to forward information about the New World to Ramusio.

In any case, Venice was already a centre of printed information about the 'East' linked to travels of merchants and others.[85] At least four editions of Marco Polo were published there 1496–c1555 (including the first edition in Italian), and nine of the the fictitious travels of 'Sir John Mandeville', 1491–1567.[86] Luigi Ronsaggio, a

---

[82] Angela Caracciolo Aricò, 'Il nuovo mondo e l'umanesimo: immagini e miti dell'editoria veneziana', in Aricò (1990), 25–33, at 25.

[83] Ambrosini (1982), especially 81n; Donatella Ferro, 'Traduzioni di opere spagnole sulla scoperta dell'America nell'editoria veneziana del cinquecento', in Aricò (1990), 93–105.

[84] Donald Lach, *Asia in the Making of Europe* (Chicago: Chicago University Press, 1965), 163–4, 180–1; Massimo Donattini, 'Giambattista Ramusio e le sue *Navigationi*', in *Critica storica* 17, 55–100.

[85] Lach (1965).

[86] Johnson, Scholderer etc (1958).

factor in Egypt and Syria who travelled in India, published his *Viaggio di Colocut* in 1539. Federici's *Viaggio nell'India Orientale* was published in 1587 (appearing in English translation in Hakluyt's famous collection only a year later), and Balbi 's *Viaggio dell'Indie Orientali* in 1590. The history of the East Indies by Lopes de Castanheda and the history of China by Gonzalez de Mendoza appeared in Venice in Italian translation in 1577 and 1586 respectively.

There was particular interest in Persia. Ambrogio Contarini's account of his mission to the Shah of Persia in the 1470s (to arrange an alliance against the Turks) was published in 1487, and again in 1524 and 1543, while Caterino Zeno's account of a similar mission, also in the 1470s, was published in 1558.[87] G. T. Minadoi's history of the wars between the Turks and the Persians was published in 1588 and again in 1594. Pietro della Valle's account of the shah, *Abbas re di Persia*, was published in 1628. and his general description of Persia in 1661.

Needless to say, the Ottoman Empire attracted even more public interest in Venice (despite the qualms of the Council of Ten). Giovio's famous account of the Turks was published four times between 1538 and 1541. Benedetto Ramberti's *Le tre cose de' Turchi*, a first-hand account by a Venetian, was published in 1539. G. P. Contarini's account of the war between sultan Selim and Venice was published in 1572. The biggest publishing success, however, was probably Francesco Sansovino's *Historia Universale de'Turchi*, first published in 1560 and reaching its eighth edition in 1600. [88]

What was published, as in the case of religion, was not always what the authorities would have liked. Three editions of Giovio on the Turks were anonymous, as if the printers were aware of the official concern with the subject which the Soranzo case reveals (above, p.84).

To sum up this section of the chapter. I have tried to suggest that the Venetians produced, circulated and received the information

---

[87] Johnson, Scholderer etc (1958).

[88] Paolo Preto, *Venezia e i turchi* (); Stéphane Yérasimos, 'De la collection des voyages à l'histoire universelle: la *Historia universale de' Turchi* de Francesco Sansovino', *Turcica* 20 (1988), 19–41.

they deserved in the sense that in certain important respects the information structure was related to, if not a simple expression of, the economic, social and political system. As Kissling has suggested, the fact that Venice was a 'mercantile state' rather than a feudal-agrarian one was reflected in its information services, dependent, especially in the fifteenth century, on a network of merchants.[89] I have illustrated this point in the last few pages, as well as adding two of my own. In the first place, I have emphasised the contribution of Venetian sub-cultures (Greek, Jewish, Slavonian and so on) to the polyglot printing for which the city was famous. In the second place, I have discussed the relation between the circulation of political information in and around Venice and the distinctive structure of the state. A regime with a Maggior Consiglio of some two thousand members cannot keep its secrets. Hence both the leakage of politically sensitive information and the recurrent attempts to stop the leaks, from prohibiting patricians from meeting foreign ambassadors to the discouragement of printed journalism.

Intellectual involution

It is time to consider changes in the system during the early modern period. Change in Venice in this period has usually been presented in terms of 'decline', whether economic, political or cultural, and assessments of the fortunes of the Venetian book trade are no exception to this rule. As early as 1603, the Senate expressed the fear that the printing industry was virtually disappearing, 'annichilando grandemente'.[90] Later historians of Venetian publishing have told an almost equally sad story. One has emphasised the decline in the numbers of printers (as of other craftsmen) in the seventeenth century. Another has treated the period from 1600 to the 1680s as one of prolonged 'crisis'.[91] William McNeill is excep-

---

[89] Kissling (1977).

[90] Quoted Brown (1891), 218.

[91] Paolo Ulvioni, 'Stampatori e librai a Venezia nel '600', *Archivio Veneto* 54 (1977), 93–124, at 108; Mario Infelise, *L'editoria veneziana nel '700* (Milan: Angeli, 1989), 9–11.

tional in his insistence that Venice remained a cultural 'metropolis' as late as 1669.[92]

Decline in a relative sense over the long term there surely was, for at least two reasons. In the first place, Venetian tolerance for other cultures and other religions, the practical live-and-let-live attitude of merchants, was undermined by the spread of the Counter-Reformation, at least from the arrival of Giovanni Della Casa as papal nuncio in 1544. The Inquisition was established in Venice in 1547, books were burned on piazza San Marco and near the Rialto in 1548, a Venetian Index was produced in 1549, and a ban on Hebrew printing issued in 1554 (lasting till 1563).

The fate of Guillaume Postel illustrates the change in climate. This unorthodox scholar returned to Venice around 1547. He was appointed chaplain of the Ospedaletto and censor of Hebrew books. He was also confessor to Madre Giovanna, a charismatic holy woman whom he believed to be the new Messiah. However, Postel was forced to leave Venice in 1549. He returned soon after, but was interrogated by the Inquisition in 1555, declared insane and imprisoned in Ravenna.[93]

Booksellers began to be interrogated on charges of smuggling heretical or otherwise pernicious books from abroad. In 1570, for example, an inquisition raid revealed copies of Machiavelli in shops of Gilio Bonfadio, Vincenzo Valgrisi, Pietro da Fino, and Gabriele Giolito. Some printers migrated to other cities such as Turin, Rome and Naples, in sufficient numbers to alarm the senate in 1601.[94] Others, such as Gabriel Giolito, shifted their investments towards the publication of devotional books in Italian for a geographically more limited market. Giolito himself translated Luis de Granada.

In the second place, the discovery of the new world undermined the importance of Venice as an information centre and commercial centre alike in the long run, by shifting the centre of gravity of

---

[92] McNeill (1974).

[93] Kuntz (1981); idem, ed., *Postello, Venezia e suo mondo* (Florence: Olschki, 1988), especially 119–36.

[94] Horatio F. Brown, *The Venetian Printing Press* (London: Nimmo, 1891), 175; Tiziana Pesenti, 'Stampatori e letterati', Arnaldi 4 (1983), pt 1, 93–129 103.

Europe westwards towards the Atlantic. The Turkish occupation of Syria and Egypt reinforced the change.[95] Lucien Febvre, writing to Henri Pirenne, once wished he could juxtapose two maps, one showing that in 1490 Venice was 'le centre privilégié du monde économique connu', the other showing that in 1600 'elle n'était plus qu'une cité périphérique'.[96] It was therefore time for another city to take over the role of Europe's centre of information and communication. The immediate successor to Venice was Antwerp, about which a Venetian envoy admitted that 'I saw Venice outdone'.[97] In similar fashion the Venetian merchant Giovanni Zonca commented in the 1560s on the *grande libertade* of Antwerp.[98] After the Spanish recapture of Antwerp and the blockade of the Scheldt, it would be the turn of Amsterdam.

All the same, the decline of Venice relative to other centres should not be treated as absolute, or exaggerated, or dated too early, or linked too closely to the numbers of printers, even if William McNeill may have been a little too generous in describing Venice as a 'cultural metropolis' in the 1660s. Rather than a steady decline or a simple continuity, what I see is an ebb and flow of different kinds of information. For example, a revival of printing took place at the end of the seventeenth century, culminating (from the information point of view) in the ten-volume encyclopaedia, the *Nuovo dizionario scientifico*, edited by Pivati and published by Milocco between 1746 and 1751.[99] From the 1750s onwards, however, the printing industry began to decline once more.[100]

Again, in the early seventeenth century, Venice seems to have been more of a centre of scientific information than ever before. Galileo was attracted to the city at the beginning of the seventeenth century, a time when a number of patricians were interested in 'nat-

---

[95] Febvre to Pirenne (1922) in Bryce Lyon, *The Birth of Annales History* (Brussels: Académie Royale, 1991), 95.

[96] Quoted Lyon, (1991), 38.

[97] Quoted John J. Murray, *Antwerp in the Age of Plantin and Breughel* (Norman: University of Oklahoma Press, 1970), 43.

[98] Marnef (1996), 3.

[99] Silvano Garofalo, *L'enciclopedismo italiano: Gianfrancesco Pivati* (Ravenna: Longo, 1980).

[100] Infelise (1989), 275–94.

ural philosophy', and it was there that he learned of the new Dutch telescope which he proceeded to imitate. At this time Paolo Sarpi was the centre of an international network of communication which included letters, visits to his convent by foreigners, and the bookshop the *Nave d'Oro*, where he met his friends and held court.[101]

The postal system continued to expand in this period. By the early seventeenth century, there were weekly couriers from Venice to Brussels (departing on Fridays), and Vienna (departing on Saturdays), as well as fortnightly couriers to Lyon and monthly couriers to Istanbul.[102] In 1684, it was explained that letters could be sent via the ordinary couriers of Venice to the Netherlands, Germany, Sweden, Denmark, Poland and Istanbul.[103] It is likely that political and geographical factors rather than economic ones underlay this expansion. It was not so much a matter of Venice setting up a system as of the imperial court, say, communicating with Istanbul through Venice.

In the sphere of clandestine publication, what we see is continuity, despite attempts at repression. The satires of Ferrante Pallavicino, who lived in Venice from about 1636 and died because he let himself be tempted away from it, were probably published in the city under false imprints. A leading printer, Marco Ginammi, published Machiavelli in 1630 and 1648, and may have published the pornographic *Alicibiade fanciullo a scuola* ('Oranges', 1652).[104] In 1653, the Senate expressed its alarm at the 'clandestine printing of impious, obscene and satirical works (*opere empie, obscene, malediche*), and forebade printers to put false places of publication on the titlepage.[105] Two years later, however, Giovanni Maria Turrini, another leading printer (who had published what he called the 'permitted works' of Ferrante Pallavicino in 1654), was accused of publishing heretical books.[106] It is likely that Meietti, who repub-

---

[101] Peter Burke (ed.) *Paolo Sarpi* (New York: Washington Square Press, 1967); Peter Burke, *Venice and Amsterdam* (second edition, Cambridge: Polity Press, 1994), 97.
[102] Ottavio Cotogno, *Compendio delle poste* (Milan: Bidelli, 1623), 208–12, 454–5.
[103] Giuseppe Miselli, *Il burattino veridico* (Rome: 1684), 172.
[104] Grendler (1977), 165–7, 285.
[105] Quoted Brown (1891), 227.
[106] Preto (1994), 173.

lished most of Sarpi's works between 1673 and 1685 (occasionally claiming to do so not in Venice but in Mirandola), reprinted the forbidden *History of the Council of Trent*.

The Venetian *poligrafi* of the sixteenth century are well known. Less familiar are their equivalents in the mid-seventeenth century, a second wave. This second group specialized in publishing books on recent history and sometimes in supplying more up-to-date information on a private basis. They included count Maiolino Bisaccioni, who lived and wrote in Venice for nearly thirty years, c. 1635–63; Giambattista Birago Avogadro, who spent most of his life there; and Girolamo Brusoni (best known as a novelist but also active as a historian). Venetian publishers (notably Ginammi, Baba, Baglioni and Combi) printed the work of a wide range of Italian historians, together with the occasional foreigner, such as Pierre Mathieu. In the age of the Thirty Years' War and the 'revolutions' of the 1640s, contemporary history seems to have sold well. Turrini published Ricci's account of the Thirty Years' War, *De bellis germanicis*, in 1649, only a year after the making of peace. The official printer Pinelli published regular accounts of Venetian naval engagements. As Appendix 4 shows, Venetian presses published a good deal about the history of central and eastern Europe, appropriately enough, since the postal service from Italy to these regions went through Venice.

Books in Greek especially liturgical books, continued to be printed by Antonio Pinelli (1603–31) and his family, and also by Andrea Giuliano (1656–87). Given its links with the Ottoman Empire, it is not surprising to find that Venice was one of the first European cities to establish coffee-houses, c1645. Florian's goes back to 1720. Newspapers were available there in the eighteenth century as they were in the 'Bottega di Cafè' on Campo San Stefano. In 1778, a witness describes another café, 'La regina d'Ungheria', as a centre of *novellisti*.[107]

The wider world was not completely forgotten. For example, Venice was one of the few places in the world where Armenian books were printed, eight of them in the sixteenth century (all by

---

[107] Preto (1994), 92.

Armenian printers), more than thirty in the seventeenth century, and still more in the eighteenth century, when the Bortali family specialized in this line of publishing.[108] Four works on the Americas by Bartolomé de Las Casas were printed by Marco Ginammi between 1626 and 1643 in both Spanish and Italian versions.[109] Two editions of the travels of Pietro della Valle in the Orient were published by Baglioni in the 1660s. G. F. Marini's account of the Jesuit missions in Tonkin and Japan were published by Storti in 1665. Three editions of the Italian translation of the *History of the Conquest of Mexico* by Antonio de Solis were published by Poletti in Venice in 1704, 1715 and 1733. The great tradition of Venetian geography was revived by Vincenzo Coronelli, who published his multi-volume world atlas with Albrizzi between 1691 and 1697, at a time when the printing industry was beginning to revive.[110] It was in Venice that the contemporary historian Birago Avogadro published his history of Africa in 1650, and Giovanni Sagredo his history of the Ottoman sultans in 1688.[111] The Englishman Paul Rycaut's history of the Turks was published in translation by Combi in 1673. The Venetian physician Nicolao Manucci, who was inspired by Marco Polo's example to see the world and who lived in India from the 1650s onwards, sent the manuscript of his history of the Mughal Empire to the Venetian senate, hoping that they would publish it.[112] A fellow-physician who travelled the same route and met Manucci in India, Angelo Legrenzi, published *Il Pellegrino nell'Asia* in Venice in 1705.[113]

However, Manucci's hopes were disappointed. Indeed, a pro-

---

[108] Baykar Sivazliyan, 'Venezia per l'oriente: la nascita del libro armeno', in *Armeni, Ebrei, Greci stampatori a Venezia* (Venice:, 1989), 23–38.

[109] Ambrosini (1982), 144–50; Angela Nuovo, 'L'editoria veneziana del xvii secolo e il problema americano', in Aricò (1990), 175–86.

[110] A. de Ferrari, 'Coronelli', DBI 29, 305–9; Teresa Colletta, 'Vincenzo Coronelli', in Colletta et al., *Libro e incisione a venezia nei secoli xvii e xviii* (Vicenza: Neri Pozzo, 1988), 1–32.

[111] G. Birago Avogadro, *Historia Africana* (Venice: Cestari, 1650); Giovanni Sagredo, *Monarchi Ottomani* (Venice: Combi, 1688).

[112] Nicolao Manucci, *Historia do Mogor* (English translation, London: 1907–8); Grossato (1994), 93–102.

[113] Grossato (1994), 103–6.

cess of what might be called 'intellectual involution' became visible quite early in the seventeenth century, if not before. 'Involution' is not a euphemism for decline, but a way of describing a shift. The city gradually became less metropolitan and more provincial. In the economic sphere, for example, Venice became a centre of regional rather than international trade.[114] From the communication point of view, the city was most important in the later period as a centre of information about itself. This was the positive aspect of involution, and a response to the increasing numbers of visitors to the city. Books published in Venice and about Venice included Gasparo Contarini's treatise on the government, with at least six Venetian editions in Latin or Italian between 1544 and 1591; the histories of Venice by Paolo Paruta (1605, 1645), Paolo Morosini (1637), and especially of Battista Nani (1662, 1663, 1676, 1679, 1686); Stringa's description of the church of San Marco (1610); Luca Assarino's *Meraviglie dell'Arsenale* (1639); Marco Boschini's *Minere della pintura* (1664), oriented towards foreign tourism; and Cristoforo Ivanovich's history of Venetian opera, *Minerva al Tavolino* (1681). Gozzi's famous *Gazzetta Veneta* (1760), one of the most famous examples of Enlightenment moral journalism, also offered information about the city.

Especially important were Francesco Sansovino's guides to the city, the little dialogue *Cose notabili*, first published in 1556, and the massive treatise *Venezia città nobilissima*, of 1581. Between them, these guides had passed through at least 38 editions by 1692, from thirteen different publishers: Calepino, Cestari, Comin, Curti, Didini, Farri, Herz, Imberti, Miloco, Rampazzetto, Salicato, Spineda, Tramontin, Valgrisi, Valvassori, Viani (Appendix 4). The dialogue appeared under various titles (*Cose maravigliose*; *Cose maravigliose e notabili*; *Cose notabili e maravigliose*) and even authors (Sansovino's name being replaced on occasion by that of Anselmo Guisconi or Girolamo Bardi). In the case of *Venezia città nobilissima*, the titlepages proclaim the superiority of each successive edition, the information being 'riformate, accommodate e grandemente ampliate', 'con nuova aggiunta', etc, thanks to the work of four different edi-

---

[114] Jean Georgelin, *Venise au siècle des lumières* (Paris and the Hague: Mouton, 1978).

tors (Giovanni Niccolo Doglioni, disguised as 'Leonico Goldioni'; Stringa; Martinioni; and Zittio). The number of copies of these works to be found in foreign libraries (notably in France) suggests their importance to foreign visitors for more than a century. They were eventually replaced by Coronelli's *Guida de'forestieri*, which had reached its fourth edition by 1700.

One might treat the fate of Sansovino's books as symbolic. His studies of the Turks were forgotten, while his guides to Venice continued to sell. There had been a time when foreigners went to Venice to learn about the contemporary world. By the seventeenth century, they were going to admire the city's past.

APPENDIX 1: SELECT ARCHITECTURAL BOOKS PUBLISHED IN VENICE

1495 Vitruvius, Latin (Pensis)
1511 Vitruvius, Latin (Tacuino)
1524 Vitruvius, Italian (Sabio)
1535 Vitruvius, Italian (Zoppino)
1537 Serlio, 4 (Marcolini)
1540 Serlio, 3 (Marcolini)
1544 Serlio, 3 (Marcolini)
1544 Serlio, 4 (Marcolini)
1546 Alberti, Italian (Vaugris)
c. 1551 Serlio, 1–2 (Sessa)
1551 Serlio, 3 (Sessa)
1551 Serlio (Marcolini)
1551 Serlio, 4 (Sessa)
1551 Serlio, 5 (Sessa)
1554 Cattaneo, 1–4 (Aldo)
1554 Palladio, Antichità (Pagan)
1556 Vitruvius, Italian (Franceschi)
1556 Vitruvius, Italian (Marcolini)
1557 Serlio (Sessa)
1558 Serlio (Sessa)
1559 Serlio, 5 (Sessa)
1560 Serlio 1–2 (Sessa)
1562 Serlio, 3 (Sessa)

c. 1562 Serlio, 4 (Marcolini)
1562 Serlio (Rampazzetto)
1565 Alberti, Italian (Franceschi)
1565 Palladio, Antichità (Varisco)
1566 Serlio, 1-5 (Francesco Senese and Zuanne Krugher)
1567 Cattaneo, 1-8 (Aldo)
1567 Vitruvius, Italian (Franceschi)
1567 Serlio, Libro estraordinario (Sessa)
1568-9 Serlio, 1-5, Latin (Francesco Senese and Zuanne Krugher)
1569 Serlio, Book 5 (Sessa)
1569 Serlio (Franceschi)
1570 Palladio, Due libri (Franceschi)
1570 Palladio, Quattro libri (Franceschi)
1570 Vignola
1576 Labacco, Architettura (Porro)
1581 Palladio, Quattro libri (Carampello)
1582 Vignola (Ziletti)
1583 Scamozzi, Antichità (Ziletti)
1584 Serlio, 1-7 (Franceschi)
1584 Vitruvius, Italian (Francheschi)
1590 Rusconi (Giolito)
1596 Vignola (Porro)
1600 Serlio, 1-7 (Franceschi)
c1600 Vignola (Doino)
1601 Palladio, Quattro libri (Carampello)
1603 Vignola (Franco)
1615 Scamozzi, Idea (Valentino)
1616 Palladio, Quattro libri (Carampello)
1618 Serlio (Franceschi)
1619 Serlio, 1-7 (Franceschi)
1629 Vitruvius, Italian (Vecchi)
1641 Vitruvius, Italian (Turrini)
1642 Palladio (Brogiollo)
c. 1648 Vignola (Remondini)
1663 Serlio, 1-6 (Combi)
1663 Serlio (Hertz)
1694 Scamozzi (Albrizzi)

Sources: STC: Michel and Michel, *Répertoire* (8 vols, Paris 1967); L. H. Fowler, The Fowler Architectural Collection (Baltimore, 1961). I should like to thank Juergen Schulz for helping me compile this list.

Appendix 2: Slavonic Texts published in Venice, 1493–1600

1493 *Breviarium Croaticum* (Torresano)
1495 *Pishtule* (Damiano)
1512 *Molitvenik* (Ratkov)
1512 *Officia BVM* (Ratkov)
1512 *Officia S. Brigittae* (Ratkov)
1519 *Psaltir* (Vukovic)
1519 *Molitvenik* (Vukovic)
1519 *Sluzhabnik* (Vukovic)
1521 Marulic, *Judit* (Fontanetto)
1522 Marulic, *Judit* (Benalio)
1522 Marulic, *Judit* (Negri)
1527 *Introductorium* (Torresano)
1527 *Molitvenik* (Vukovic)
1527 *Sluzhabnik* (Vukovic)
1528 *Bukvar* (anon)
1528 Misali (Bindoni)
1536 *Molitvenik* (Vukovic)
c1536 *Sobornik* (Vukovic)
1537 *Oktoich* (Vukovic)
1538 *Sobornik* (Vukovic)
c.1538 *Molitvenik* (Vukovic)
1543 *Pishtule* (Sessa)
1546 *Psaltir* (Vukovic)

1547 *Molitvenik* (Vukovic)
1549 Dimitrovic, *Sedam piesni* (Bascarini)
1549 Drzic, *Tirena* (anon)
1551 Drzic, *Pjesni* (anon)
1554 *Sluzhabnik* (Vukovic)
1556 Lucic, *Skladanya* (Marcolini)
1560 *Molitvenik* (Vukovic)
1561 *Breviarium* (Torresani)
1561 *Horarium* (Giunta)
1561 *Psaltir* (Vukovic)
1561 *Triody* (Vukovic)
1562 *Kato* (Temperica)
1562 *Missale* (anon)
c1565 Divkovic, *Nauk karstianski* (anon)
1566 *Chasoslovec* (Jakov iz Kamene Reke)
1567 Gradic, *Libarze* (Guerra)
1568 Hektorovic, *Ribanja* (Camotio)
1569 Hektorovic, *Piesni* (anon)
1569 Zoranic, *Planine* (Farri)
1569 *Psaltir* (Zagurovic)
1569 *Sluzhabnik* (Zagurovic)
1570 *Trebnik* (Zagurovic)
c1570 *Sluzhabnik* (Zagurovic)
1571 *Officia BVM* (Barom)
1571 *Officia S. Brigittae* (Barom)
1571 *Svjatki* (Barom)
1572 *Razlicnie potrebi* (Jakov)
1580 *Psaltir* (Vukovic)
1580 Zlataric, *Aminta* (Guerra)
1582 Jerkovic, *Bogoljubna* (Rampazetto)
1584 Krnarutic, *Vazetye Sigetta* (d'Albe)
1585 Lucic, *Robinja* (Mazoletto)
1585 *Nauk Katolicaski* (anon)
1586 Krnarutic, *Pirama i Tizbe* (Bindoni)
1586 Marulic, *Judit* (Bindoni)
1586 *Pishtole* (Rampazetto)
1595 Vrancic, *Dictionarium* (Moreto)

1596 *Pishtole* (anon)
1597 *Molitvenik* (Rampazetto)
1597 Zlataric, *Elektra/Aminta* (Aldus)
1599 Cubranovic, *Jeghiupka* (Salicato)

Source: Josip Badalic, *Jugoslavia usque ad annum 1600* (Baden-Baden, 1959).

APPENDIX 3: TEXTS IN SPANISH PUBLISHED IN VENICE

1523 *Celestina* (anon)
1528 Delicado, *Lozana*
1531 *Celestina*
1533 *Amadís* (Pedrazano)
1534 Oviedo, *Summario*
1534 *Primaleón* (Pedrazano)
1548 Avila, Comentario (Çornoça)
1552 Avila, Comentario (Marcolini)
1552 Nuñez, *Clareo y Floriseo* (Giolito)
1553 Ulloa (ed) *Processo de cartas de amores* (Giolito)
1553 Ulloa (trans) *Sentencias y dichos* (Giolito)
1553 anon, *Questión de amor* (Giolito)
1553 Guevara, *Libro aureo* (Giolito)
1553 Homer, *Ulyxea* (Giolito)
1553 Ariosto, *Orlando*, trans Urrea (Giolito)
1553 Boscán, *Obras*, with Garcilaso de la Vega (Giolito)
1553 San Pedro, *Carcel de Amor* (Giolito)
1553 *Celestina*, ed Ulloa (Giolito)
1553 Mexia, *Silva* (Giolito)
1555 Medina, *Arte del navegar* (Pederzano)
1558 Giovio, *Impresas* (Giolito)
1566 Urrea, *De la verdadera honra* (Grifo)
1567 Petrarch, *Sonetos* (Bevilacqua)

1568 Leone Ebreo, *Diálogos*, trans Costa
1568 Montemayor, *Diana* (Comin)
1569 Ulloa, Commentarios (Farri)
1574 Montemayor, *Diana* (Comin)
1626 Las Casas, *Relación* (Ginammi)
1644 Las Casas, *Conquista* (Ginammi)

Sources: Antonio Palau Dulcet: Rumeu (1973)

APPENDIX 4: SELECT SEVENTEENTH-CENTURY WORKS ON RECENT HISTORY

1605 Paruta, HV (Nicolini)
1623 Mathieu, Francia (Fontana), rpr 1624, 1628, 1629
1623 Morosini, Historia de la Repubblica Veneta (Pinelli: new edition 1637)
1625 Mathieu, Guerre, trans Canini (Barezzi: Fontana), rpr 1628
1627 Pieri, Guerra di Fiandra (Ciotti)
1630 Davila, Guerre (Baglioni); new eds 1634, 1638, 1642, 1650, 1664, 1692
1633 Noris, Guerre di Germania (Pinelli)
1634–8 Bisaccioni, Guerra in Alemagna (Baba)
1638 Pallavicino, Successi del mondo in 1636 (Tomasini)
1638 Pomo, Guerre di Ferdinando II (Sarzina)
1640 Bentivoglio, Fiandra (Baba), new ed. 1668
1640 Strada, Guerra di Fiandra (Baba)
1642 Bisaccioni, Gustavo Adolfo (Pavoni)
1642–6 Zilioli, Historie (Turrini)
1643 Tesauro, Campeggiamenti (Garzoni)
1644 Birago, Disunione
1645 Contarini, Guerra da Selim (Combi)
1645 Paruta, Historia Veneta (Giunti)
1646–8 Gualdo Priorato, Guerre di imperatori (Bertani)
1647 Giraffi, Rivolutioni (Baba)
1648 Birago, Mercurio veridico (Leni)

1649 Ricci, De bellis germanicis (Turrini)
1652 Bate, Moti d'Inghilterra
1653 Birago, Sollevationi (Turrini)
1653 Bisaccioni, Guerre civili (Storti), rpr 1655
1654 Birago, Turbolenze di Europa (Ginammi)
1655 Gualdo Priorato, Rivolutioni di Francia (Baglioni)
1655 Ricci, Res italicae (Turrini)
1656 Brusoni, Historia d'Europa (Turrini)
1657 Brusoni Historia Universale (Storti)
1661 Brusoni, Historia d'Italia (Storti)
1662 Nani, HRV (Combi), rpr 1663, 1676, 1686
1668 Bentivoglio, Fiandra (Miloco)
1671 Bianchi ('Vimini'), Guerre Civili di Polonia (Pinelli)
1671 Brusoni, Historia d'Italia (Storti), new ed. 1676
1672 Rycaut.Imperio Ottomano, trans Belli (Combi)
1673 Brusoni, Historia dell'ultima guerra tra Venezia e Turchi (Curti)
1679 Nani, HRV, part 2 (Combi), rpr 1686
1679 Valier, Guerra di Candia (Baglioni)
1681 Gazzotti, Guerre d'Europa (Pezzano)
1684 Camuccio, Assedio di Vienna (Poletti)
1685 Armi cesaree nell'Ungheria (Cagnolini)
1687 Giustiniani, Armi imperiali (Curti)
1689 Brandano, Guerre di Portogallo (Baglioni)
1691 Locatelli, Veneta guerra in Levante (Albrizzi)

Sources: *Catalogue of Seventeenth-Century Italian Books in the British Library* (3 vols, London: British Library, 1986): Michel and Michel, *Répertoire* (8 vols, Paris 1967).

Appendix 5: Editions of Sansovino

1556 ['Anselmo Guisconi'] Tutte le cose notabili che sono in Venetia (no publisher)
1560 Tutte le cose notabili che sono in Venetia (Rampazzetto)
1561 Delle cose notabili che sono in Venetia (Comin)
1562 Delle cose notabili che sono in Venetia (Farri)
1563 Delle cose notabili che sono in Venetia (Calepino)
1564 Delle cose notabili che sono in Venetia (Calepino)
1565 Delle cose notabili che sono in Venetia (Franceschi)
1565 Delle cose notabili che sono in Venetia (Rampazzetto)
1566 Delle cose notabili che sono in Venetia (Franceschi)
1566 Delle cose notabili che sono in Venetia (revised by Doglioni and Zittio: Cestari)
1567 Delle cose notabili che sono in Venetia (Franceschi)
1572 Delle cose notabili che sono in Venetia (Viani)
1581 Venetia città nobilissima (Farri)
1583 Delle cose notabili che sono in Venetia (Valvassori)
1587 Delle cose notabili che sono in Venetia (Zoppini)
1587 Delle cose notabili che sono in Venetia (Valgrisi, 24o)
1587 Delle cose notabili che sono in Venetia (Valgrisi, 8o)
1592 Delle cose notabili che sono in Venetia (Zoppini)
1601 Delle cose notabili che sono in Venetia (Salicato)
1601 [under name of 'Bardi'] Venetia città nobilissima (Salicato)
1602 Venetia città nobilissima (Spineda)
1602 Delle cose notabili che sono in Venetia (Spineda)
1603 Cose maravigliose, revised by 'Goldioni' (Imberti)

1604 Venetia città nobilissima, revised by Stringa (Salicato)
1606 Delle cose notabili che sono in Venetia (Salicato)
1612 Cose maravigliose e notabili, revised by 'Goldioni' (Imberti)
1624 Cose maravigliose e notabili, revised by 'Goldioni' (Imberti)
1629 Cose notabili et maravigliose, revised by 'Goldioni' (Herz)
1641 Cose notabili et maravigliose, revised by 'Goldioni' (Herz)
1641 Cose maravigliose e notabili, revised by 'Goldioni' (Imberti)
1649 Cose notabili et maravigliose, revised by 'Goldioni' (Herz)
1655 Cose notabili et maravigliose, revised by 'Goldioni' (Herz)
1662 Cose notabili et maravigliose, revised by 'Goldioni' (Herz)
1663 Venetia città nobilissima, revised by Martinioni (Curti)
1666 Cose notabili et maravigliose, revised by 'Goldioni' (Cestari)
1671 Cose notabili et maravigliose, revised by 'Goldioni' (Cestari)
1675 Cose notabili et maravigliose, revised by 'Goldioni' (Cestari: Miloco)
1692 Cose notabili et maravigliose, revised by 'Goldioni' (Didini)
1692 Cose notabili et maravigliose, revised by 'Goldioni' (Tramontin)

Sources: STC: Michel and Michel, *Répertoire* (8 vols, Paris 1967); and information from Juergen Schulz.

6: THE AGE OF THE BAROQUE

1. The Problem

Historians of the sixteenth and eighteenth centuries have traditionally described their periods as the 'Renaissance' and the 'Enlightenment'. No such conventional label is available to historians of the seventeenth century. Some speak of the age of the 'scientific revolution', others of the 'baroque age'. In so doing they follow the tradition of studying the *Zeitgeist,* the 'spirit' of the age. The art historian Heinrich Wölfflin included the poetry of Torquato Tasso and the music of Giovanni Pierluigi da Palestrina in his concept of baroque art. Oswald Spengler went still further, drawing parallels between 'the differential calculus and the dynastic principle of politics in the age of Louis XIV'. The Spanish historian José Maravall was only a little more cautious when he described the baroque as a historical structure characterized by four main traits: a culture which was controlled (*dirigida*), appealing to the masses (*masiva*), urban, and conservative.

Parallels between the arts are generally attractive and sometimes illuminating, but they are always speculative and inevitably arbitrary, even in cases where the same individual was active in more than one art, as in the cases of John Vanbrugh in architecture and the theatre, or Paolo Sarpi in the study of nature and of history. More dangerous is the attempt to describe a whole historical period with a label, like baroque, derived from art history. Still more misleading is the habit of turning the baroque into a histori-cal agent, almost a person, and declaring that 'it' did or aspired to do something.

Behind this imprecise language lies a major problem, the as-sumption of the cultural homogeneity of an age. To many histori-ans, myself included, the assumption seems almost self-evidently false. It ignores, for example, the many differences between elite and popular culture. It may be the case that as Maravall argues, the baroque was a 'mass' movement in the sense that the Church was using the new dramatic style to reach a wide audience, but it was only very slowly that certain baroque motifs were incor-porated into popular art. Cultural distinctions and cultural con-flicts cannot be ignored. Historians such as Victor Tapié and Josef Polišenský have described European culture in the early seven-teenth century not as single but as double. Classicism and baroque have often been defined as opposite as well as rival styles, in terms of regularity versus irregularity, simplicity versus complexity, re-straint versus exuberance, clarity versus difficulty, repose versus movement, balance versus imbalance, reason versus unreason, and so on.

Classicism is most easily defined by a concern for rules, for fol-lowing the model of antiquity, especially the trinity of ancient authorities, Aristotle, Cicero and Vitruvius. Baroque is more elu-sive. Condemned by contemporary critics for breaches of rules, it is better defined more positively in terms of emphases on certain themes – death, for example, the vanity of human endeavour, il-lusions, and instability. We might speak of a baroque world-view characterized by an unusual preoccupation with the contrast be-tween appearance and reality (*être/paraître, ser/parecer, Sein/Schein*). As the title of Calderón's famous and much-imitated play puts it, *Life is a Dream*. A recurrent theme in the literature of the time is disillusion (*desengaño*). A striking example occurs in a play by An-dreas Gryphius in which the figure of a beautiful woman turns into the image of Death himself before the eyes of her lover.

To speak in this general way about common themes is more precise than Spengler but it still raises problems. The problem of dating, for example. Some historians of literature and art describe the age of the baroque as running from 1580 to 1670 or 1680, from Montaigne to Bernini (this chapter will follow them). Maravall, on the other hand, prefers the dates 1605–50. Others allow the baroque to continue to 1750. It is not easy to define the criteria according to which the dates are chosen. A second problem is the assumption that art and literature 'reflect' the life of the time. Is it not possible that they compensate for what is lacking in the life of the time? Or might it be the case that art sometimes influenced life?

All the same, the idea of an age of the baroque has its attractions and its advantages, notably as a complementary opposite to an emphasis on national cultures. So let us use the term 'baroque age', on three conditions. In the first place, it is important to look closely at the vocabulary used by contemporaries, especially the key metaphors through which they interpreted their experiences, crossing the frontier between art and life. In the second place, it is prudent to move gradually outwards from the history of the arts into other cultural domains. In the third place, in order to build bridges between creative individuals such as Bernini and Newton and the age in which they lived, it is essential to examine their contemporary reception. These considerations have shaped the approach adopted in this chapter.

2. Theatre and Music

In the seventeenth century, all the arts reveal the influence of the drama, the art of appearance or illusion *par excellence* and also the art of surprise. The drama may be described as a multi-media event, whether it took place in the streets or in a purpose-built theatre (theatres were constructed in increasing numbers in Italy, Spain, England and elsewhere from the late sixteenth century onwards). In these theatres the painted scenery (*Scheinarchitektur*, as the Germans call it), became increasingly elaborate, and so did various 'special effects', such as thunder and lightning, fires and floods, or rapid changes of scene. Italian specialists in theatrical machinery were much in demand, as in the cases of Giacomo

Torelli and Giovanni Burnacini at the rival courts of Louis XIV and the emperor Leopold I in the 1660s.

A variety of dramatic forms flourished at this time. Tragedies were written by Pierre Corneille and Jean Racine, and (for reading rather than for performance), by the Germans Andreas Gryphius and Kaspar von Lohenstein. Religious drama was represented by the Spaniard Pedro Calderón, most famous for his play *La vida es sueño* (c. 1638), and the Dutchman Joost van Vondel. Comedy was represented by Jean-Baptiste Molière and William Congreve. Pastoral poetry and the pastoral romance (from Sannazzaro to Sidney) was now replaced by the pastoral drama, notably by Tasso's *Aminta* and the *Pastor Fido* of Giambattista Guarini, which were translated into many European languages (from English and French to Croat and modern Greek), in the course of the seventeenth century. The preoccupation with theatricality in this period may be illustrated by the vogue for the drama in the drama. Shakespeare's *Hamlet* (c. 1600), and Corneille's *Illusion comique* represent plays within plays. Jean Rotrou's *Saint Genest* (1645) concerns an actor who is asked by the daughter of the emperor Diocletian to play the role of a Christian martyr.

A new style of music emerged in Italy around the year 1600. Claudio Monteverdi's *seconda pratica,* as he called it, was concerned above all with the expression of emotions, especially violent emotions. However, the new style did not please everyone. The *seconda pratica* was attacked by the critic Giovanni Maria Artusi because the new music did not give pleasure to the ear. The new style was most appropriate to musical dramas, to the new genre which we know as 'opera', including Monteverdi's *Orfeo* (first performed in 1607), his *Arianna* (performed 1608), and his *Incoronazione di Poppea* (1642). The first German opera, *Daphne,* by Heinrich Schütz, followed the model of Monteverdi, while the expatriate Italian Jean-Baptiste Lully developed an alternative style (more dignified but less dramatic) for the French court, and the Englishman William Purcell synthesized the Italian and French styles in his *Dido and Aeneas* (1689) and his *Faerie Queene* (1692). The sacred oratorio was another dramatic form of music which flourished in this period, from Schütz to Handel. Yet another was the cantata, from Marc-Antoine Charpentier to Johann Sebastian Bach.

3. *Architecture, Sculpture and Painting*

Classical architecture continued the High Renaissance tradition of Greek and Roman forms. Baroque architecture, on the other hand, was more innovative, like the so-called 'Mannerist' architecture which preceded it. Both mannerist and baroque architects broke the classical rules. However, they broke them in different ways. Mannerist architects preferred light and elegant forms, while their baroque successors preferred weight. In the famous formula of the Swiss art historian Heinrich Wölfflin, the baroque style was characterized by 'Mass and movement' (*Massigkeit und Bewegung*). Façades, for example, were sometimes undulating rather than flat. The wide new streets and avenues of major cities could best be appreciated from a moving carriage. In all these respects baroque architecture might be described as more 'dramatic' than the architecture of the Renaissance which preceded it. The example of Rome's Piazza San Pietro, Piazza Navona and Piazza del Popolo shows how cities were coming to resemble stages, the scenery including fountains and Egyptian obelisks erected in order to symbolize the triumph of Christianity over paganism.

Another important feature of the architecture of the period was its eclecticism. Francesco Borromini and Guarino Guarini drew on Gothic forms as well as classical ones, although Borromini in particular was often criticized for this practice. Christopher Wren went further, declaring that as far as architectural forms were concerned, 'not only Roman and Greek but Phoenician, Hebrew and Assyrian' were all acceptable. Johann Bernhard Fischer von Erlach, architect to the Habsburg emperors, published a history of architecture (the *Entwurff*, 1721), in which Islamic and Chinese buildings took their place alongside Greek and Roman exemplars.

In sculpture as in architecture we see a concern with triumphalism, with *Massigkeit* (gigantic funeral monuments, for example), with drama, and, especially in the work of GianLorenzo Bernini, with movement. Bernini's *David*, in contrast with Michelangelo's statue in repose, captures the moment immediately before the hero launches the stone from his sling. In similar fashion, his *Apollo and Daphne* represents the god in hot pursuit of a nymph who is just on the point of being transformed into a laurel tree.

In painting, it is the variety of styles practiced around 1600 which attracts attention, as it did in the seventeenth century. The critic Gianpietro Bellori, for instance, distinguished three styles, praising the Carracci brothers for their judicious combination of art and nature, in contrast to the *maniera* of the Cavaliere Arpino, which neglected nature, and also to that of Caravaggio, who neglected art.

Of the three styles, the most innovative was that of Caravaggio. It was not always appreciated: the painter was criticized in his own time for despising beauty and searching for deformity. A painting of the death of the Virgin was rejected by the church for which it was painted on the grounds that Mary looked like a peasant. In similar fashion, Rembrandt was sometimes criticized for his naturalism, for choosing an ugly washerwoman, for instance, as his model for a nude.

However, the theatricality of Caravaggio, in his *Conversion of St Paul* (c. 1601), for example, or of Rubens (whether his huge canvases were celebrating St Ignatius Loyola or Marie de' Medici), contrasts with the understated style of Rembrandt or of Jan Vermeer. More generally, the Dutch 'art of describing' in paint (landscapes, townscapes, interiors of houses, vases of flowers and so on), may be contrasted with the Italian art of narrative, the *istoria*. To describe such contrasts, there developed an increasingly rich vocabulary for speaking about style. In painting, for example, the Venetian critic Marco Boschini criticized the more traditional brushwork of Raphael as *secco e duro*, reserving his praise for free, spontaneous, sketchy, apparently unfinished work, a *forma senza forma* characterized by dramatic *colpi di pennello*. Outside Italy, this spontaneity may be illustrated by the work of Velázquez and the later Rembrandt (an Italian patron, Don Antonio Ruffo of Messina, sent back Rembrandt's *Blind Homer* to be completed).

In architecture, sculpture and painting alike, the seventeenth century may be described as a time of increasingly acute competition between styles and consciousness of styles. However, this did not always mean that practitioners of one style disapproved of all the others. Bernini, for example, admired the work of the French classicist Nicolas Poussin. Bernini himself, like the Carracci and other artists, was also capable of switching between styles according to the occasion, working in the grand manner for public commissions and in a more naturalistic manner to portray his mistress Constanza Bonarelli.

4. Literature

The poets Torquato Tasso and Giambattista Marino were criticized in much the same ways as their contemporaries Caravaggio and Monteverdi. The critics singled out for disapproval their unexpected or obscure metaphors, violent contrasts, and breaches of the rules, often for the purpose of surprise, or to use Marino's term, *maraviglia*. In literature as in painting and architecture the seventeenth century was marked by a battle between styles, in this case Ciceronianism versus anti-ciceronianism, or as contemporaries used to say 'Attic' versus 'Asiatic'. The 'new' models came from Roman literature of the so-called 'silver' age, especially Seneca and Tacitus. These models, characterized by a looser structure and a predilection for maxims or epigrams, were followed by the Flemish humanist Justus Lipsius, for example, in his Latin prose, and in the vernacular, in their essays, by Michel de Montaigne and Francis Bacon.

In the case of dramatic writing, there was a similar battle over the so-called 'rules' attributed to Aristotle, regarding the unities of time, place and action. Racine, for example, obeyed the rules, while Corneille's *Le Cid* (1636) was condemned by the newly-founded French Academy for breaking them. The Academy also formulated linguistic rules in its famous dictionary (published from 1694 onwards), which followed the model of the *Dictionario* (1612) of the Florentine Academia della Crusca.

More generally, we may contrast the aesthetics of classicism with the aesthetics of baroque. On the classical side, we find writers continuing to stress the importance of 'imitation' and of the precepts of Aristotle's *Poetics* and Horace's *Art of Poetry*, reformulated by the new Horace, Nicolas Boileau, in his *Art poétique* (1674). It was Boileau who criticized his colleague Saint-Amant, author of a biblical epic, *Moïse Sauvé*, for faults of taste such as describing 'les choses du monde plus affreuses, des crapaux et des limaçons qui bavent, le squelette d'un pendu'.

On the baroque side, there was a greater stress on what the English called 'wit', the French, *esprit*, the Spaniards, *agudeza* and the Italians *argutezza*, in other words the art of verbal surprise. The theorists of this alternative style included Baltasar Gracián in his *Arte de ingenio* (1641) and Emanuele Tesauro, in *Il cannocchiale aristotelico* (1655). The title of Tesauro's instructions for the production of *ingeniosi concetti* is itself an excellent example of the *argutezza* he recommended. Following these models, many European writers devised anagrams, acrostics, chronograms, or poems in the shape of wings, for example, or an altar complete with steps.

In the historical writing of this period we may observe a similar contrast of styles. On one side, there was the elaborately rhetorical style of Agostino Mascardi, for instance, or Famiano Strada. A professor of rhetoric at the Sapienza, a Latin poet and a writer on ethics and the passions, Mascardi was and remains best-known as a historian. His *Arte istorica* (1636) expounded the theory of a rhetorical history, while his *Congiura del conte Fieschi* (1629) provided an example of the practice. As for Strada, he taught rhetoric at the Collegio Romano but is best known for his history of the revolt of the Netherlands, *De bello belgico decades*, written at the request of the Duke of Parma, published in 1632–47, and translated into Dutch, French, Italian, English and Spanish before the end of the century.

On the other side, the plain style was taken to the limit by Dutch historians such as Pieter Bor and Leeuw Aitzema, who inserted official documents into their narrative where Mascardi or Strada would have inserted speeches. Even in Italy, as Benedetto Croce once noted, a number of historians of this period, such as Maiolino Bisaccioni or Vittorio Siri, wrote in a style which was deliberately 'antiumanistico e antiletterario'.

Historical writing illustrates very clearly the preoccupation with the distance between appearance and reality which we have noted as a characteristic of the period. For example, the writings of Paolo Sarpi, notably his *Istoria del Concilio di Trento* (1619), abound with terms such as *pretesto, colore, guerra occulta,* or 'una arte di governo coperta di manto della religione'. Again, in his *Guerre civili di Francia* (1631), Enrico Davila contrasts the *apparenze esterne* of tranquillity before the wars with the *discordie* or *insidie occulte* or *nascoste*. In his *History of the Great Rebellion,* Edward Hyde Earl of Clarendon wrote of the 'outward visible prosperity' of England in the 1630s as hiding conflicts which became apparent in the civil wars of the 1640s.

The metaphors of the theatre, the mask and the cloak recur (obsessively, one is tempted to say), in the literature of this period. Montaigne wrote of life as theatre, while Shakespeare and Vondel described the world as a stage. The French magistrate Jacques-Auguste de Thou wrote of 'those who use religion to make a Spanish cloak to cover their ambition'. His friend Sarpi wrote in 1609 that 'I am forced to wear a mask' (*Personam coactus fero*). John Milton called Sarpi 'The Great Unmasker of the Trentine Council'. In his *Maximes* (1665), the French duke de La Rochefoucauld used a similar metaphor, that of veils: 'Quelque soin que l'on prenne de couvrir ses passions par des apparences de piété et d'honneur, elles paraissent toujours au travers de ces voiles'. Another favourite metaphor was that of 'anatomy', cutting through surfaces to reveal structures. The early twentieth-century sociologist Karl Mannheim was surely correct in insisting on the importance of these metaphors in the seventeenth century and their relation to the later theory of ideology.

5 Secrets of State, Reason of State

What the political anatomists revealed were 'secrets of state', *mystères d'état* or *arcana imperii,* a phrase borrowed from the Roman historian Cornelius Tacitus. They analysed what they called 'the prudence of governments' (*prudentia regnativa, prudencia de estado*), 'civil prudence' (*prudentia civilis*), or 'political prudence'. The Piedmontese writer Giovanni Botero devoted the second part of his treatise *Della Ragione di Stato* (1589) to this subject, while the classical scholar Justus Lipsius stressed the importance of different kinds of prudence in his anthology of ancient writers, *Politicorum Libri Sex* (1589), described by a fellow-scholar as a work of philosophy the like of which 'has not been written or seen in a thousand years' (the book went through fifteen editions in ten years, and was translated into seven languages).

Lipsius, who taught at the universities of Leiden and Leuven, in the northern and southern Netherlands respectively, during the religious wars, discussed topics such as deception, distinguishing white lies (*deceptiunculae*) from major deceits (*magnae fraudes*), such as perfidy or injustice. Torquato Accetto discussed the techniques and also the pleasures of deceit in *Della dissimulazione onesta* (1641). The many treatises on courts and courtiers, in the tradition of Baldassare Castiglione's famous *Cortegiano* (1528), continued to discuss the presentation of self but they now placed increasing emphasis on dissimulation and disguise.

Putting their precepts into practice, some writers disguised their own ideas – or more often, Machiavelli's – in the form of a commentary on the many political maxims to be found in Tacitus, as in the case of Scipione Ammirato's *Discorsi sopra Cornelio Tacito* (1594) and scores of later works. They frequently asserted that the *arcana imperii* were not to be revealed to 'the vulgar'. All the same, they contributed to this process of vulgarization by publishing their reflections. Many writers preferred to carry out this task by discussing the major events of the reigns of Roman emperors, especially Tiberius, as described by Tacitus, whether in homage to the prestige of ancient Rome or because they followed their own counsels of prudence. However, some of them were also prepared to draw parallels between the actions of Roman emperors and those of the rulers of their own time. In his brief Protestant phase, Lipsius, for instance, compared the duke of Alba, who was governing the Netherlands for Philip II and persecuting heretics, to the cruel emperor Tiberius.

The main topics discussed in this genre of political treatises were violence and deceit, force and fraud, the opposite but complementary qualities of the lion and the fox which Machiavelli had recommended to his prince. On one side, there was the necessity of using severe measures against rebels for example, a practice not infrequently compared to that of a physician who amputates a limb in order to preserve life. On the other, there were the advantages of simulation and dissimulation, exemplified (once again) by Tiberius, by Cesare Borgia (as Machiavelli had noted), and by Louis XI of France, who is supposed to have coined the maxim 'who can't feign can't reign' (*qui nescit dissimulare, nescit regnare*).

The means by which rulers acquire or keep power, especially in emergencies came to be known as *ragion di stato*. The phrase probably began as a euphemism, a way of avoiding Machiavelli's over-frank discussion of 'necessity' at a time when that author's works were banned in the Catholic world and attacked by the Protestants. However, 'reason of state' became a fashionable term in the decades following the publication of Botero's book on the subject in 1589. By this time the topic was, according to Botero, a constant subject of discussion in the courts of some princes, the opinions of Niccolò Machiavelli and Cornelius Tacitus being frequently quoted.

The novelty of the phrase 'reason of state' in the 1590s may be judged from the fact that the German and Latin translations of Botero did not use it. It spread rapidly thereafter, particularly in Italian, Latin (*ratio status*), Spanish (*razón de estado*) and French (*raison d'état*). It might be said that the late sixteenth century saw the rise or constitution of a 'discourse' on reason of state, in the sense of a more or less closed intellectual universe structured around a small number of concepts, authorities, assumptions and examples. It reveals an increasing interest on the part of the authors of treatises on politics in what rulers actually did rather than what they ought to do, the rise of what was sometimes referred to in this period as 'political science' (*scientia politica*).

Some of these authors claimed that this science could be reduced to rules, others, like the Spanish commentator on Tacitus, Alamos de Barrientos, asserted that 'Strictly speaking, political prudence cannot be called a science, because its conclusions are not evident and certain at all times'. The parallel with the literary debates of the time on the importance of rules will be obvious enough, while a still closer parallel comes from moral philosophy. The equivalent of Alamos in ethics was the position of the so-called 'casuists' (predominantly but not exclusively Jesuits), who claimed that 'cases of conscience' could not be reduced to general rules but had to be studied on their own terms. An 'empiricist' ethics, one might call it, in contrast to the idea of natural law associated in particular with the Dutch scholar Hugo Grotius and his *De Iure Belli et Pacis* (1625), which argued that the rules governing international relations had a validity independent of the existence of God.

The authors of the treatises walked an intellectual tightrope, praising severity but condemning cruelty, and arguing against lying but in favour of dissimulation. Some of them, notably the Spanish Jesuit Pedro de Ribadeneira, distinguished two kinds of reason of state, the true and the false. The latter, otherwise known as 'devilish' or 'hellish' reason (*ragion del diavolo, ragion d'inferno*) was associated with the doctrines of Machiavelli. If it began as a euphemism, 'reason of state' ended as a dirty word, associated with hypocrisy and murder and mocked on the seventeenth-century stage. Whether they loved it or hated it, however, writers on politics were preoccupied with the topic of the extraordinary and often dramatic measures which rulers took in emergencies, *coups d'état*, as the French scholar Gabriel Naudé called them (apparently for the first time), in a treatise on the subject that he published in 1639.

6 Neostoicism

Let us turn from the public to the private sphere. In this domain one of the most important changes was the rise of 'Neostoicism', in other words the revival of interest in a group of ancient philosophers, notably Epictetus, Plutarch, Marcus Aurelius and above all Seneca. The key idea of these philosophers was that of 'constancy' (*constantia* in Seneca's Latin), in other words tranquillity of mind, the capacity to stand upright against what Hamlet called 'the slings and arrows of outrageous fortune'. Linked ideas included self-discipline; non-attachment to worldly things – travelling light through life, as Seneca described it; and the distinction between the few matters which were really important and the rest (*adiaphora* or 'indifferent things').

Stoic philosophy was known in the Middle Ages and still better in the Renaissance. However, it was in the later sixteenth and early seventeenth centuries that an interest in stoicism became a fashion in the sense of spreading beyond a circle of intellectuals and colouring, if not penetrating, the everyday life of some European elites. Central to the process of the reception of stoicism was Justus Lipsius. Lipsius made his reputation with his Latin dialogue *On Constancy* (1584). By the early seventeenth century the dialogue had been translated into Dutch, French, English, German, Spanish, Italian and Polish.

The example of Lipsius was followed by the French magistrate Guillaume Du Vair, who translated Epictetus into French and published his own dialogue *On Constancy* (1595). Michel de Montaigne abandoned his early enthusiasm for stoic ideas, but his follower Pierre Charron remained close to stoicism in his book *On Wisdom* (1601). The Italian moralist Virgilio Malvezzi wrote stoic meditations on the lives of Romulus, Tarquin, David and others which were popular not only in Italy but also in Spain and England. In Spain, Francisco de Quevedo produced a translation of Epictetus into Spanish verse and also an introduction to stoic philosophy. In Germany, the poet Martin Opitz wrote a poem, *Zlatna*, on tranquillity of mind. The stoic movement extended to art and artists. Rubens, for instance, belonged to the circle of Lipsius, while Borromini owned a bust of Seneca and committed suicide by falling on his sword in the ancient Roman style.

The stoic concern with self-control led to a more acute interest in the nature of the emotions, or to use the favourite term of the period, the 'passions'. Descartes, for example, wrote a treatise on the subject, while the painter Charles Lebrun published a book on the art of representing the passions. The art of dissimulation, which depended on the concealment of the emotions, was recommended to private individuals as well as to rulers. As Gracián put it, 'El más plático consiste en disimular. Lleva riesgo de perder el que juega a juego descubierta' (The most useful thing to do is to dissimulate. The man who shows his cards risks losing the game).

7 The World of Nature

As in the case of music and painting, a new style of science (or as it was called at this time, 'natural philosophy'), was coming into existence at the beginning of the seventeenth century, and some contemporaries remarked on the change. The astronomer Johan Kepler, for instance, entitled one of his books *Astronomia nova* (1609). In a letter to Galileo in 1632, the philosopher Tommaso Campanella claimed to see a 'new age', announced by 'new worlds, new stars, new systems, new nations'. The English poet John Donne wrote that 'new philosophy calls all in doubt'. The intellectual system of Aristotle, a framework for so many European thinkers since the thirteenth century, was more and more frequently questioned. The importance of René Descartes, in his *Discourse on Method* (1637) and other works, was that he offered a system to replace that of Aristotle, and did so in a series of works written with a clarity which was coming to be seen as a characteristically French style.

The preoccupation with the difference, indeed the contrast between appearance and reality can be found in the natural sciences of this period no less than in the arts. Anatomists increasingly dissected animals and humans in order to understand the structure of their bodies. In physics, Galileo distinguished between what he called 'primary' and 'secondary' qualities. The secondary qualities, such as colour, were perceptible by the senses in everyday life, but the real or primary qualities were only accessible to reason or to observation aided by such new instruments such as the telescope, the microscope and the barometer. The deep structures of reality were now viewed as mathematical, as Isaac Newton argued in his *Mathematical Principles of Natural Philosophy* (1687). This belief explains the importance attributed at this time to precise measurement, weighing air for example.

It is with good reason that some historians apply the phrase 'the mechanization of the world picture' to this period. Galileo and Newton studied the mechanics of the heavens. Kepler declared that 'the machine of the universe is not similar to a divine being but similar to a clock'. Descartes explained light and colour in essentially mechanical terms, and viewed animals and human bodies as automata. The English philosopher Thomas Hobbes concurred. 'What is the heart but a spring', he wrote, 'and the nerves, but so many strings: and the joints, but so many wheels?'.

To mathematics was joined the method of 'experiment', a term which is related to that of everyday 'experience' but gradually diverged from it in this period as natural philosophers, in the famous phrase of Francis Bacon, 'put Nature to the question', contriving artificial situations in order to test hypotheses. The Florentine Accademia del Cimento was founded in 1657 by two followers of Galileo. The French philosopher Blaise Pascal tested the traditional claim that 'Nature abhors a vacuum' by having a barometer taken to the top of a mountain. The mercury level was lower at the top than at the bottom of the mountain, a variation explained more easily by the weight of the air than by any constant abhorrence of a vacuum.

Again, it was thanks to his experiments with prisms that Newton was able to show that what we perceive as 'white' light is in fact a mixture of rays of different colours. Yet again, a useful way of distinguishing between traditional 'alchemy' and the new 'chemistry' of this period might be to define the latter in terms of a concern with precise quantities. Mathematics and systematic experiment, in short 'reason', were replacing the authority of tradition in one intellectual field after another.

The new philosophy was clearly on a collision course with the Catholic Church, if not with all the Christian churches. Galileo was in fact summoned before the Roman Inquisition on two occasions, being warned in 1616 and condemned to house arrest in 1633. To this day many issues in his trial are still debated – whether certain individuals bore grudges against him, whether he misunderstood his warning, whether the main issue was his support of the Copernican view that the sun was in the centre of the universe, or his belief that the universe was made up of atoms. In a brief account it is best to focus on the main principles involved. Galileo was not the sort of scholar who simply wanted to carry on his research without interference. He had strong views about the theological implications of scientific discoveries. He wanted the Church to support the Copernican theory, and spent a good deal of effort on this 'cultural propaganda'.

The crucial issue in his campaign was the interpretation of the Bible, which seemed in certain passages to contradict the heliocentric theory of Copernicus. Galileo argued that the Bible was not always to be taken literally because its statements were simplified in order 'to accommodate them to the capacities of the common people' (the term 'accommodation' was a traditional one in theology). He quoted Augustine on the need to interpret the bible 'in context' (another traditional term), and claimed that the text could not be understood without the aid of another book, the 'book of nature'.

The official attitude, expressed by cardinal Bellarmine, was that Galileo should content himself 'di parlare ex suppositione e non assolutamente'. In other words, it was permissible to support the heliocentric theory as a hypothesis which 'saves the appearances' better than Ptolemy's epicycles. However, to say that the sun is really in the centre of the universe ran the danger of 'rendere false le scritture sante'. With hindsight we become aware of a paradox: that the Church now supports Galileo's theology, while the community of scientists support Bellarmine's philosophy of science in the sense of emphasizing their inability to speak with certainty of what underlies appearances.

The success of the mathematical method in the study of nature led to a fashion for applying it, especially in its geometrical form, to every intellectual field. The late seventeenth century saw the rise of what was sometimes called 'political arithmetic' or 'political anatomy', in other words the use of 'statistics' (the word is derived from 'state'), especially population statistics, in the service of governments. The Dutch philosopher Baruch Spinoza presented his conclusions on ethics as 'proved by the geometrical method' (*ordine geometrico demonstrata*). The French Jansenist Pierre Nicole published an *Essai géometrique sur la grace générale*. Emmanuele Tesauro's *Canocchiale aristotelico* included what the author called 'teoremi ... per fabricar concetti arguti'. A Scottish philosopher, John Craig, attempted to be the Newton of history with his *Mathematical Principles of Christian Theology* (1699), which included geometrical 'rules of historical evidence'.

A generation ago, historians such as Herbert Butterfield summed up all these developments in natural philosophy in the dramatic phrase, 'The Scientific Revolution'. Today, their successors (Steven Shapin, for example), have become increasingly uncomfortable with the phrase. They do not deny that the changes described above occurred, but they wish to place them in a wider context. On one side, they argue that the interest in precise measurement and the view of the universe as a machine were not novelties in the seventeenth century, even if such views and interests were spreading more widely at that time. On the other side, they point to the persistence (or even the revival), of studies of magic, astrology, alchemy and what contemporaries called 'the occult philosophy', which attracted some of the greatest names in what we call 'science'. Kepler, for example, was interested in astrology, while Newton devoted a great deal of his time to alchemy.

These occult interests cannot be dismissed as 'survivals'. They made a contribution to what we think of as 'modern' science, 'our' science. The 'mechanical philosophy' described above did not replace traditional ideas either simply or smoothly. Kepler and Newton adopted it in some intellectual domains but not in all. The new philosophy was resisted by scholastic philosophers (of whom there were many in the seventeenth century), and also by the Platonists, from the Cambridge professor Henry More to the Cistercian monk Juan Caramuel Lobkovic. Leibniz, whose interests were eclectic (like the architecture of Wren and Borromini), is perhaps the most famous example of a philosopher who resisted the attractions of the mechanistic world-view.

Leibniz was not the only eclectic. The German Jesuit Athanasius Kircher, for instance, was a polymath or (as they said in the seventeenth century), a 'polyhistor', who wrote on the arts and sciences alike, from music to magnetism and from alchemy to hieroglyphs. The Swede Olaf Rudbeck was the Protestant equivalent of Kircher. Their intellectual edifices may be described as 'baroque' not only in the sense that they were massive (however weak the foundations seemed to later generations), but also, more precisely, because they incorporated alternative antiquities. Kircher was fascinated by Egypt and China, while Rudbeck studied the 'barbarian philosophy' of the 'Goths', in other words the ancient Scandinavians.

8. Baroque and the Counter-Reformation

Given the coexistence in this period of two styles, two tastes, two sensibilities, and two world-views, it is natural to ask whether the division between them was associated with the social or religious or political divisions of the time. A generation ago Victor Tapié and Josef Polišenský both gave a strong affirmative answer to this question. For example, they suggested that baroque (with its stress on the marvellous), was Catholic, while classicism (with its stress on simplicity), was Protestant. They argued that the baroque style was linked to both the negative and positive aspects of the Counter-Reformation.

The negative or repressive side, the 'Counter'-Reformation in the strict sense, involved a crusade against heresy and immorality which extended to art and music as well as literature and drama. It is not difficult to document the progress of this crusade. Painters such as Paolo Veronese (in 1573) as well as poets and playwrights found themselves summoned to the tribunals of the Inquisition, and the idea of an Index of prohibited images, on the model of the *Index Librorum Prohibitorum,* was seriously discussed. Critics scrutinized paintings to see that they contained nothing against the faith, and condemned art and music alike for 'lasciviousness'. The distinction between the sacred and the profane became an increasingly sharp one, while profane elements in religious works were increasingly regarded as intolerable. This shift in attitude had serious consequences for art and music as for literature. Masses based on secular themes like the tune *L'homme armé* were coming to offend the pious, and so were comic scenes in the background of religious paintings or the sub-plot of religious plays.

The positive aspect of the movement, the 'Catholic Reformation', included the rise of new forms of devotion. Attempts have often been made to link these new devotions to the rise of new styles of painting, sometimes baroque and some times 'mannerist'. The controversy between them revealed the speculative and even arbitrary nature of such connections. So did the long controversy over baroque as a Jesuit style. In fact the Jesuits built in a variety of styles in this period, including Gothic, exemplifying the advice of St Ignatius (quoting St Paul) that they should be 'all things to all men'.

In the 1930s, the French art historian Emile Mâle attempted a more precise approach to possible links between painting and the Counter-Reformation, examining changes in iconography after the Council of Trent and emphasizing both the representation of new saints, Ignatius Loyola and Teresa of Avila for example, and the new emphasis on death, visions and ecstasies. Mâle also showed how art was used as a form of apologetics, illustrating doctrines and practices, from the sacrament of confession to trans-substantiation, which the Protestants had attacked.

Caravaggio's *Ecstasy of St Francis* and his *Conversion of St Paul* exemplify Mâle's thesis, and so does Bernini's *Ecstasy of St Teresa*, which illustrates a passage from her autobiography. Again, Bernini's *Cathedra Petri* was a dramatic statement of papal primacy. The Protestants had challenged Rome: architecture and sculpture had to emphasize the papal definition of reality. The Jesuits helped spread the baroque style even if they did not create it. Examples given earlier in this chapter illustrate the importance of Jesuits such as Famiano Strada, Athanasius Kircher and Baltasar Gracián in seventeenth-century European culture. Tesauro too was a Jesuit for more than twenty years. Corneille and Calderón were both pupils of the Jesuits, while Rubens was close to the Jesuits and decorated their church in Antwerp.

9. Baroque, Court and Nobility

If we turn from religious to secular patronage, it is to find that scholars have often linked the baroque style to courts and in particular to absolute monarchies. Rubens was employed by Queen

Marie de'Medici in France and by James I (who would have liked to have been an absolute monarch) in England. Many plays were presented at courts. Indeed, some contemporaries viewed the court itself as theatre. The Italian visitor Primi Visconti, for instance, described Louis XIV as an actor and his court as 'la plus belle comédie du monde'. Natural philosophers were invited to court, like Galileo at the court of the Medici in Florence. In this setting they were encouraged to present dramatic experiments and to show the 'marvels' of nature. Some rulers (Louis XIV included) spent a good deal of money on the acquisition of rare animals, vegetables or minerals for their collections, at least in part to display themselves as powerful enough to control these miniature universes and enlightened enough to take an interest in natural philosophy.

It has sometimes been argued that the baroque style is noble, while classicism, on the other hand, is bourgeois. Simplicity in the arts is likely to attract the bourgeoisie, so the argument goes, because it is congruent with the bourgeois values of sobriety and utility. Louis XIV's minister Jean-Baptiste Colbert, who came of merchant family, criticized the sculptor Pierre Puget for wasting government money on figureheads for ships. In the Dutch Republic, a state virtually governed by merchants, the plain or classical style was dominant. On the other side, the association between baroque and nobility can be explained by adapting some ideas from the American sociologist Thorstein Veblen. The baroque style is one of conspicuous ornament (implying that the patron has enough wealth to waste) and also of conspicuous difficulty (implying that the patron has the leisure and the education to decode the meaning).

At a macro-level, the geography of baroque and classicism seems to confirm these contrasts. Classicism was dominant in England (where the relative absence of baroque has often been noted), as it was in the Dutch Republic, in North Germany and in Scandinavia, all of which were predominantly Protestant areas. As another American sociologist, Robert Merton, has argued, natural philosophy flourished more among Protestants (or as he put it, thinking of England, among 'Puritans'), than among Catholics. The difficulty of defining Puritanism has led to the modification of the 'Merton thesis', as it is called, but the contrast between the career of natural philosophy in the Protestant and Catholic worlds is even more striking when studied at a European level than in the case of England alone. The absence of major Iberian contributions to natural philosophy in this period is conspicuous indeed, while Galileo, as we have seen, had problems with the Church.

As for the association between classicism and bourgeoisie, one should remember that the two greatest commercial cities of the seventeenth century, Amsterdam and London, were situated in the classical half of Europe (even if Amsterdam Town Hall and St Paul's cathedral may appear more baroque than classical to some viewers today). By contrast, baroque was dominant in Italy, Spain, Central Europe and in the Southern Netherlands. The last example is a particularly telling one because the Netherlands was culturally homogeneous in 1500 but had developed two contrasting cultures by 1650, Protestant, scientific and classical in the north, Catholic, rhetorical and baroque in the south, or to make the point still more simply, Rembrandt versus Rubens.

In this cultural geography of contrasts, one major country is particularly difficult to place: France. Viewed from a distance, France appears to contradict our arguments by combining Catholicism with classicism. In close-up, however, we find neither pure Catholicism nor pure baroque, but an artistic, a social and a religious mixture. The Protestants (known as Huguenots), accounted for ten per cent of the French population, while the Jansenists (a group which included Pascal and at one time Racine), have been described as 'Catholic Puritans'. It may not be coincidence that both Pascal and Racine came from the so-called *noblesse de robe*, a social group of lawyers, judges and officials on the frontiers between the nobility and the bourgeoisie.

This hybrid culture was attracted by both classicism and baroque. Baroque writers such as Quevedo and Gracián had many editions in French translation. The French had baroque artists of their own, such as the sculptor Pierre Puget or the painter Simon Vouet. Bernini's baroque project for the Louvre was seriously considered, by Louis XIV if not by Colbert. However, the Louvre as it was built in the seventeenth century is a masterpiece of the classical style. One might speak of a shift towards classicism in France in the seventeenth century, coinciding with a growing interest in experiment and in the mechanical philosophy and leading to a decline of the baroque.

10. *Hispanophilia, Hispanopobia*

The influence of Italian culture on other parts of Europe in the age of Bernini, Caravaggio, Galileo, Marino, Monteverdi, and Sarpi is well-known. However, the Spanish influence and the reaction against it also deserve to be noted. A number of Spanish words were adopted into other languages at this time: Italian examples include *complimenti, creanza, disinvoltura,* and *etichetta,* all terms referring to good behaviour. Spanish literature was widely known in translation. *Don Quixote,* for example, was translated into English, French, German, Italian and Dutch in the course of the seventeenth century. Mateo Alemán's picaresque novel *Guzmán de Alfarache* was translated into French, Italian, German, English and even Latin. Quevedo's *Dreams* was translated into French, German, English, Dutch and Italian. Gracián's *Oracle* was translated into French, Italian and English. A political emblem-book, Saavedra's *Idea de un príncipe christiano* (1640), was translated into six languages by the end of the century (Italian, Latin, German, Dutch, French and English).

Corneille's play *Le Cid* took its theme from Spanish history and was inspired by a play on the same subject by a Spanish playwright, Guillén de Castro. Three Spanish saints inspired devotion all over Catholic Europe: Teresa, Ignatius (both canonized in 1622), and Francis Xavier. Teresa's autobiography was translated into Italian, French, Latin, Flemish, English and Polish.

Spanish influence was particularly strong in Central Europe. In his youth, Rudolf II spent eight years at the court of Philip II. In Prague in the early seventeenth century, leading noble families such as the Dietrichsteins, the Lobkovics and the Žerotíns were pro-Spanish in both their politics and their culture. Zdeněk Lobkovic, for example, owned Spanish paintings and books, including a copy of Cervantes. Rodrigo Arriaga, a Spanish Jesuit and a leading philosopher, lived in Prague for some forty years and was rector of the Carolinum. Juan Caramuel Lobkovic, as his name suggests, was half Spanish and half Czech. The German writer Grimmelshausen's *Simplicissimus* (1669) was a picaresque novel about the Thirty Years' War that followed Spanish models.

As in the case of Renaissance Italy, Hispanophilia provoked the opposite reaction of Hispanophobia, all the more violent because Spain was an imperial power. Jacques-Auguste de Thou's remark about 'those who use religion to make a Spanish cloak to cover their ambition' has already been quoted, and it is worth adding that the remark was made at a time when Philip II was intervening in the French religious wars in the hope of obtaining the kingdom for his daughter Isabella. Paolo Sarpi hated and feared what he called the 'Catholicon', an alliance between Spain, the pope and the Jesuits. Tommaso Campanella denounced what he called *la superbia spagnola*. Campanella used the verbs *hispanizare* and *spagnolare* to refer to those who imitated Spanish customs and fashions. In other words, when Benedetto Croce blamed 'il gusto spagnuolo' for the decline of Italian taste in this period, he was doing little more than echo judgments that had been made in the seventeenth-century itself.

Some contemporaries preferred the French style, which according to Carlo García in his *Antipatia de franceses y españoles* (1617) was not only the rival but the opposite of the Spanish style, whether in clothing, speech, or even ways of walking or drinking. The German Martin Opitz, for example, sometimes wrote in French, and the metre of some of his German verses imitates the French alexandrines. In both Rome and Venice, there were French and Spanish factions, showing their allegiance by their style of dress (the architect Borromini, for instance, wore Spanish clothes). The French critic Jean Chapelain, the man who censured Corneille's *Cid* for breaking the rules of drama, condemned Spanish and baroque culture together in one sentence: 'les modernes espagnols ont corrompu leur style et sont tombés dans les figures bizarres et forcés'.

11. *Baroque and Cultural Crisis*

It is time to turn from the cultural geography of the baroque age to its chronology. This chronology was not uniform: in Central Europe, for example, the baroque style in the arts was still flourishing in the eighteenth century. The main problem, however, concerns the period 1580–1680. What events and what trends shaped the attitudes and values of different groups, separating this period from what went before and what came after?

A series of diverse but complementary answers may be given to this question. For example, the preoccupation with mortality so characteristic of the art and literature of the period may well have been a response to the plagues of 1576, 1630 and the 1660s, just as the macabre sensibility of the late Middle Ages may be viewed as a reaction to the Black Death. The many civil wars of the period also had important cultural consequences. Lipsius presented stoic philosophy as a response to the troubles of his time, and Du Vair agreed that it was a remedy for 'public calamities'. In Central Europe, Neostoicism was at its height in the age of Opitz and Gryphius, during the Thirty Years' War. The vogue for the discourse of reason of state may also be explained as a response to the civil wars of the previous generation, as well as a reaction to the rise of 'absolute' monarchy (unconstrained by law).

More intellectually ambitious, some historians (whether Marxists, like Eric Hobsbawm and Rosario Villari, or anti-Marxists like Roland Mousnier and Hugh Trevor-Roper), have been attracted by the idea of what they call the 'general crisis' of the seventeenth century. Strictly speaking, the term 'crisis' – originally a medical metaphor – signifies a short period of turbulence followed by structural change. The problem in this instance is to decide when the crisis of the seventeenth century occurred. Some scholars locate the crisis in the middle of the century, pointing to the political upheavals of the 1640s in England, France, Catalonia, Naples, Palermo, Portugal, the Ukraine, and so on, 'revolutions' which were already attracting attention at the time, in Luca Assarino's *Rivolutioni di Catalogna* (1644), for instance, Giambattista Birago Avogadro's *Rivolutioni di Portogallo* (1646), or Alessandro Giraffi's *Rivolutioni di Napoli* (1647).

Other scholars, following the literary historian Paul Hazard, speak of a 'crisis of European consciousness' and date it to the years 1680–1720 or thereabouts. The essential point they make is that this period was characterized by what the British historian Keith Thomas has called a 'decline of magic', part of the longer trend which Max Weber described as the 'disenchantment of the world'. As famine and disease declined and the expectation of life increased, the upper classes abandoned their traditional beliefs in magic and witchcraft. Trials for witchcraft, for example, declined sharply in England, France, and the German-speaking parts of Europe. In his *Pensées à l'occasion de la comète* (1681), the sceptical Calvinist Pierre Bayle argued forcefully that it was presumptuous of humans to assume that comets and other extraordinary natural phenomena were messages warning them of future disasters. In a more secure and sceptical world, the theatrical style of the baroque no longer seemed as appropriate as before.

To this already substantial list of cultural changes around the year 1700 might be added still others. The so-called 'battle of the books', for instance, at the end of the seventeenth century, in which the 'moderns', such as Charles Perrault, undermined the authority of classical antiquity and redefined its place in contemporary culture. On the international scene, Italian or Spanish cultural models gradually yielded to French or English ones. Madeleine de Scudéry's romances *Cyrus* and *Clélie*, for instance, written in the 1650s, were translated into English, German, Italian and Spanish. In Italy, Molière was translated in the 1680s, Racine in the 1690s. French began to be taught in colleges for nobles at about this time, while French words were increasingly adopted into other languages. John Dryden's *Marriage à la Mode* (1673) mocked fashionable Englishmen and women who used French terms such as *grande monde, risque* or *épuisé*. Courtly Germans introduced such words as *galanterie, goût* and *politesse* into their conversation, irritating Christian Thomasius into writing an explosive tract against *The Imitation of the French* (1686). Like Italophobia and Hispanophobia in before it, Francophobia was an admission of the cultural hegemony of the foreigner.

In any case, for whatever reason, we see an increasingly powerful reaction against the grandiloquence and obscurity of the baroque style in the arts. In 1644, for instance, Gianpietro Bellori attacked the architecture of his day as capricious and individualistic. 'Ciascuno … si finge da se stesso in capo una nuova Idea, e larva di Architettura a suo modo … deformando gli edifici … freneticavano angoli, spezzature, e distorcimenti di linee'. A generation later, the English diplomat William Temple attacked what he called 'Gothic' verse, in other words 'a raving or rambling sort of wit or invention, loose and flowing, with little art or confinement to any certain measures or rules'.

In the eighteenth century, criticisms of this kind became more and more common. In 1718, for instance, the Dutch critic Arnold Houbraken criticized Rembrandt because he did not 'execute his pictures carefully'. In architecture, Colen Campbell, one of the leaders of the Neo-Palladian movement in Britain, exclaimed: 'How affected and licentious are the works of Bernini and Fontana! How wildly extravagant are the designs of Borromini!' Around the middle of the century, the term 'baroque' came into use to refer to music or architecture which was considered bizarre or capricious. The word would not lose its pejorative meaning until the beginning of the twentieth century.

Given this major cultural shift, it is surely understandable that Giambattista Vico's *Scienza Nuova* (first published in 1725), should have remained largely unappreciated in its author's own time. Its obscure and poetic style encouraged its first readers to treat this treatise on the philosophy of history as a work of the late baroque, while its author appeared to be a polymath in the declining tradition of Kircher and Rudbeck. It was only in the nineteenth century that Vico ceased to be dismissed as a pre-Cartesian and came to be perceived instead as post-Cartesian, a former enthusiast for Descartes who formulated penetrating criticisms of his philosophy.

This chapter has tried to demonstrate the problems involved in applying a single adjective, 'baroque', to the culture of the whole of Europe over the century 1580–1680. The binary opposition of 'baroque' and 'classicism' is better, but still fails to accommodate all the varieties of elite culture, let alone popular culture. The best that can be said of the concept 'the age of the baroque' is that it remains suggestive. What it suggests, as I have tried to show, is a multitude of more or less precise connections between different forms or domains of behaviour, from the arts to styles of religious and political culture.

References

Alpers, S., The Art of Describing, Chicago 1983.

Biagioli, M., Galileo Courtier: the Practice of Science in the Culture of Absolutism, Chicago 1993.

Butterfield, H., Origins of Modern Science 1300–1800, London 1951.

Casini, P., L'universo-macchina: origini della filosofia newtoniana, Bari 1969.

Clark, G. N., The Seventeenth Century, Oxford 1929.

Croce, B., Storia dell'età barocca, Bari 1929.

Evans, R. J. W., The Making of the Habsburg Monarchy, Oxford 1979.

Haskell, F., Patrons and Painters: a Study in the Relations between Italian Art and Society in the Age of the Baroque, London 1963.

Hauser, A., A Social History of Art, 2 vols, London 1951.

Klaniczay, T., Renaissance und Manierismus, Berlin 1977.

Kühlmann, W., Gelehrtenrepublik und Fürstenstaat: Entwicklung und Kritik des deutsche Späthumanismus in der Literatur des Barockzeitalters, Tübingen 1982.

Labrousse, E., Bayle, Oxford 1983.

Mâle, E., L'art religieux après la concile de Trente, second edn. Paris 1949.

Maravall, J., Culture of the Baroque, English translation Manchester 1986.

Meinecke, F., Machiavellism: the doctrine of raison d'état and its place in modern history, English translation, London 1957.

Merton. R. K., 'Science, Technology and Society in Seventeenth-Century England', Osiris 4 (1938), 360–420.

Mousnier, R., Les XVIe et XVIIe siècles, Paris 1953.

Nicolson, M. H., The Breaking of the Circle: Studies in the Effect of the New Science upon Seventeenth-Century Poetry, Evanston 1950.

Oestreich, G., Neostoicism and the Early Modern State, Cambridge 1982.

Polišensky, J. V., The Thirty Years' War. 1970.

Porter, R. and Teich, M., eds, The Scientific Revolution in National Context, Cambridge 1992.

Rossi, P., I filosofi e le macchine, Bari 1962.

Rousset, J., La littérature de l'âge baroque en France, Paris 1953.

Shapin, S., The Scientific Revolution, Chicago 1996.

Tapié, V., The Age of Grandeur: baroque and classicism in Europe, English translation, London 1960.

Thomas, K. V., Religion and the Decline of Magic, London 1971.

Tuck, R., Philosophy and Government 1572–1651, Cambridge 1993.

Villari, R., Elogio della dissimulazione, Rome and Bari 1987.

Villari, R., ed., Baroque Personae, English translation, Chicago 1995.

Wölfflin, H., Renaissance and Baroque, English translation Ithaca NY, 1966.

Yates, F., The Rosicrucian Enlightenment, London 1972.

7: THE REPUBLIC OF LETTERS AS A COMMUNICATION SYSTEM

This article argues that the concept of the 'Republic of Letters' or 'commonwealth of learning' is just as useful for writing the intellectual history of the modern period, 1750–2000 as it is in the case of the early modern period, to which the term is generally confined. The rise of nationalism and specialization in the nineteenth century was sufficient to modify but not to destroy the community of scholars. Examining the Republic not only as an imagined community but also as a system of communications, the author distinguishes four periods, that of the horse-drawn commonwealth (1500–1850); the age of steam (railways and steamships and the steam press) (1850–1950); the age of jet travel (1950–90) and the age of the personal computer and the Internet (1990–). Divisions between parts of the commonwealth and disruptions to it will be discussed, but it will be argued that reactions to these problems revealed the survival of solidarity.

KEYWORDS commonwealth of learning; communication; imagined community; network; Republic of Letters; scholarship.

The early modern European 'Republic of Letters' or 'commonwealth of learning', from the Renaissance to the Enlightenment, has been the object of a number of recent studies, designed as contributions to the history of learning.[1] In what follows, by contrast, the Republic will be studied as a communication system.[2] Focusing on communication leads to an alternative periodization, extending the idea of the Republic beyond the late eighteenth century, the moment when books and articles on this topic usually come to an end. The rise of the Internet has encouraged some scholars to speak of the revival of the Republic, but this article will argue that the 'digital Republic' is simply the last of four phases in the history of an institution that has endured for some 500 years. The four phases will be distinguished in terms of changes in the communication system, thinking both of physical communication, the movement of people and things, and of the media – oral, written, printed, electronic and so on.

I

The idea of the Republic of Letters goes back to the Renaissance itself. The Latin phrase *respublica litterarum* is first recorded in 1415, in a letter written by a Venetian humanist.[3] This commonwealth of scholars was essentially what Benedict Anderson, thinking of the nation, called an 'imagined community'.[4] It was sometimes described, in Friedrich Gottlieb Klopstock's *Die Deutsche Gelehrtenrepublik* (1774) for example, by means of an extended political metaphor in which the Republic possessed a senate, laws and so on.

As in the case of the nation, what Anderson calls 'print-capitalism' assisted the rise of the community. It is surely significant that the phrase *respublica letterarum* only became widespread in the age of Erasmus, half a century after the invention of printing. Erasmus became the centre of a network of correspondents thanks

---

[1] Studies include, in chronological order, Bots, *Republiek der Letteren*; Kühlmann, *Gelehrtenrepublik und Fürstenstaat*; Neumeister and Wiedemann, *Respublica litterarum*; Goodman, *The Republic of Letters*; Goldgar, *Impolite Learning*; Bots and F. Waquet, *La République des Lettres*.

[2] This aspect is stressed by Bots and Waquet, *Commercium*; Ultee, 'Letters'.

[3] Fumaroli, 'The Republic of Letters'.

[4] Anderson, *Imagined* Communities.

to a reputation that was based on his published books.[5] Anderson's argument may be carried a little further by observing that the learned journal was an invention of the later seventeenth century. Journals such as the *Giornale de'letterati* of Rome, *Nouvelles de la République des Lettres* of Rotterdam, *Bibliothèque Universelle et Historique* of Amsterdam, *Acta Eruditorum* of Leipzig, and so on, held the commonwealth together by offering news about the world of learning, including obituaries of scholars and, above all, reviews of new books.[6] The simultaneity stressed by Anderson in the case of the nineteenth-century newspaper could be found in the seventeenth century among the learned readers of the *Nouvelles de la République des Lettres,* edited by a Frenchman in exile in the Netherlands and addressed to an international community of scholars.[7]

The commonwealth may be regarded not only as an imagined community but also as a system of communication, since customs and institutions existed that facilitated collaboration between scholars or at least co-operation at a distance. These customs and institutions included writing letters in Latin that broke through the barriers of the European vernaculars, making gifts of publications and information, and visiting fellow-scholars when travelling. In the early seventeenth century, for example, scholars visiting Venice would place the learned friar Paolo Sarpi on their itinerary as well as Piazza San Marco.

European libraries were often open to foreign visitors. The entrance to the Bodleian Library Oxford still bears the old inscription 'For the republic of the learned' (*Reipublicae Letteratorum*), although some foreign scholars complained that they were not made welcome, especially when they asked to see manuscripts. At a time of religious conflict, often turning into war, Protestant scholars were allowed to use the Vatican Library.[8] Many Catholic and Protestant

---

[5] Anderson, *Imagined* Communities 36; Jardine, *Erasmus*; Burke, 'Erasmus'.

[6] The function of integration is stressed in Schneider, *Friedrich Nicolais Allgemeine Deutsche Bibliothek.*

[7] On simultaneity, Anderson, *Imagined Communities* 145, 194. On leading journals, Bost, *Un intellectuel*; Gardair, *Giornale de'letterati*; Laeven, *Acta Eruditorum.*

[8] Jaumann, *Europäische Gelehrtenrepublik*; A. Grafton, 'A Sketch Map'.

scholars also managed to maintain good personal and epistolary relations with each other.

By the eighteenth century, the commonwealth had expanded beyond Europe and had set up outposts in Batavia (now Djakarta), Calcutta (now Kolkata) and in the Americas, notably in Mexico City, Lima, Boston, Philadelphia and Rio de Janeiro, where an Academy of Sciences was founded in 1772.[9] The rise of global or at least intercontinental knowledge communities did not begin with the WorldWideWeb, even if this rise has been accelerating in the last 20 years.

It is possible that we now tend to see this learned community through rose-tinted spectacles, the spectacles of nostalgia. As a corrective, two Anglophone scholars recently portrayed the republic in a more realistic fashion, emphasizing rivalries and conflicts, priority disputes, accusations of plagiarism and so on.[10] From the social point of view the commonwealth remained restricted, virtually confined to upper- and middle-class males (though Countess Eva de la Gardie was a member of the Swedish Academy).

In theory, the community was egalitarian, based on equal exchange, and attempts were made to abolish or at least to suspend social distinctions among scholars. In the Royal Swedish Academy of Sciences, for instance, all members were addressed as *herr*, despite the fact that some had titles of nobility. In practice, of course, some scholars were more equal than others. There were masters and disciples, teachers and students, patrons and clients. The commonwealth was not isolated from the rest of society, the hierarchical society of the old regime, even if in some respects it represented a criticism of it.

II

Most studies of this community, real or imagined, come to an end either around 1750, with the *Encyclopédie*, or in 1789, with the French Revolution, or at the latest around 1800, with the Napo-

---

[9] On Boston and Philadelphia, Fiering, 'The Transatlantic Republic'.
[10] Daston, 'Ideal and Reality'; Goldgar, *Impolite Learning*.

leonic wars, speaking of the fragmentation or even the collapse of the republic.[11] In what follows, I shall argue that this ending is premature. There are of course some good reasons, if not sufficient reasons, for this collective decision on the part of the community of historians. Two main reasons that might be summed up in as many words: nationalism and specialization.

The Napoleonic wars had a negative impact on scholarship, disrupting communication. Although the French and British began by following the 'axiom', as the President of the Royal Society of London, Joseph Banks, puts it, 'That the science of two Nations may be at Peace while their Politics are at war', collaboration soon broke down. Banks, for instance, was surprised that a Frenchman declined to visit him in 1793. 'I cannot conceive', he wrote, 'that any one would consider as a political necessity to debar me from the acquaintance of a learned man because he is of a nation with which we are at war'.[12] The Institute in Paris asked Banks to ensure that the French expedition to map the Australian coastline was not hindered and he did so, but he was unable to have a British explorer released in return.[13] The famous remark, by an English medical scientist, Edward Jenner, that 'The sciences are never at war' was going out of date at the very moment (1803) that it was made.

The harmony of the commonwealth of learning was increasingly threatened not only by wars but also more insidiously by the shift from cosmopolitanism to nationalism.[14] In the context of learning, one might even speak of the 'nationalization' of knowledge at this time, in the sense of the rise of a view of scholars as representatives of their nation and their recruitment into the service of the nation-state. Money was often forthcoming from nineteenth-century governments for great national scholarly enterprises such as national museums, national libraries, dictionaries of national biography,

---

[11] Goldgar, *Impolite Learning* and Bots and Waquet, *La République*, end in 1750. Goodman, *The Republic of Letters*, ends with the Revolution. On *éclatement*, Bots and Waquet, *La République* 58; on *écroulement*, Masseau, *L'invention de l'intellectuel* 122–7.
[12] Beer, The *Sciences*; Daston, 'Ideal and Reality'; Banks qtd. in Gascoigne, *Science* 155.
[13] Gascoigne, Science 159.
[14] Meinecke, *Weltbürgertum*.

national geographical or geological surveys, or histories of the nation and its language and literature. On the other hand, scholarly enterprises that lacked this national resonance received less official support.[15]

A second point in favour of the traditional end of the story of the commonwealth of learning around the year 1800 concerns the long trend towards intellectual specialization, the fragmentation of the old republic into separate provinces or communities of specialists.[16] Like nationalism, specialization created obstacles to communication between scholars. Divisions between disciplines were increasingly institutionalized, embodied in departments, or institutes with walls separating them from other 'academic tribes and territories'.[17] The commonwealth, like the campuses of which it was now composed, became an archipelago of disciplinary islands. As a result of these changes, the phrase *république des lettres* gradually became restricted to *belles-lettres*.[18]

Despite nationalism and specialization, a case can be made for the re-instatement of the idea of the commonwealth of learning to describe scholarly communication in the West (and increasingly over the whole globe) since 1800.[19] The history of the commonwealth of learning may be divided into four periods of extremely unequal length. The first period, a long early modern period that extends from about 1450 to 1850, might be described as the age of the horse-drawn commonwealth, because books, letters and scholars themselves all required horse-power in order to travel. The same point can of course be made about the Middle Ages, although the idea of a commonwealth of learning was not yet circulating.

The second period, 1850–1950, might be called the age of steam, marked by travel by railways and steamships, and by printing with the steam press. The third period, from about 1950 to 1990, was

[15] Burke, *Social History*, 192–7.
[16] Bots and Waquet, *République* 159.
[17] Becher, *Academic Tribes*; Burke, *Social History* 160–83.
[18] Bots and Waquet, *République* 159; Veblen, *The Higher Learning* 48.
[19] Cf. Karady, 'La république des lettres'; Callisen and Adkins, 'Pre-digital Virtuality' (my thanks to the authors for letting me read this paper before its publication).

the age of air, with a scholarly 'jet set' engaging in constant travel, while international telephone calls became easier and cheaper. The fourth is the electronic age, the age of the personal computer and the use of e-mail, not to mention increasing feelings of guilt about carbon footprints.

As the first age has received the lion's share of scholarly attention, what follows will concentrate on the last 150 years, without forgetting survivals from one age into another – or indeed long-term trends, notably the more or less continuous increase in the population of the commonwealth and the growing formalization and institutionalization of relations between its members.

III

In some ways the second or steam age of the commonwealth of learning was a continuation of the first. The practice of letter writing continued to be important. Indeed, the international postal service was becoming faster, cheaper and more reliable at this time, thanks not only to the railways, which transported letters as well as people, but also to the Bern Postal Conference of 1874. However, the letter was now supplemented by the offprint, a kind of scholarly visiting card that might be sent in order to initiate or maintain relations with a foreign colleague.[20]

The steamship helped to transform the commonwealth because it allowed the transatlantic barrier to be broken by the 1840s, making possible, for instance, the lecture tours in the USA made by Charles Lyell, Matthew Arnold, T.H. Huxley and a number of British popularizers of science. Australia now moved within reach: the British Association for the Advancement of Science held its 84th annual meeting in Melbourne in 1914. The German scholars Karl Lamprecht, Ferdinand Tönnies, Ernst Troeltsch, Max Weber and Werner Sombart all sailed to the USA in 1904 on the occasion of the Universal Exposition at St Louis and stayed to deliver lectures. A regular exchange of visiting professors between Berlin and Harvard was inaugurated at this time. By the 1920s, Rockefeller fel-

---

[20] Hagstrom, *The Scientific Community* 30.

lowships were giving some young European physicists the opportunity to work in the USA.[21]

The commonwealth was transformed by the rise of the international congress. Congresses of this kind were a nineteenth-century invention, successful enough to be averaging around 30 a year by the end of the century. The first International Congress of Historical Sciences, for instance, was held in Paris in 1900, the location having been chosen to coincide with the world fair of that year, which also attracted congresses of mathematicians, physicists, chemists, botanists, geologists, meteorologists and psychologists.[22] The statisticians had held their first international congress in 1853, the chemists in 1860, the medics in 1867, the geographers in 1871, the art historians, the orientalists and the meteorologists in 1873, the geologists in 1878, and so on. The simultaneous rise of the railway and the international congress can hardly be coincidence. Communication between scholars was assisted by the rise of three competing languages of international scholarship: first French, which was already beginning to replace Latin in the late seventeenth century; then German, from the early nineteenth century onwards; and finally English.[23]

These developments had their price: the decline of local knowledge societies, for instance—antiquarian, archaeological, literary and so on—associated with traditional media of communication such as the letter, the lecture and the annual volume of printed proceedings. The rise of formal standards such as peer-group review for the publication of articles in learned journals tended to exclude the contributions of outsiders, widening the gap between amateurs and professionals.[24]

The major fault-line was between what C.P. Snow, in 1959, called 'the two cultures'.[25] By Snow's time, incidentally, scientists

---

[21] Brocke, *Wissenschaftsgeschichte und Wissenschaftspolitik* 185–6; Weiner, 'The Refugees' 194, 196.
[22] Erdmann, *Towards a Global Community*.
[23] On German as a learned lingua franca, Ammon, 'Deutsche als Wissenschaftssprache'.
[24] A vivid example in Hesketh, 'Diagnosing Froude's Disease'.
[25] Snow, *Two Cultures*.

were more likely than their colleagues in the humanities to view themselves as a community, sometimes described as an 'invisible college'.[26] The Anglo-Hungarian polymath Michael Polanyi, consciously adapting the older usage, referred to 'the republic of science'.[27]

The scientific republic was divided into an ever-increasing number of disciplines, which were also described as communities on occasion. The idea of 'the crystallographic community', for instance, or 'the protein community' now competed with the wider unit, though it was of course possible for individuals to consider themselves members of both the wider and the narrower groups.[28] One reason for preferring the phrase 'commonwealth of learning' to 'Republic of Letters', especially when speaking of the nineteenth and twentieth centuries, is the association of the term 'commonwealth', at least to British ears, with a loose federation permitting multiple identities.

In the twentieth century, these divisions were accompanied by other disruptions to communication. Needless to say, the rise of Fascism and Nazism and the two world wars were disasters for the world of learning as for the world in general. Some scholars expressed a strong nationalism. Ninety-three German professors wrote a letter in defence of the burning of the library at the University of Leuven in 1914.[29] In the USA, the sociologist Albion Small broke off relations with his former friend and colleague Georg Simmel. In Belgium, the historian Henri Pirenne broke with Karl Lamprecht. Pirenne himself was arrested and deported to Germany following a protest against the German takeover of the University of Ghent.[30]

However, some reactions to these disruptions revealed the wider solidarity of the commonwealth. After the war, the League of Nations was concerned with international cooperation at a scholarly as well as a political level. An International Research Coun-

---

[26] Crane, *Invisible Colleges.*
[27] Polanyi, *Science Faith;* cf. Jouvenel, 'Republic of Science'.
[28] Law, 'The Development of Specialties'. Cf Crawford, 'The Universe'.
[29] Johnson, *Kaiser's Chemists* 1812.
[30] Lyon, *Henri Pirenne* 247–8, 258–62; cf. Chickering, *Karl Lamprecht.*

cil for Science was inaugurated in Brussels in 1919 and a League of Nations Committee on Intellectual Co-operation in 1922 (its members including Henri Bergson and Albert Einstein). An International Astronomical Union was founded in 1922.[31] Pirenne worked for the revival of the International Historical Congresses and for the re-admission of German scholars to the community of historians. He presided over the Brussels Congress in 1923 where he presented comparative history as an antidote to nationalism. Another Belgian, the bibliographer Paul Otlet, spent much of his life trying to improve the communication of world knowledge and the prospects of peace among nations, founding the Mundaneum (1919) in Brussels for these purposes and working with the Committee on Intellectual Co-operation. Otlet's attempt to reconstruct the old commonwealth of learning was not successful, but it does illustrate the resurgence of the ideal.[32]

The rise of Fascism and Nazism led of course to the great intellectual exodus of the 1930s: the flight of scholars, most of them Jewish and German speaking. The continuing solidarity of the commonwealth was revealed by the reception of these scholars in Britain, Sweden, Turkey, the USA, South America, New Zealand and elsewhere.

IV

In the third age of the Republic, approximately 19501990, the growing ease of air travel encouraged the proliferation of small international conferences on specific themes. The grand international disciplinary congresses mentioned earlier survived into this period, becoming larger and larger, but precisely for this reason the real work was increasingly done elsewhere.

In the age of the Cold War, the Iron Curtain obviously divided the commonwealth, as the division between Catholics and Protestants had done in the age of the early modern religious wars. Once again, however, scholarly communication continued across

---

[31] Kevles, 'Reorganization'.
[32] Discussed in Levie, *L'homme*. Cf Laqua, 'European Internationalism (s).

the divide. At the official level, to take historical studies as an example, the curtain was sometimes drawn back sufficiently to allow conferences, between French and Polish historians, for example, as well as an annual conference of economic historians at Prato where, at the urging of the mayor of the city (usually a member of the PCI), historians from what the magazine *Encounter* used to call 'the other shore' were always well represented.

Again, compensating to some degree for existence of the Curtain, the new period began with the foundation of UNESCO (1946), which succeeded the League of Nations Committee but was given more resources than its predecessor. The English scientist Joseph Needham and the American knowledge manager Vannevar Bush were among those who helped insert the 'S for Science' into UNESCO (originally planned as an organization for culture and education). Another English scientist, Julian Huxley, became the first director-general. UNESCO also supported the International Political Science Association (1949), the International Sociological Association (1949), the International Social Science Council (1955) and two multivolume world histories: the *History of Mankind* (1963–6), quickly condemned as ethnocentrically western, and its successor the *History of Humanity* (1994–2009), in which the regional sections were generally written by scholars from the region concerned.

In this third age the rise of the Common Market, European Community and European Union made an obvious impact on the commonwealth of learning. An obvious example is CERN (Conseil Européen pour la Recherche Nuclé aire, 1954, now The European Organization for Nuclear Research), driven, it is true, by financial necessity, because particle accelerators do not come cheap, but helping create a European community of scientists, or at least of particle physicists. Again, international competition in space, so visible in the 1950s and 1960s, the age of Sputnik and the American moon landing, was replaced by collaboration, driven once again by financial necessity.

On the side of the humanities international organizations, more modest in scale, include the European Consortium for Political Research (1979); and the Consortium of European Research Libraries (1992) coming together to record all books printed in Europe in

1455–1830 and known — in a possibly sardonic allusion to CERN — as CERL. The European Science Foundation (1974) gives money for projects in both the humanities and the natural sciences, thus serving what it calls 'the European research community', the commonwealth of learning under a new name.

Institutes on the model of the Institute of Advanced Study at Princeton (1930) were founded in this period in Wassenaar (Netherlands Institute for Advanced Study, 1970), Berlin (the *Wissenschaftskolleg*, 1980) and in Uppsala (the Swedish Collegium for Advanced Study, 1985) encouraging the internationalization of learning by the traditional means of prolonged face-to-face encounters between scholars from different countries.

V

The fourth age is obviously difficult to see in historical perspective since it began relatively recently, when the Berlin Wall fell and the WorldWideWeb was christened. However, it is already clear that the 'Digital Republic of Learning' differs in important respects from its predecessors. The Republic of Letters was always a 'virtual community', but the acceleration of communication has made its members more conscious of interaction at a distance than they used to be.[33] Electronic conferencing allows participants to ask speakers questions by e-mail. Research is being transformed by the rise of e-research centres like the ESRC National Centre for e-Social Science (2006), allowing collaboration at a distance and giving a new meaning to the old idea of an 'invisible college'. A project such as the Census of Marine Life, involving individuals from over 80 nations but carried out between 2000 and 2010, was scarcely conceivable in the pre-electronic age.[34]

Optimists have described these trends in terms of 'the flattening of the world' in the sense of 'connecting all the knowledge centres on the planet together in a single global network', on in which participants are placed 'on a more equal footing than at any previous

---

[33] Darnton, *Case* 13, 58, 106; Callisen and Adkins, 'Predigital Virtuality'.

[34] Crawford, Shinn, and Sörlin, *Denationalizing Science* 4; Snelgrove, *Discoveries*.

time in the history of the world'.[35] The trend to this kind of collaboration has been assisted not only by the thaw of the political Ice Age but also by the rise of English as the new Latin.

However, this learned lingua franca encourages inequalities as well as assisting communication. Unlike Latin in the early years of the *respublica litterarum,* English is the first language of many scholars, giving them a competitive advantage. The intellectual playing field is still far from level. The rise of global English or 'globish' encourages the 'unequal exchange of texts', because many more studies are translated from English than are translated into it.[36] Indeed, scholarly books and articles in English cite texts in other languages much less often than the other way round. Scholars in some countries, from Sweden to Brazil, are under pressure from the heads of universities to publish in English rather than in their own language in order to raise the international prestige of their institutions.[37]

The fact that English is the language of major search engines such as Google has increased its dominance still further, alarming some users of other languages, such as the French, among them former president Jacques Chirac and also Jean-Noël Jeanneney, the president of the Bibliothèque Nationale de France, whom Chirac consulted in 2005 about the possibility of a French search engine (launched later, under the name Quaero).[38]

The impact of technological change on the everyday life of scholars is multiple and still difficult to assess. For example, video-conferencing established itself in the 1990s, and gives a new meaning to the sense of simultaneity discussed above, although it remains unclear whether this new technique, or institution, will replace meetings in 'real space' or merely supplement them.

Libraries have been transformed, losing first their card catalogues, replaced by computers; and then their journals, increasingly accessible online. The future of the book, or more exactly the paper

---

[35] Thomas Friedman, qtd. in Hannerz, *Anthropology's World* 114.
[36] Swaan, *Words of the World* 41–59. Cf. Crystal, *English as a Global Language;* Nerrière, *Parlez Globish;* McCrum, *Globish* 210–54. More sceptical, at least so far as the long term is concerned, Ostler, *The Last Lingua Franca.*
[37] Hannerz, *Anthropology's World* 113–30.
[38] Jeanneney, *Quand Google défie l'Europe.*

book, begins to look uncertain.[39] The offprint, whether handed out or sent by post, is being replaced by the e-mailed article, published or unpublished. The author of an article submitted to an e-journal may elicit reactions from a number of readers before acceptance, in the place of the traditional two or three anonymous critics.

The rise of blogging has affected the world of learning as well as other places. According to an enthusiast, 'Scholars who blog are engaging in more than personal publishing; they are shaping a new "third place" for academic discourse, a space for developing the social networks that help drive the more visible institutions of research'.[40] Even more important has been the rise of electronic databases, whether scholars create their own or use ready-made ones via search 'engines' such as Google. Working online transforms scholarly space as well as time. The importance of these innovations in the history of communications is not only the speeding up of the process of finding information but also the fact that personal computers can be used in so many locations.

In some important respects, then, the old distinction between centres of knowledge located in major cities such as Paris, London or New York and the provinces is finally being eroded. Marshall McLuhan's celebrated phrase 'the global village' remains an exaggeration but it has become more accurate now than it was in his own day (he died in 1980). On the other hand, theory, in the social as well as the natural sciences, is still produced for the most part in the West, despite calls for social theory to incorporate the social experience of all parts of the world in its generalizations.[41]

In the social history of the commonwealth of learning, the most remarkable — indeed, unforeseeable — development has been the democratization of intellectual cooperation that is most vividly illustrated by Wikipedia. Its articles are often inaccurate, but that criticism can be made of printed encyclopaedias as well. What is distinctive about on-line encyclopaedias is their rapid, indeed continuous revisability. Together with other e-institutions, Wikipedia shows that the commonwealth is not dead but alive and well, even

---

[39] Darnton, Case 43–58; Grafton, 'Codex in Crisis'.
[40] Halavais, 'Scholarly Blogging' 117.
[41] Connell, *Southern Theory*.

if it is — like the rest of us — far from perfect.

Despite the latest revolution, the last word should perhaps go to continuity. In an age of databases, some scholars still write information on 5x3 inch record cards and store them in shoeboxes, to the surprise of their research students, who now come from the digital generation. Intellectual progress still depends on personal encounters and dialogues. A recent study was surely right to emphasize the persistence of orality in academic life, even in our own time.[42] Sociologists of knowledge have suggested that 'at the research frontier, the transmission of new approaches and skills almost always requires direct face-to-face contacts'.[43] Despite the rise of writing, print and electronic communication, academic life still depends on the most traditional of the media: the spoken word.

References

Ammon, Ulrich. 'Deutsche als Wissenschaftssprache [German as a Learned Language].' *Sprache und Sprachen in der Wissenschaften* [Language and Languages in the Sciences]. Herbert Ernst Wiegand, ed. Berlin: de Gruyter, 1999. 668–85.

Anderson, Benedict. *Imagined Communities: Reflections on the Origin and Spread of Nationalism.* 1983: Rev. ed. London: Verso, 1991.

Becher, Tony. *Academic Tribes and Territories.* 1989: 2nd ed. Buckingham: Open University Press, 2001.

Beer, Gavin R. DE. *The Sciences Were Never at War.* London: Nelson, 1960.

Bost, Hubert. *Un intellectuel avant la lettre: le journaliste Pierre Bayle* [An Intellectual Before Intellectuals: The Journalist Pierre Bayle]. Amsterdam: APA-Holland UP, 1994.

---

[42] Waquet, *Parler comme un livre.*
[43] Hoch and Platt, 'Migration'.

Bots, Hans. *Republiek der Letteren: Ideaal en Werkelijkheid* [The Republic of Letters: Ideal and Reality]. Amsterdam: APA-Holland UP, 1977.

Bots, Hans and Françoise, Waquet. *Commercium litterarium, 1600–1750: la communication dans la République des lettres* [Literary Exchanges, 1600–1750: Communication in the Republic of Letters]. Amsterdam: APA-Holland UP, 1994.

– – –. *La République des Lettres* [The Republic of Letters]. Paris: Belin, 1997.

Brocke, Bernhard Vom, ed. *Wissenschaftsgeschichte und Wissenschaftspolitik im Industriezeitalter: Das 'SystemAlthoff'. in historische Perspektive* [TheHistory of Science and Science Policy in the Industrial Age: The 'Althoff System' in Historical Perspective]. Hildesheim: Lax, 1991.

Burke, Peter. 'Erasmus and the Republic of Letters.' *European Review,* 7 (1999): 5–17.

– – –. *A Social History of Knowledge.* Vol. 2, From the Encyclopédie to Wikipedia. Cambridge: Polity Press, 2011.

Callisen, Christian T., and Barbara Adkins. 'Pre-digital Virtuality: Early Modern Scholars and the Republic of Letters.' *The Long History of New Media: Technology, Historiography, and Contextualizing Newness.* David W. Park, Nicholas W. Jankowski, and Steve Jones, eds. New York: Peter Lang, 2011. 55–72.

Chickering, Roger. *Karl Lamprecht: A German Academic Life (1856–1915).* New Jersey: Humanities Press, 1993.

Connell, Raewyn. *Southern Theory.* Cambridge: Polity Press, 2007.

Crane, Diana. *Invisible Colleges: Diffusion of Knowledge in Scientific Communities.* Chicago: University of Chicago Press, 1972.

Crawford, Elisabeth. 'The Universe of International Science, 18801939.' *Solomon's House Revisited: The Organisation and Institu-*

tionalization of Science. Tore Frängsmyr, ed. Canton MA: Science History Publications, 1990. 251–69.

Crawford, Elisabeth, Terry Shinn, and Sverker Sörlin. *Denationalizing Science: The Contexts of International Scientific Practice.* Dordrecht: Kluwer, 1993.

Crystal, David. *English as a Global Language.* Cambridge: Cambridge University Press, 1997.

Darnton, Robert. *The Case for Books.* New York: PublicAffairs, 2009.

Daston, Lorraine. 'The Ideal and Reality of the Republic of Letters in the Enlightenment.' *Science in Context,* 4 (1991): 367–86.

Erdmann, Karl Dietrich. *Towards a Global Community of Historians: The International Historical Congresses and the International Committee of Historical Sciences, 1898–2000.* Oxford: Oxford UP, 2005.

Fiering, Norman. 'The Transatlantic Republic of Letters.' *William and Mary Quarterly,* 33 (1976): 642–60.

Fumaroli, Marc. 'The Republic of Letters.' *Diogenes,* 143 (1988): 129–52.

Gardair, Jean-Michel. *Le 'Giornale de'letterati' de Rome (1668–81)* [The 'Journal of the Learned' of Rome (1668–81)]. Florence: Olschki, 1984.

Gascoigne, John. *Science in the Service of Empire.* Cambridge: Cambridge UP, 1988.

Goldgar, Anne. *Impolite Learning: Conduct and Community in the Republic of Letters, 1680–50.* New Haven: Yale UP, 1995.

Goodman, Dena. *The Republic of Letters: A Cultural History of the French Enlightenment.* Ithaca: Cornell UP, 1994.

Grafton, Anthony. 'A Sketch Map of a Lost Continent: the Republic of Letters.' *Worlds Made by Words: Scholarship and Community in the Modern West.* Cambridge, MA: Harvard University Press, 2009. 934.
– – –. 'Codex in Crisis: The Book Dematerializes.' *Worlds Made by Words: Scholarship and Community in the Modern West.* Cambridge, MA: Harvard University Press, 2009. 288–326.

Hagstrom, Warren O. *The Scientific Community.* New York: Basic Books, 1965.

Halavais, Alex. 'Scholarly Blogging: Moving Toward the Visible College.' *Uses of Blogs.* Axel Bruns and Joanne Jacobs, eds. New York: Peter Lang, 2006. 117–26.

Hannerz, Ulf. *Anthropology's World.* London: Pluto, 2010.

Hesketh, Ian. 'Diagnosing Froude's Disease: Boundary Work and the Discipline of History in Late-Victorian Britain.' *History and Theory,* 47 (2008): 373–95.

Hoch, Paul, and Jennifer Platt. 'Migration and the Denationalization of Science.' *Denationalizing Science: The Contexts of International Scientific Practice.* Elisabeth Crawford, Terry Shinn, and Sverker Sörlin, eds. Dordrecht: Kluwer, 1993. 133–52.

Jardine, Lisa. *Erasmus Man of Letters: The Construction of Charisma in Print.* Princeton: Princeton UP, 1993.

Jaumann, Herbert, ed. *Die Europäische Gelehrtenrepublik im Zeitalter des Konfessionalismus* [The European Republic of Learning in the Age of Confessionalism].Wiesbaden: Harrassowitz, 2001.

Jeanneney, Jean Noël. *Quand Google défie l'Europe: plaidoyer pour un sursaut* [When Google Challenges Europe: A Wake-Up Call]. Paris: Mille et une Nuits, 2005.

Johnson, Jeffrey A. *The Kaiser's Chemists: Science and Modernization in Imperial Germany*. Chapel Hill, NC: University of North Carolina Press, 1990.

Jouvenel, Bertrand De. 'The Republic of Science.' *The Logic of Personal Knowledge: Essays Presented to Michael Polanyi*. London: Routledge and Kegan Paul, 1961. 131–41.

Karady, Victor. 'La république des lettres des temps modernes. L'internationalisation des marchés universitaires occidentaux avant la Grande Guerre [The Republic of Letters in Modern Times: The Internationalisation of Western University Markets Before the Great War].' *Actes de la Recherche en Science Sociale*, 121 (1988): 92–103.

Kevles, Daniel J. 'The Reorganization of International Science in World War I.' *Isis*, 62 (1971): 47–60.

Kühlmann, Wilhelm. *Gelehrtenrepublik und Fürstenstaat: Entwicklung und Kritik des deutschen Späthumanismus in der Literatur des Barockzeitalters* [Republic of Learning and Absolute Monarchy: the development and critique of German late humanism in the literature of the age of the baroque]. Tübingen: Niemeyer, 1982.

Laeven, A. Hubert. *Acta Eruditorum*. Amsterdam: APA-Holland University Press, 1986.

Laqua, Daniel. European Internationalism (s), 1880–1930: Brussels as a Centre for Transnational Cooperation. Ph.D. thesis. University of London, 2008.

Law, John. 'The Development of Specialties in Science: The Case of X-ray Protein Crystallography.' *Perspectives on the Emergence of Scientific Disciplines*. Gerard Lemaine, ed. The Hague: Mouton, 1976. 123–52.

Levie, Françoise. *L'homme qui voulait classer le monde: Paul Otlet et le mundaneum* [The Man Who Wanted to Classify the World: Paul Otlet and the Mundaneum]. Brussels:Impressions Nouvelles, 2006.

Lyon, Bryce D. *Henri Pirenne: A Biographical and Intellectual Study.* Ghent: Story Scientia, 1974.

Masseau, Didier. *L'invention de l'intellectuel dans l'Europe du XVIIIe siècle* [The Invention of the Intellectual in Eighteenth-Century Europe]. Paris: Presses universitaires de France, 1994.

McCrum, Robert. *Globish: How the English Language Became the World's Language.* London: Viking, 2010, 210–54.

Meinecke, Friedrich. *Weltbürgertum und Nationalstaat* [1908: English trans. Cosmopolitanism and the National State]. Princeton: Princeton University Press, 1970.

Nerrière, Jean-Paul. *Parlez Globish.* Paris: Eyrolles, 2004.

Neumeister Sebastian, and Conrad Wiedemann, eds. *Respublica litterarum* [The Republic of Letters]. Wiesbaden: Harassowitz, 1987.

Ostler, Nicholas. *The Last Lingua Franca: English Until the Return of Babel.* London: Penguin Books, 2010.

Polanyi, Michael. *Science Faith and Society.* 1948: 2nd ed. Chicago: University of Chicago Press, 1964.

Schneider, Ute. *Friedrich Nicolais Allgemeine Deutsche Bibliothek als Integrationsmedium der Gelehrtenrepublik* [Friedrich Nicolai's "General German Library" as a Means of Integrating the Republic of Learning]. Wiesbaden: Harassowitz, 1995.

Snelgrove, Paul V.R. *Discoveries of the Census of Marine Life.* Cambridge: Cambridge University Press, 2010.

Snow, Charles P. *The Two Cultures.* 1959: new ed. Cambridge: Cambridge UP, 1998.

Swaan, Abram De. *Words of the World: The Global Language System.* Cambridge: Cambridge UP, 2001.

Ultee, Maarten. 'Letters and the Republic of Letters.' *Seventeenth Century,* 2 (1987): 95–112.

Veblen, Thorstein. *The Higher Learning in America.* New York: Huebsch, 1918.

Waquet, Françoise. *Parler comme un livre. L'oralité et le savoir (XVIe-XXe siècle)* [To speak like a book. Orality and knowledge (16th-20th centuries)]. Paris: Albin Michel, 2003.

8: HISTORICAL
REFLECTIONS ON URBAN
VIOLENCE[1]

This article considers changes in urban violence over the long term, comparing and contrasting pre-industrial cities (especially but not exclusively in early modern Europe) with the mega-cities of the contemporary world (especially São Paulo). It emphasizes the dislocation and relocation of violence within the city, and the gradual professionalization of violence over the centuries.

Studies of modern urban violence appear in increasing numbers, even if they do not keep up with the violence itself. What seems to be lacking, however, is a serious attempt to consider this phenomenon over the long term. It is often assumed that the urban violence of our time is unique, if not in quantity, then at least in the main forms it takes. By contrast, this article offers traditional parallels for much of what is generally considered characteristically modern. The purpose of the parallels is not to assert a simple thesis of continuity, *plus ça change plus c'est la même chose*, but rather to try to define in a more nuanced manner what part of the 'cultural

---

[1] The original version of this article was published as 'Urban Violence and Civilization', *Braudel Papers* 11 (1995), 1–8. My thanks to Norman Gall for suggesting that I write this article and for feeding me with books and questions thereafter. The article has been extensively revised to take account of research since 1995 as well as to incorporate some new ideas.

repertoire' of violence is really peculiar to our time.

Given the dimensions of the topic, it is inevitable that these reflections take the form of an essay – impressionistic, personal and provisional. These reflections come from a historian of early modern Europe who has been inspired by urban sociology and anthropology, notably that of the Chicago school and especially Robert Park, the famous American journalist turned academic (Park, 1916). The emphasis will fall on the early modern European city, but the nineteenth century, Asia and the Americas will be discussed from time to time.

Needless to say, it will not be assumed that cities had a monopoly of violence. Psychologists tell us that aggression is part of human nature. In the case of early modern Europe, the subject of a good recent survey, travelers on main roads risked becoming victims of 'highwaymen', women working in the fields risked being raped, and male villagers risked being involved in tavern brawls (Ruff, 2001, 141; cf. Muchembled, 1989; Österberg, 1991).

In the case of cities, it is necessary to discriminate between types of violence, locales of violence, and occasions of violence. The emphasis in what follows will be on differences. A geography of modern violence is both necessary and possible, contrasting the USA, for instance, with Japan, where, despite the tradition of inter-personal violence associated with the samurai, aggression today seems to be turned inwards and expressed by suicide, including the suicides of children and adolescents. As for the contrast between 'traditional' and 'modern' cities, it will sometimes be reaffirmed, sometimes denied and often qualified.

In what follows eight problem areas will be discussed – 1, the perpetrators of violence; 2. the victims of violence; 3, the timing of violence; 4, the locales of violence; 5, the motives of violence; 6, the technology of violence; 7, the repertoires of violence and 8, the management of violence. In each case an attempt will be made both to compare and to contrast the mega-cities of our time, especially São Paulo (which I happen to know relatively well), with pre-industrial cities, especially the larger cities of early modern Europe (ranging from 100,000 to 1,000,000 inhabitants).

1. The perpetrators

In the case of the contemporary city, an initial distinction to make is that between violence by amateurs and by professionals. On one side there are the 'crowds' to whom responsibility for riots is usually attributed (though it would be unwise to assume that no professionals take part). On the other, we find the trained specialists in violence. They may be urban guerrillas ('terrorists') or 'strong-arm men' – *capangas* and *capoeiros* in nineteenth-century Brazil, *goondas* in India and so on (the army and the police will be considered in section 8 below). In between the two come rival groups or 'gangs' of young men, so visible today in Los Angeles or Rio de Janeiro. Violence is not exactly their job, but it is a regular part of their lives.

All three groups had their analogues in the early modern city. Riots were common and crowds have been studied by many historians, especially since the classic studies of revolutionary Paris (Lefebvre 1934; Rudé, 1959). The professionals of violence included the retainers of noblemen and the men known in early modern Italy as *bravi* (Walker, 1998). It seems that the young men of the pre-industrial city fought for and identified with their district, like the Castellani (from the Castello area) and the Nicolotti (around the church of St Nicholas) in Venice, so that gangs were hardly necessary. However, violent groups with distinctive names and territories can be found by the 1840s, if not before, with the 'Bowery Boys' of New York, as an early example (Asbury 1928, the inspiration for the film directed by Martin Scorsese in 2002).

In all cases, amateur or professional, traditional or modern, what stands out is the predominance of YAMs – a convenient abbreviation for 'Young Adult Males' – a group which, at least when unmarried, had less to lose than older colleagues with wives and children and more money and leisure to spend on fighting as well as on drinking and organizing festive events, from charivari to Carnival (Burke 1978, 29; Ruff 2001, 125).

There are also some contrasts to be noted. One is the prominent place of women in early modern urban riots, especially food riots, in England, France, Netherlands and elsewhere, riots in which women could act with relative impunity from later prosecution (Davis 1973, 86–7; Walter 1980, 62–3; Dekker 1982, 51–2). A second contrast between our own time and the early modern world concerns the role of elites. The cases of rape which came before the courts of Renaissance Venice not infrequently involved young noblemen (Ruggiero 1980). In England too, in the sixteenth and early seventeenth centuries, the propensity to violence among young noblemen is easy to document (Stone 1965, 223–34). The rise of the habit of dueling in the sixteenth and seventeenth centuries alarmed contemporaries, who viewed it as a rise in violence (Billacois 1986, Kiernan 1988).

Can we speak of noble 'hooligans'? If by this term we mean perpetrators of more or less gratuitous violence, then the answer will be 'sometimes but not always'. A more structured form of political violence was important among the upper classes in Italian city-states. There were frequent conflicts, virtually private wars, between factions (Guelphs and Ghibellines, Black and White Guelphs, etc), as well as between families. In early modern times, the practice of vendetta was general 'respectable', rather than associated with criminals (Mafia, Triads), as it seems to be today.

In many places and periods, urban violence has been associated with a 'faction' in the sense of a group structured by the vertical solidarity of patrons and clients, as opposed to the horizontal solidarity of a social class. In the case of the political conflicts in ancient Rome, for instance, Cicero, like his enemies, had armed clients, veterans and slaves in his service (Lintott 1968, 1982). In twelfth-century Nishapur, a dispute between two Muslim schools of law (Hanafi and Shafi'i), mobilized two factions who are said to have destroyed the city in their battles (Bulliet 1972). Reading this account, it is hard not to think of Tehran in the age of the *ayatollahs*.

2 The victims

As in the case of the perpetrators, young adult males often predominate among the victims of violence. In São Paulo in 1994, for instance, about 93% of the victims of homicide were male and about 75% were aged between the ages of 15 and 49. Another striking feature of modern urban violence, especially collective or crowd violence, is the choice of outsiders as victims, whether one thinks of the endemic 'Paki-bashing' in contemporary London, the regular attacks on Turkish or Moroccan immigrants in Germany, or the sudden outbursts of violence against Tamils in Colombo in 1983, Sikhs in Delhi in 1984, and so on (Das 1990).

It has been asserted that in India, so-called 'communal riots' go back only to the end of the nineteenth century, to the Talla riot in Calcutta in 1897. In other parts of the world the tradition is much older. There were ethnic riots in American cities in the nineteenth century, by the Irish in New York, for example (Gordon 1993). There were riots against foreigners in London in the sixteenth, seventeenth and eighteenth centuries (Lindley 1983, 111–12). In Paris and elsewhere in France in 1572, the Catholics turned on the Protestant minority and massacred them (Davis 1973, Crouzet 1990). In Spanish cities, attacks on the Jewish and Muslim minorities were already common in the late Middle Ages (Wolff 1971, Nirenberg 1996).

Victims need not be people. Violence against physical objects is common, from the iconoclasm of the Reformation to the so-called 'vandalism' of the French Revolution, to say nothing about our own day, from the wrecking of telephone boxes to the toppling of statues of Lenin and Stalin following the collapse of the Berlin Wall (Christin 1991, Gamboni, 1996). Another kind of victim is a political regime. The barricades in Paris in 1789, 1848 and 1871 offer famous examples – though the local tradition of the barricade goes back at least as far as 1588, when rebels proclaimed that Henri III might be king of France, but that Henri duke of Guise was king of Paris (Descimon 1990).

3. Timing

It may be useful to distinguish 'endemic' from 'epidemic' violence, or to avoid the tempting but dangerous analogy with disease, violence that is either 'structural' or 'conjunctural'. For instance, a study of violence in India comments on the 'normal, structural violence embodied in everyday life in Gujarat' (Das 1990, 215). In similar fashion, a historian of seventeenth and eighteenth-century cities in the Netherlands, one of the most peaceful parts of Europe in the period, has remarked that 'In Amsterdam, violence by small crowds was ... considered an everyday occurrence', whether the occasion of rioting was religion, taxes or the price of food (Dekker 1989).

In traditional cities, as in traditional societies more generally, violence was more intense during festivals, times when the population of the city swelled with country people come to see the show, when work was forbidden, so that the people were on the streets, when drink flowed more freely than usual, and so on (Ruff 2001, 163–82). Some of the festive events involved violence, especially against animals, from the 'bear-baiting' of Elizabethan London to the bull-fighting to be found in the South of France and in Italy as well as in Spain in the early modern period (Mitchell 1991, Bennassar 1993, Shubert 1999). Violence against humans was also planned on particular occasions, as in the case of the so-called 'fist wars' in Venice (Davis 1994).

More often, violence was an unintended consequence of a festival. Festive football matches such as the Florentine *calcio* sometimes ended in fights. In seventeenth-century London, Shrove Tuesday was regularly marked by attacks on brothels by apprentices (Lindley 1983, 109–110; Harris 1986). As for Carnival, an Englishman in Venice at the end of the sixteenth century noted that on the Sunday night seventeen people had been killed and innumerable people injured, and that he had been told that there were murders every night of Carnival. This in a city of fewer than 200,000 inhabitants, though it may have swelled to 300,000 at this time of year (Sir Robert Dallington quoted in Burke 1978, 315).

On occasion, violence escalated and produced an incident that passed into popular memory or indeed into History with a capital H. 'Evil May Day' was the name for an attack on Germans in sixteenth-century London which took place on 1 May, a major English festival, at that time still associated with the rites of spring rather than organized labour. The celebration of the feast of Corpus Christi in Barcelona in June 1640 marked the beginning of a long revolt against control from Madrid (Elliott 1963, 445–51).

In today's world, on the other hand, despite the regular Sunni-Shia conflicts at Moharram (Das 1990, 16–19), violence seems to have less to do with festivals. This is true even for Carnival, at least relatively speaking. The 1995 statistics for violence during the Brazilian Carnival showed S. Paulo with 74 homicides (one per 130,000 inhabitants); Rio with 44; and Belo Horizonte, Porto Alêgre, and Salvador with five apiece (*Veja*, 8 March 1995, 29). These figures are rather low compared with sixteenth-century Venice! In Rio at the beginning of the twentieth century, fighting regularly took place during Carnival, but the two deaths in a battle between two groups of revellers in the district of Botafogo in 1902 seem to have been exceptional (Soihet 1993, 78, 88, 98, 146–8). In the case of violence as in that of other forms of leisure activity, the weekend has replaced traditional festivals, and in Europe at least, hospitals expect to be busy on Saturday night.

A special case of festive violence is associated with elections. Elections were frequent occasions of violence in ancient Rome and eighteenth-century England, as they are in certain parts of India even today (Bhan 1995, 21, 93, 150). Why violence has deserted elections in Brazil, for instance, or Venezuela, while remaining massive in these countries on other occasions, is a difficult question.

There remains the problem of chronology over the long term. It is generally considered that violence, especially homicide, declined in European cities, as indeed in Europe generally, from the late Middle Ages to the nineteenth century, to rise again, but less steeply, from the later twentieth century onwards (Chesnais 1981). Take the case of Amsterdam, for instance. From 47 homicides a year per thousand people in the later fifteenth century, the figure gradually declined to less than 2 a year by 1800, returning to 6 or more by the 1990s (Spierenburg, 1996). The trend might be linked to the famous hypothesis of the sociologist Norbert Elias about the 'civilizing process', his argument that westerners had become more and more self-controlled over the long term, from the twelfth century to the twentieth (Elias 1939). Elias and his followers later introduced the idea of the 'de-civilizing process' to account for changes from the 1930s onwards (Mennell 1990).

At a time when other European cities were relatively quiet, the beginning of the twentieth century, Spanish cities witnessed a cycle of political violence, culminating in the Civil War. In 1909, for example, the inhabitants of Barcelona lived through their 'tragic week', with anarchists throwing bombs. Between 1917 and 1923, about a thousand people died for political reasons in Barcelona (Thomas 1961, 67). By this time, of course, political violence in the cities of Germany, Italy, Russia and elsewhere was becoming commonplace. Since 1940 the Catalans, like the Spaniards in general, have escaped from this cycle of violence (with significant exceptions, such as the actions of ETA). Has the memory of the civil war been sufficient to keep the peace in Spanish cities? How long can this memory continue to remain effective?

4. Locales

Contemporary students of the city often consider it as an arena or set of arenas for different kinds of activity. In this sense we might speak of 'fields of violence' in the city. The subject has occasionally been discussed, (Ramalho Massena, 1986; Das 1990, 10–14), but it surely deserves more attention.

Zones where violence is predictable might be described as 'hot'. In Belfast, for example, until the recent truce, the Shankill Road was on of these zones. In Europe generally, hot zones are often peripheral because the poor are pushed out of the centre, while in the Americas they are often central because of the decay of the inner city. Other hot areas or stages for the performance of violence include taverns (especially towards closing time), factories (the scene of strikes and picketing), prisons, police stations, the roads in which traffic is most dense, and sports stadia and their vicinities (the violence of the fans spilling onto the streets).

The expectation of violence has left a good many traces on the contemporary urban landscape. In Chicago, for example, the heavily guarded houses of the Black Muslim leaders are extremely visible (or at any rate they were in the 1980s). They are urban fortresses. The hills or *morros* of Rio, dense with *favelas,* may also be regarded as fortresses, or as 'no-go areas', as they say in Belfast, into which the police do not dare to enter. Another outward sign of the expectation of violence is the modern condominium in São Paulo, New York, Los Angeles and other cities, with its spatial segregation, its high walls or railings and the security guards at the gate, as well as guard dogs and alarms. Chains across the street have sometimes been used to protect residents of São Paulo from violence (Caldeira, 1992, 196ff, 268).

All this has happened before. No-go areas of more traditional cities included the so-called 'rookery' of nineteenth-century London, and its equivalent in seventeenth-century Palermo, rabbit-warrens of narrow streets that were unsafe for the forces of order to enter. By the eighteenth century, if not earlier, guides for visitors were drawing attention to the more dangerous regions of major cities such as Paris. 'Hot' areas included bridges, which were often the scene of ritualized confrontations between the young men of different districts, as in the famous cases of Venice and Pisa. They were a sort of 'No Man's Land', or in the language of the anthropologist Victor Turner, a 'liminal' space (Turner 1969, Burke 1993, Davis 1994).

As for urban fortresses, Italy witnessed the rise of private towers from the year 1000 onwards; the 194 'noble towers' recorded in Bologna, the forest of towers still to be seen by tourists to San Gimignano, and so on (Gozzadini 1875, Martines 1973, Heers 1990, 281ff). Even in Renaissance Florence a grand building like the Palazzo Medici was built for defence as well as display, its doors massive, its windows high and protected by grilles. There were chains in the streets in medieval Toledo and sixteenth-century Perugia, in these cases probably to repel cavalry charges (Heers 1990, 89).

The most obvious difference between cities as theatres of violence then and now seems to be the presence or absence of public executions. As Michel Foucault and others have pointed out, the practice of beheading, hanging or otherwise killing criminals in public declined in Europe in the nineteenth century. Before that time, even children were familiar with the sight of the heads of traitors or the hanging bodies of robbers on public display. Whether or not this familiarity increased their own propensity for violent behaviour will be discussed in a later section.

Another contrast concerns the theatre itself and the area around it. In the nineteenth century, theatre riots were not uncommon. The audience often smashed the seats to demonstrate their disapproval of changes in the programme, while the Astor Place riot of 1849 in New York, a demonstration against the British actor William Macready, led to at least 22 deaths and many injuries (Levine 1989, 64–5). Today, this kind of violence has migrated from the theatre to the football stadium.

5. Motives

Is urban violence rational or irrational? In attempting to answer this question it does not seem useful to distinguish between periods. No age, not even the Enlightenment, can plausibly claim to be more rational than another.

However repellent we may find it, we surely have to admit that violence may often be rational in the sense of an efficacious means to certain ends. Take the case of political assassination. Often counter-productive it may be over a longer period, violence usually works in the short term, especially when the victims are taken by surprise.

In the case of collective violence, the traditional interpretation, from the descriptions by sixteenth-century observers to the theories of Gustave Lebon, has stressed the irrationality of the mob (Lebon 1912). This kind of 'spasmodic' interpretation, as he called it, was vigorously attacked by the late Edward Thompson in a now famous article on the eighteenth-century English crowd, suggesting that it was a rational, moral agent and even that riots were a form of collective bargaining (Thompson 1971).

Thompson's critique of the prejudices and also the metaphors common among observers of 'mobs' continues to be valuable, but we must not take his model of the English food riot and apply it indiscriminately to urban riots in general. Many of them were and are less rational as well as more lethal. The need for villains and scapegoats, the need to purify the community from 'pollution' by outsiders, perceived as less than human, and the possibility for individuals to lose their sense of responsibility, to transcend themselves in the crowd – these features of riots surely require anthropological and psychological as well as sociological analysis (Lefebvre 1934, Douglas 1966, Kakar 1990, Blok 1991). In short, collective violence may be expressive rather than instrumental.

The parallel between the violence in today's ethnic riots and that to be found in traditional cities such as Paris during the religious wars of the sixteenth century is indeed striking (Davis 1973, 59–60). In the religious wars, both sides saw themselves as re-enacting the history of the chosen people in the Old Testament, purifying the land of unbelievers (Crouzet 1990). In similar fashion the Sinhalese who massacred Tamils in Sri Lanka in 1983 re-enacted stories from their epic the *Mahavamsa,* notably the slaughter of demons by prince Vijaya. In this way they dehumanized their enemies before taking violent action against them (Kapferer 1988, 29–39).

The idea that urban violence is a symptom of underlying problems also deserves to be taken seriously. Some recent studies of riots in Karachi, for instance, have stressed the effect on the inhabitants of the city of regular shortages of water and power and the collapse of other public services fraying nerves and encouraging the search for scapegoats. A similar point has been made about violent responses to breakdowns of the public transport system in Rio and São Paulo (Das 1990, 189, 192, 207; Moisés and Stolcke 1980).

In traditional cities, food crises had similar effects, at least on occasion. Bakers rather than shortages were blamed for increases in the price of bread. Again, in late medieval Spanish cities, attacks by Christians on the quarters inhabited by Jews and Muslims became more frequent after the 'Black Death' of 1347–8, as if non-Christians were blamed for the plague. The rumour of the kidnapping of children by the authorities, which led to violence in

Paris in 1750, has been perceptively interpreted by two French historians as a symptom of discontent with the monarchy (Farge and Revel 1988). An anthropologist working on Africa once described accusations of witchcraft as a 'social strain-gauge' (Marwick 1964). In similar fashion, we might describe collective violence in the city as an indicator of social tensions.

'Festive violence', as the Russian critic Mikhail Bakhtin called it, deserves a separate discussion (Bakhtin 1965). It has already been illustrated by Carnival and fist wars.

In the case of Brazil in the twentieth century, one thinks especially of violence against public property, the so-called 'quebra-quebra', whether directed against street lights (as in Rio in 1904), or against public transport (as in Rio and São Paulo in 1974). The traditional explanation for this violence is neatly summed up in a carnival song, the *Maxixe Aristocrático* by José Nunes:

Quebra, quebra, quebra e
Requebra
Vamos de gosto quebrar
Vamos de gosto quebrar.
('Break, break, break and break again, let us break out of sheer enjoyment').

However, like the 'spasmodic' theory of riot, this analysis raises more problems than it solves. Is the smashing (however joyous) fundamentally expressive, an end in itself? Is it a relief for the psychological tensions provoked by the problems of the transport system? Or is it a conscious strategy, an attempt to force the municipal authorities to improve the system?

The violence of football fans inside and outside the stadium in Britain and elsewhere would seem to be a more clear-cut example of expressive or festive violence, following predictable patterns or 'rules' but sometimes getting out of control. (Marsh 1978).

At this point it may be worth raising the question of *machismo* as a possible key to the propensity to certain kinds of violence, honour killings for instance, in certain places and among certain groups. Spanish political violence has already been discussed; one wonders whether it has anything to do with the cultural values traditionally expressed in the bull-fight, the claim that the spectacle is for real men and that its critics are effeminate themselves and encourage effeminacy in others (Mitchell 1991, 92–6). The high homicide statistics from Latin countries have already been noted. However, the violence is not a Latin monopoly. Take the case of the Middle East. Homicides are relatively frequent in Cairo and Alexandria, for instance, to say nothing about Iraq. Perhaps we can speak of a Middle Eastern *machismo* (Gilsenan 1996, 201, 206, 295).

We return to the role of the YAMs. In certain places and times, at least, aggression is part of their definition of their masculinity. The language of insult may be revealing in this respect. In Britain, the violence of football fans not infrequently follows the exchange of ritualized insults such as 'wankers' (masturbators), which is a way of asserting that the other side are not real men. One might compare the incident in Amritsar in 1984, when the army occupied the temple and the Sikh women taunted their men with questions like 'Where is the starch in your moustache now?' The assassination of Mrs Gandhi soon followed (Das 1990, 140).

In the context of the cultural roots of violence, something should be said about representations. For the last half century a debate has been going on about the consequences of the many representations of violence on television, and whether this encourages boys in particular to imitate in real life the actions they see on the screen. The debate was revived in the USA by the Columbine incident, in the small town of Littleton Colorado, in 1999, when two students killed a teacher and twelve of their classmates, as it had been in Britain in 1996, when one teacher and sixteen children were killed in a school in Dunblane (it is curious that both incidents took place in small towns, not in proverbially violent mega-cities).

From an early modern perspective, however, televised violence seems distanced rather than close. Like adults, early modern children were familiar with violence as they were familiar with death, in unmediated forms. In cities, they regularly witnessed public executions as well as bear- and bull-baitings, to say nothing of spontaneous violence on occasions when they were standing by. As in the case of the ancient Romans who went to see gladiators kill and die in the Colosseum, these experiences may at the very least have reduced inhibitions by making violence familiar.

However, violence itself may be a representation. The theatrical element in public executions has been noted (Dülmen 1985). A similar point may be made about terrorism. It was the nineteenth century that saw the rise of urban 'terrorism' in the sense of actions deliberately carried out to spread terror and confusion among the spectators and thus allow anarchists or other groups to seize power. Actions of this kind were obviously facilitated by new technologies of violence, notably bombs.

6. Technology

The contrast between ancient and modern is at its most obvious in the field of technology.

In ancient Rome, stones are among the weapons most frequently mentioned in the sources. In medieval Italy, by contrast, urban warfare was more technologically sophisticated, witness the use of boiling oil in the sieges of noble towers, or the use of cavalry in the streets (the police horses of today give us some idea of their impact on pedestrians). At a more everyday level, the fact that in medieval and early modern Europe, many men regularly carried knives made it easy for minor brawls to turn lethal. There was a Dutch proverb, 'A hundred Netherlanders, a hundred knives' (Deursen, 1978–80, 110). We might speak of a 'knife culture', the equivalent of the 'gun culture' of the USA since 1800 (Hofstadter 1970, Bellesisles 2000).

By the sixteenth century, however, technological innovation in the means of violence was already worrying the authorities. The rapier, for instance, made duelling more lethal. Even more dangerous was the spread of the arquebus and its use in cities, in Genoa, for instance, or in Paris, for the assassination of Admiral Coligny in 1572, for example.

In the nineteenth century the bomb entered the arsenal of urban violence, associated with the anarchists in particular. Today, we witness the diversification of high-tech violence – machine-guns and long-range rifles in Rio, rocket launchers in Bagdad, semtex bombs in London, poison gas in Tokyo. From the quantitative point of view, however, the crucial change is the spread of cheap firearms.

'The transfer of technology and techniques between groups deserves to be noted, for instance between Brazilian urban guerrillas with political aims and the organization of drug-dealers known as *Comando Vermelho,* a transfer which resulted from contacts between guerrillas and criminals in the prisons of Rio (Amorim 1993, 44, 46, 68). This was not the first case of this kind of transfer: in nineteenth-century Spain, bandits learned from and imitated the techniques of the guerrillas against Napoleon.

7 Repertoires

The sociologist Charles Tilly and others have analyzed collective action, including violent action, in terms of what they call 'repertoires' that vary from one culture to another (Tilly 1986). In this respect as in others, comparisons and contrasts between the early modern period and our own day are in order. Repertoires include the technologies discussed in the previous section, but also the symbolic, ritual or theatrical aspects of violence, the 'scripts' that the actors follow (cf Farge and Zysberg 1979).

Ritualized violence, both official and unofficial, varies from one culture to another, understandably enough, since the function of ritual is essentially to express the central values of a particular culture. Tarring and feathering victims, for instance, instead of lynching them or as a prelude to lynching them, is a form of ritualized violence associated with the American South in particular. In early modern Europe, unofficial or popular 'executions' were often modeled on official ones, including dragging bodies or corpses to or from the place of execution and the display of heads on pikes.

Violence against property also took ritualized forms and care was often taken to distinguish it from looting, for example by smashing or burning furniture thrown from the windows of the victim's house into the street, as happened to unpopular officials or nobles in the revolt of Naples in 1647, among many other instances (Burke 1983). In some cases this form of violence was so regular and predictable that it may be described as 'ritual pillaging', as in the case of sixteenth century Rome during the brief interregna between the death of a pope and the election of his successor (Ginzburg 1987).

In the case of early modern violence, it should also be borne in mind that in cities as well as in the countryside, many people were accustomed to killing chickens, pigs and other animals, disemboweling them, cutting them into pieces, castrating them and so on. On occasion, similar techniques were employed on humans.

In contrast to the volume of work on early modern Europe, studies of recent history generally have little to say about the repertoires or the dramaturgy of violence. The study of the kidnapping of Aldo Moro by the Red Brigades is an exception in this field (Wagner-Pacifici 1986). A study of the ritualized violence of political demonstrations might also be illuminating, identifying recurrent elements such as pelting the police with missiles or burning cars and attempting to identify inflections in the use of this 'vocabulary' in different locales.

8. Management

A contrast between traditional and modern also emerges from an analysis of what might be called the 'management' of violence – often though not always a euphemism for repression. Today, attempts at controlling the means of violence, especially small arms, are generally made at national level, as in the case of the ban on privately-owned firearms in Britain following the Dunblane incident in 1996. In early modern Europe, on the other hand, arms control was local. When Cosimo de'Medici became Duke of Tuscany in 1537, for example, he banned crossbows and other offensive weapons from Florence and ordered the guards at the gates of the city to ensure that these weapons did not enter the city (Ruff 2001, 50).

The traditional European system was to rely on amateurs to keep order in cities; the watch, the militia, the Dutch *schutterij*, and so on, often figures of fun because of their ineffectiveness. In London, for instance, public order depended on the often ineffective watch and in case of emergency the militia or 'trained bands'. Even so, compared to the countryside, cities were safe havens thanks to these amateur forces, or in the case of Paris from 1667 onwards, professionals (Lindley 1983, Ruff 2001, 90–1).

Certain public rituals were expected to support these efforts to keep the urban peace. As a number of scholars have pointed out, public executions, for example, were a form of morality play, warning the public of the consequences of crime (Foucault 1975, Spierenburg 1984, Dülmen 1985). In similar fashion, instruments of torture were displayed in the streets of Rome at Carnival. Public festivals were supposed to act as a safety-valve, a form of controlled disorder, although the calendar of riots was well known and on one occasion at least, in Sicily in 1648, the authorities discussed the question whether Carnival was a cause of violence or a cure for it (Burke 1978, 203). A similar point might be made about dueling as a form of ritualized violence. In the long term it marked a stage in the 'civilizing process' in the sense of imposing rules on the informal fighting which had preceded it. In the short term, however, as we have seen, the custom of dueling may have increased violence.

If violence did break out, there was little the authorities could do in the early stages, apart from ordering a curfew. In Catholic countries crucifixes and the Blessed Sacrament were used on occasion as an instrument of crowd control, for example in Naples and Palermo during the revolts of 1647. When the priests came out, the rioters obediently stopped what they were doing and dropped to their knees – but unfortunately not for very long (Burke 1983, 198–9).

In the last resort, if the Blessed Sacrament did not work, it was necessary to call in the army to restore order. The shift from the relative impunity of rioters to their treatment as an 'enemy' was a dramatic one. Townspeople were always alarmed to hear of the approach of an army. It mattered little whether the army was an enemy or 'friendly', since the fear of sacking, looting, raping, and torturing was the same. No wonder that the billeting of troops in

the houses of civilians was used as a punishment, as well as a solution to the problem of what to do with the troops in peacetime
(Elliott 1963, 387–417).

This system began to change only when governments constructed permanent barracks for soldiers, from the end of the seventeenth century onwards, and organized professional police forces,
in the nineteenth century. Since then the technology of methods of
crowd control has changed a good deal; we live in the age of police
vans, anti-riot gear, plastic bullets, tear gas, specially trained para-
military forces and so on.

It is not at all infrequent for attempts at management to have
turned into attacks on crowds by the forces of 'order'. In nineteenth-century Britain, the troops were ordered to charge a peaceful demonstration on one notorious occasion, in St Peter's Fields
in Manchester in 1819, an event remembered with bitter humour
as the massacre of 'Peterloo' on the model of Waterloo. The attack
on a demonstration in St Petersburg by Cossack cavalry on 'Black
Sunday' in 1905 is equally well known. Turning back to São Paulo,
one thinks of the violence of police against strikers early in the
twentieth century, or the notorious attack on the crowd in the main
square of the city, the Praça da Sé on 1 May 1919, or more recently
the violence of the military police during the military dictatorship
and even later. The military police are recorded to have killed 1,104
people in São Paulo in 1991 (Sevcenko 1992; Barcellos, 1992; Caldeira 1992, 159).

These reflections may be concluded and summarized in the
form of three theses.

1. Urban violence is not new but it does not take the same forms
at all times. It is necessary to distinguish varieties, types, actors,
victims, occasions, technology, and so on.

2. The dislocation and relocation of violence within the city deserves emphasis. Brazilian elections and carnivals, for instance,
are no longer major sites of violence, but displacement does not
mean disappearance. In Europe too, festive violence has moved
from traditional sites such as the bridge to new ones such as the
stadium.

3. Over the long term, violence seems to have been professional-

ized. Traditional urban violence was mainly the work of amateurs, at a time when the majority of adult males carried weapons, while today (with the significant exception of ethnic riots) it is mainly the work of professionals. The proportion of the population taking active part in violence has probably diminished. In that limited sense, despite the scale of the problem of violence in contemporary cities, we may still speak, like Norbert Elias, of a 'civilizing process'.

References

Amorim, Carlos 1993: *Comando Vermelho*. Rio.

Asbury, Herbert 1928: *The Gangs of New York*. New York.

Bakhtin, Mikhail M. 1965: *Rabelais and his World,* English trans. Cambridge Mass.

Barcellos, Caco 1992: *Rota 66*. São Paulo.

Bellesisles, Michael 2000: *Arming America: The origins of a National Gun Culture*. New York.

Bennassar, Bartolomé 1993: *Histoire de la tauromachie*. Paris.

Bhan, Susheela 1995: ed., *Criminalization of Politics*. Delhi.

Billacois, François 1986: *Le duel dans la société français des xvie-xviie siècle*. Paris.

Blok, Anton 1991: The Meaning of "Senseless" Violence, rpr in his *Honour and Violence,* Cambridge, 2001, 103–14.

Brown, Richard M. 1969: Historical Patterns of Violence in America, in *Violence in America,* ed. H. D. Graham and Ted R. Gurr, Cambridge, Mass., 35–64.

Bulliet, Richard W. 1972: *The Patricians of Nishapur.* Cambridge Mass.

Burke, Peter 1978: *Popular Culture in Early Modern Europe.* Revised ed., Aldershot 1994.
Burke, Peter 1983: The Virgin of the Carmine and the Revolt of Naples in 1647, rpr *Historical Anthropology of Early Modern Italy.* Cambridge.
Burke, Peter 1993: Cities, Spaces and Rituals in the Early Modern World, in *Urban Rituals in Italy and the Netherlands,* ed. Heidi de Mare and Anna Vos, Assen, 29–38.

Caldeira, Teresa Pires do Rio (1992) *City of Walls: Crime, Segregation and Citizenship in S. Paulo.* Dissertation, Berkeley.

Chesnais, Jean-Claude 1981: *Histoire de la violence.* Paris.

Christin, Olivier 1991: *Une révolution symbolique: l'iconoclasme Huguenot et la réconstruction catholique,* Paris.

Crouzet, Denis 1990: *Les guerriers de Dieu: la violence au temps des troubles de religion (vers 1525–vers 1610).* Paris.

Das, Veena 1990: ed., *Mirrors of Violence.* Delhi.

Davis, Natalie Z. 1973: The Rites of Violence, *Past & Present* 59 (1973), 51–91.

Davis, Robert C. 1994: *The War of the Fists: Popular Culture and Public Violence in Late Renaissance Venice.* New York.

Dekker, Rudolf 1982: *Holland in Beroering.* Baarn.
Dekker, Rudolf 1989: Some Remarks about Collective Action and Collective Violence, *Tijdschrift voor Sociaalgeschiedenis* 15, 158–65.

Descimon, Robert 1990: Les barricades de la fronde Parisienne:

une lecture sociologique, *Annales ESC* 45, 397–422.

Deursen, Theo van (1978–80) *Plain Lives in a Golden Age,* English trans. Cambridge 1991.

Douglas, Mary 1966: *Purity and Danger.* London.

Dülmen, Richard van 1985: *The Theatre of Horror,* English trans. Cambridge 1990.

Elias, Norbert 1939: *The Civilizing Process,* English trans. 2 vols, Oxford 1981–2.

Elliott, John H. 1963: *The Revolt of the Catalans.* Cambridge.

Farge, Arlette and André Zysberg 1979: Les théâtres de la violence à Paris au 18e siècle, *Annales E. S. C.* 34, 984–1017.
Farge, Arlette and Jacques Revel 1988: *The Rules of Rebellion,* English trans., Cambridge 1991.

Foucault, Michel 1975: *Surveiller et punir,* English trans. *Discipline and Punish,* London 1978.

Gamboni, Dario 1996: *The Destruction of Art: Iconoclasm and Vandalism since the French Revolution,* London.

Gilsenan, Michael 1996: *Lords of the Lebanese Marches: Violence and Narrative in an Arab Society.* London.

Ginzburg, Carlo (1987) Ritual Pillages, English trans. in Edward Muir and Guido Ruggiero (eds) *Microhistory and the Lost Peoples of Europe,* Baltimore 1991, 20–41.

Gordon, Michael 1993: *The Orange Riots: Irish Political Violence in New York City, 1870 and 1871.* Ithaca.

Gozzadini, Giovanni 1875: *Delle torri gentilizie di Bologna.* Bologna.

Harris, Tim 1986: The Bawdy House Riots of 1668, *Historical Journal* 27, 537–56.

Heers, Jacques 1990: *La ville au moyen âge.* Paris.

Hofstadter, Richard 1970: America as a Gun Culture, *American Heritage* 21.

Kakar, Sudhir 1990: Some Unconscious Aspects of Ethnic Violence in India, in Das, 135–45.

Kapferer, Bruce 1988: *Legends of People, Myths of State: Violence, Intolerance and Political Culture in Sri Lanka and Australia.* Washington.

Kiernan, Victor 1988: *The Duel in European History.* Oxford.

Le Bon, Gustave 1912: *La révolution française et la psychologie des revolutions.* Paris.

Lefebvre, Georges (1934) 'Foules révolutionnaires', rpr in his *Etudes sur la Révolution Française,* Paris 1954, 371–92.

Levine, Lawrence W. (1989) *Highbrow/Lowbrow: the Emergence of Cultural Hierarchy in America,* Cambridge, Mass.

Lindley, Keith (1983) Riot Prevention and Control in Early Stuart London, *Transactions of the Royal Historical Society* 33, 109–26.

Lintott, Andrew W. 1968: *Violence in Republican Rome.* Oxford.
Lintott, Andrew W. 1982: *Violence, Civil Strife and Revolution in the Classical City, 750–330 BC.* London.

Marsh, Peter et al, 1978: *The Rules of Disorder.* London.

Martines, Lauro 1973: (ed.) *Violence and Civil Disorder in Italian Cities 1200–1500.* Berkeley.

Marwick, Max 1964: Witchcraft as a Social Strain-Gauge, rpr in Marwick, ed., *Witchcraft and Sorcery*, Harmondsworth, 1970, 280–95.

Mennell, Stephen 1990: Decivilizing Processes, *International Sociology* 5, 205–23.

Mitchell, Timothy 1991: *Blood Sport: A Social History of Spanish Bullfighting*. Philadelphia.

Moisés, José Alvaro, and Verena Stolcke 1980: Urban Transport and Popular Violence, *Past & Present* 86, 174–92.

Muchembled, Robert 1989: *La violence au village: sociabilité et comportements populaires en Artois (du 15e au 17e siècle)*. Turnhout.

Nirenberg, David 1996: *Communities of Violence: Persecution of Minorities in the Middle Ages*, Princeton.

Österberg, Eva, 1991: Violence among Peasants, in *Mentalities and Other Realities*, Lund, 89–112.

Park, Robert E. 1916: 'The City', rpr his *Human Communications*, Glencoe, 13–51.

Ramalho Massena, Rosa Maria 1986: A distribuição espacial da criminalidade violenta na região metropolitana do Rio de Janeiro, *Revista Brasileira de Geografia* 48, 285–330.

Rudé, George 1959: *The Crowd in the French Revolution*. Oxford.

Ruff, Julius R. 2001: *Violence in Early Modern Europe 1500–1800*. Cambridge.

Ruggiero, Guido 1980: *Violence in Early Renaissance Venice*. New Brunswick.

Sevcenko, Nicolau 1992: *Orfeu extático na metrópole: S.Paulo, socie-dade e cultura nos frementes anos 20*. São Paulo.

Shubert, Adrian, 1999: *Death and Money in the Afternoon: a History of Spanish Bullfighting*. Oxford.

Soihet, Rachel 1993: *Subversão pelo Riso: o Carnaval Carioca 1890–1945*. Dissertation, Niteroi.

Spierenburg, Pieter 1984: *The Spectacle of Suffering*. Cambridge.
Spierenburg, Pieter 1996: Long-Term Trends in Homicide, in Eric A. Johnson and Eric H. Monkkonen (eds) *The Civilization of Crime: Violence in Town and Country since the Middle Ages*, Urbana, 63–105.

Stone, Lawrence 1965: *The Crisis of the Aristocracy*. Oxford.

Thomas, Hugh 1961: *The Spanish Civil War*. 3rd edition, Harmonds-worth 1977.

Thompson, Edward P. 1971: The Moral Economy of the English Crowd in the Eighteenth Century, rpr his *Customs in Common*, Har-mondsworth 1993, 185–258.

Tilly, Charles 1969: Collective Violence in European Perspective, in *Violence in America*, ed. H. D. Graham and T. R. Gurr, Cambridge, Mass., 5–34.
Tilly, Charles 1986: *The Contentious French*. Cambridge, Mass.

Turner, Victor 1969: *The Ritual Process: Structure and Anti-Structure*. London.

Wagner-Pacifici, Robin E. 1986: *The Moro Morality Play: Terrorism as Social Drama*. Chicago.

Walker, Jonathan 1998: *Bravi* and Venetian Nobles, c. 1550–1650, *Studi Veneziani*, n.s. 36, 85–114.

Walter, John 1980: Grain Riots and Popular Attitudes to the Law, in *An Ungovernable People,* ed. John Brewer and John Styles, London, 47–84.

Wolff, Philippe 1971: 'The 1391 Pogrom in Spain', *Past & Present* 50, 4–18.

9: IMAGINING IDENTITY IN THE EARLY MODERN CITY

$\text{C} \mathcal{O} \!\!\!\!\!\! \Longleftrightarrow \!\!\!\!\!\! \mathcal{O} \mathcal{O}$

This chapter might be described as a series of variations on a theme from Georg Simmel, especially from his famous essay of 1903 on 'The Great City and the Life of the Spirit' (or however one should translate *Geistesleben*), in which he suggested that like the money economy, the big city is associated with impersonality in social relations. One of Simmel's most vivid illustrations of the trend was the development of a new transport system of buses and trams in which people sit opposite one another for considerable periods of time without speaking, as in the London Underground today.

Simmel placed most emphasis on the negative side of this development, the sense of isolation. 'One nowhere feels as lonely and lost as in the metropolitan crowd.' 'We frequently do not even know by sight those who have been our neighbours for years.' But it is worth remembering that he also noted the positive side of anonymity, the fact that the big city 'grants the individual a kind and an amount of personal freedom which has no analogy whatsoever under other conditions'.[1] We might say that the medieval proverb, *Stadtluft macht frei*, had been given a new meaning.

---

[1] Georg Simmel, 'The Metropolis and Mental Life' (1903), trans. in *Cities and Society*, edited by Paul K. Hatt and Albert J. Reiss, Glencoe, Ill., 1959, 635–46, at pp. 640, 642.

I

The isolation of the individual in the city was very much an idea of the period, expressed in the paintings of Kirchner such as 'Street, Berlin 1913' with its faceless figures in the background, or outside Germany in Manet's *Café in the Place du Théâtre-Français* (1881) with its solitary customer.

A few years after Simmel, his analysis of the city was taken up and also taken further by North American sociologists, especially the Chicago school. Robert Park, who had once studied with Simmel, agreed with him that the city is not based on primary or face-to-face groups. Human relations are 'impersonal'. If Kirchner now appears to be illustrating Simmel, we might say that Edward Hopper translated into paint the ideas of Park and his colleague Louis Wirth. Speaking of his famous picture *Nighthawks* (1942), Hopper once commented that 'Unconsciously, probably, I was painting the loneliness of a large city.'[2]

As for Park, he went on to describe the new urban society with a mixture of detachment and excitement. 'The individual's status is determined to a considerable degree by conventional signs – by fashion and "front" – and the art of life is largely reduced to skating on thin surfaces and a scrupulous study of style and manners.'[3] If this sounds like Erving Goffman, there is no reason for surprise, since Goffman was a later representative of the Chicago tradition.[4]

To this point Park added another about the social and cultural heterogeneity of the city, the 'urban mosaic', as he called it. It was not just its size but its segmentation that 'encourages the fascinating but dangerous experiment of living at the same time in several different contiguous, but otherwise widely separated worlds.'

To amplify: because you are not known in most parts of the city, you can experiment with alternative identities outside your neigh-

---

[2] Quoted in Edward Hopper, Exhibition Catalogue, London 2004, p.19.

[3] Robert Ezra Park, 'The City: Suggestions for the Investigation of Human Behavior in the Urban Environment', in Park, Ernest W. Burgess and Roderick D. McKenzie, *The City*, Chicago 1925, 1–46, at pp. 40–1.

[4] Erving Goffman, *The Presentation of Self in Everyday Life*, New York 1958.

bourhood, invent and re-invent yourself, 'pass' for what you are not. It is like a mild version of the freedom conferred by invisibility. It offers a dramatic contrast to the 'little community', secure but constraining, where the history of individuals and their families is well known. Borrowing Benedict Anderson's famous phrase, we might say that the city, no less than the nation, is an 'imagined community of which the members 'will never know most of their fellow-members'.[5]

From Simmel and Park and others such as Louis Wirth and Harvey Zorbaugh, who worked both in and on Chicago, there has developed a sociological, anthropological and also a literary tradition of interpretations of the city. The generalist Lewis Mumford, and more recently the writer Jonathan Raban, the sociologist Richard Sennett, and the Swedish anthropologist Ulf Hannerz all stand in this tradition.[6] But there are contrasts. Where Mumford, for instance, stressed the dark side of urban life, Raban emphasized its positive aspects.

In his *Soft City* (1974), Raban suggested that the city 'threatens you with absorption into total anonymity.' But he also saw the positive side, which he calls the 'softness' of the city. 'It awaits the imprint of an identity. For better or worse, it invites you to remake it, to consolidate it into a shape you can live in'. Like Park, Raban noted the segmentation of the city and gave the example of Ronald Kray as a successful confidence trickster. 'The secret lay in keeping his audiences separated'.[7] The hetereogeneity or 'fluidity' of the city offers opportunities for different performances in different settings and before different audiences.[8]

In what follows, I should like to suggest that the awareness of anonymity and also of its consequences, both positive and negative, actually goes back a long way before Simmel. Although it was not yet elaborated sociologically, this awareness already formed

---

[5] Benedict Anderson, *Imagined Communities* (1983), second ed., London 1991.
[6] Lewis Mumford, *The Culture of Cities*, New York 1938; Jonathan Raban, *Soft City*, London 1974); Richard Sennett, *The Fall of Public Man*, Cambridge 1977; Ulf Hannerz, *Exploring the City*, New York 1980.
[7] Mumford, p. 266. Raban, pp. 165, 9, 74.
[8] Hannerz, p. 114.

part of the urban experience. The theme was already an important one in the cultural and social history of Europe between the Renaissance and the Enlightenment. It was linked to two major socio-cultural trends of the period, the rise of what it is convenient to call 'individualism' and the change in the social system from one based on inherited status to one with a place for a combination of wealth and good behaviour.

II

Today, critics of urban life often look back at the past with nostalgia as the time when communities still existed. But the idea of the anonymity of the city goes back further than they generally realize. It was indeed a commonplace. Like so many early modern commonplaces, it went back to the ancient world.

In ancient Rome, which reached a million people, it used to be said that a great city was a great wilderness (*magna civitas, magna solitudo*). This Latin proverb, quoted by Francis Bacon in one of his essays, was actually a translation from a Greek comedy.[9]

However, it is from the sixteenth century onwards, with the rise of large cities, remarks on urban anonymity are recorded again and again, whether the context is Venice, Amsterdam, Paris or London. In the 1540s, a Welsh visitor described Venice as follows: 'No man there marketh another's doings or ... meddleth with another man's living ... No man shall ask thee why thou comest not to church ... to live married or unmarried, no man shall ask thee why. For eating of flesh in thine own house, what day soever it be, it maketh no matter.'[10] This passage surely tells us something about Wales.

This description of the big city was, or became, a literary topos. In 1741, for instance, a native of the Canaries contrasted the Spain of the Inquisition with Paris, where 'no one asks where you are going, or questions who you are, nor at Easter does the priest ask if

---

[9] Quoted in Strabo, *Geography, eremia megale stin e megale polis*, referring to Megalopolis in Arcadia (16.738: Loeb edn, 8 vols, London 1960–9, vol.7, p. 201).
[10] William Thomas, *History of Italy* (1549), edited by George B. Parks, Ithaca 1963, p. 83.

you have been to confession'.[11] The 18th-century journalist Sébastien Mercier agreed: 'La liberté religieuse est au plus haut degré possible à Paris: jamais on ne vous demandera aucun compte de votre croyance: vous pouvez habiter trente ans sur une paroisse sans y mettre le pied.' (Religious liberty is possible in Paris in the highest degree: you will never be asked about your beliefs: you may live in a parish for thirty years without putting your foot in the church).

When James Boswell, a Scot who migrated to London, first saw the London shops open on Good Friday, he remarked rather primly 'that one disadvantage arising from the immensity of London was, that nobody was heeded by his neighbour; there was no fear of censure for not observing Good-Friday, as it ought to be kept'. Four years later, however he had come to appreciate the advantages of London and was noting 'The freedom from remark, and petty censure, with which life may be passed' in the city.[12]

Another view of the city that recurs at this time is the one that we know best today from Walter Benjamin's famous description of the *flâneur*. This description has some early modern parallels, linked to the Renaissance or baroque idea of the city as a stage. Here I call three witnesses, Descartes, Steele and Fielding. Descartes appreciated not only the Dutch Republic but Amsterdam in particular for its freedom. As he explained to his friend Jean-Louis Guez de Balzac in a letter of 1631, 'Je vais me promener tous les jours parmi la confusion d'un grand peuple, avec autant de liberté et de repos que vous sauriez faire dans vos allées' (I go for a walk every day in the confusion of a great centre of population, with as much freedom and relaxation as you do walking in your garden). The philosopher sometimes took the time to observe his fellows: 'si je fais quelquefois réflexion sur leurs actions, j'en reçois le meme plaisir, que vous feriez de voir les paysans qui cultivent vos campagnes.' (If I sometimes reflect on their actions, I receive the same pleasure

---

[11] Quoted in Henry Kamen, *Inquisition and Society in Spain*, Bloomington Ind. 1985, p. 258.
[12] James Boswell, Life of Johnson (1792), edited by G. B. Hill, 6 vols., Oxford 1934–50,14 April 1775, 1 April 1779.

as you do in observing the peasants who work on your estate). He came back to the subject a few years later in the *Discourse on Method,* saying that in Amsterdam he could live 'aussi solitaire et retiré que dans les déserts les plus écartés' (in as much solitude and retirement as in the most distant deserts), among 'la foule d'un grand peuple ... plus soigneux de ses propres affaires que curieux de celles d'autrui' (the crowd of a great centre of population ... more concerned with its own business than curious about that of others).[13]

Again, a number of *The Spectator* (no. 454, 1712) written by Richard Steele, was devoted to the pleasure of observing London. Fielding too delighted in looking at and listening to the London of his day. 'Here you have the Advantage of solitude without its Disadvantage, since you may be alone and in Company at the same time; and while you sit or walk *unobserved*, Noise, Hurry and a constant Succession of Objects entertain the Mind.'[14]

So far the commonplaces discussed might be described as topoi of enthusiasm. However, this enthusiasm was not shared by everyone. Let us turn to negative reactions to the city. In a history of Paris written in the late seventeenth century, we read that 'dans Paris chacun vit avec tant de liberté, que d'ordinaire de fort honnêtes gens demeurent en même logis sans se connoître.' (in Paris everyone lives with such freedom, that it is normal for respectable people to live in the same house without knowing one another).[15] This was another topos. Mercier may be cited once again: 'On est étranger à son voisin, et l'on n'apprend quelquefois sa mort que par le billet d'enterrement.' (People are strangers to their neighbours and on occasion learn of their death only by reading the notice of burial). And still closer to Simmel, 'Nous sommes ... condamnées dans cette ville immense à nous voir sans nous connaî-

---

[13] René Descartes, *Oeuvres Philosophiques,* vol. 1, edited by Ferdinand Alquier, Paris 1963, pp. 292, 601.

[14] Fielding quoted in Roy Porter, *London: a Social History* (1994), second ed. Harmondsworth 1996, p. 203.

[15] Henri Sauval, *Histoire des antiquités de la ville de Paris* (1724), rpr Farnborough 1959, vol. 1, p. 62. Cf Peter Burke, 'Reflections on the Pre-Industrial City', *Urban History Yearbook* (1975), 13–21, at p. 19.

tre.' (In this immense city we are condemned to see one another without knowing one another).[16]

The novelist Rétif de la Bretonne, who grew up in rural Burgundy before coming to Paris to make his fortune, quoted his father's reaction to the city: 'que de monde! Il y en a tant que personne ne s'y connaît, même dans le voisinage, même dans sa propre maison.' (So many people! There are so many that people do not know one another, not even in the neighbourhood or even in the same house).[17]

The same point was made about London, a little later. Wordsworth wrote in *The Prelude* (book 7) that people lived in London 'Even next-door neighbours, as we say, yet still/Strangers, nor knowing each the other's name', while the early sports writer Pierce Egan wrote in his *Life in London* (1821) 'The next door neighbour of a man in London is generally as great a stranger to him as if he lived at the distance of York.'

Another early modern topos, neutral rather than positive or negative, anticipated Robert Park on the urban mosaic. The seventeenth-century satirist Jean La Bruyère, a master of the art of distanciation, noted with what we might call an anthropological eye the different sub-cultures of the city. 'La ville est partagée en diverses sociétés qui sont comme autant de petites républiques, qui ont leurs lois, leurs usages, leur jargon et leurs mots pour rire.' (The city is divided into different cultures which are like so many tiny republics, with their own laws, customs, jargon and jokes). Hence an individual in a *quartier* he does not know 'se trouve là comme dans un lays lointain' (might just as well be in a distant country).[18] In similar fashion, Joseph Addison described London as 'an aggregate of several nations', with their own 'customs, manners and interests'. For instance, 'the inhabitants of St James's, notwithstanding they live under the same laws

---

[16] Sébastien Mercier, *Tableau de Paris* (1781), new ed., 12 vols., Amsterdam 1783–8, vol. 1., pp. 3, 61, 281, vol. 3, pp. 87–91.

[17] Rétif de la Bretonne (1796–7) *Monsieur Nicolas*, rpr 6 vols., Paris 1959, vol.1, pp. 179–80.

[18] Jean La Bruyère, *Caractères* (1688), edited by Georges Mongrédien, Paris 1960, p. 182.

and speak the same language, are a distinct people from those of Cheapside.'[19]

III

So far this chapter has summarized perceptions of the city that were expressed in commonplaces but may have been no less deeply felt for all that. Were these generalizations accurate? They were not and are not the whole story. In the 1960s, the sociologist Herbert Gans criticized the arguments of Simmel and his followers, notably Louis Wirth, by pointing to the existence of urban 'villages', ethnic neighbourhoods like the Italians in certain quarters of New York.[20] The judicial records of Paris, London, Rome and other cities show that quasi-villages of this kind existed in early modern times and that the neighbours might know a great deal about the so-called 'private' life of the individuals in their street.[21] Again, members of a particular social group, such as urban patricians, might know one another all too well, and one reason for the famous dominos that the Venetian nobles wore in the Carnival season in the eighteenth century was to hide their identity from colleagues who knew their faces. Even Venice might be a village for the patriciate.

High rise buildings already existed and there was a world of furnished rooms for recent arrivals to the city in particular, where it is quite possible that people living on one floor did not know the names of lodgers living on another, but these buildings were outnumbered by those of the quasi-villages. It is likely that people were most impressed by the anonymity of certain parts of the city because it was unusual, and failed to notice the village-like neighbourhoods because they were normal. On the other hand, urban

---

[19] Joseph Addison and Richard Steele, *The Spectator* (1711–12), edited by Donald F. Bond, 5 vols., Oxford 1965, no. 403, 12 June 1712.

[20] Herbert Gans, *The Urban Villagers*, New York 1962.

[21] David Garrioch, *Neighbourhood and Community in Paris 1740–90*, Cambridge 1986; Peter Burke, *Historical Anthropology of Early Modern Italy: Perception and Communication*, Cambridge 1987, pp. 95–109; Laura Gowing, *Domestic Dangers: women, words and sex in early modern London*, Oxford 1996.

villages were and are unlike rural villages because it was so easy to step outside them, as Park noted, and enter another social world. How did people respond to this segmentation?

It is well known that the early modern period was a time of increasing preoccupation with individual identity, with self-presentation or 'self-fashioning', a term launched by the critic Stephen Greenblatt in his study of the English Renaissance but one that could equally well be used of other parts of Europe, witness the many autobiographical texts and other 'ego-documents', as the Dutch call them, produced at this time.[22] Most of these ego-documents were produced in cities, and the self-consciousness they express may be regarded a response to the rise of cities.[23]

To return to Boswell and the London journal he began keeping immediately before his arrival in the city in 1762.[24] Boswell was a perfect example of *homo goffmanicus* or *homo greenblatticus*, since he was obsessed with self-presentation and self-fashioning. 'I have discovered that we may be in some degree whatever character we choose.' (21 Nov 1762). 'I was now upon a plan of studying polite reserved behaviour, which is the only way to keep up dignity of character' (1 Dec 1762). It has been argued that Boswell's *Journal* is an untrustworthy source because its protagonist (like the Boswell of the *Life of Johnson*) is a literary persona, but in the context of the present argument, one might say that its very unreliability makes the text more valuable, embodying as well as describing self-fashioning.

Boswell tells us that he bought a sword on credit as a deliberate experiment, entering the most fashionable swordsmith's in London and choosing an expensive item. Then, finding that he did not have the five guineas with him he asked if he could take the sword away with him all the same. The point for Boswell was to see 'what effect my external appearance and address would have'

---

[22] Stephen Greenblatt, *Renaissance Self-Fashioning,* Chicago 1980; Rudolf Dekker, 'Presser's Heritage: Ego-Documents in the Study of History', *Memoria y Civilización* 5 (2002), pp. 13–37.

[23] Cf. James Amelang, *The Flight of Icarus: Artisan Autobiography in Early Modern Europe,* Stanford 1998.

[24] James Boswell, *London Journal,* edited by F. A. Pottle (1951), rpr London 1973.

(1 Dec 1762). His experiment worked. In the language of Robert Park, the provincial was learning how to skate on thin ice.

The fiction of the early modern period includes a number of figures who behaved rather like Boswell. It is of course risky to make use of fiction as a historical source, or indeed as a sociological one (though Robert Park recommended Zola's novels as a way of understanding cities better).[25] We obviously have to be careful not to read romances or novels, poems or plays as simple descriptions of social reality rather than as satire (say) and not to read the 'I' of the text as an expression of the true opinions of the author. All the same, fiction is an invaluable source for the history of the social imagination, as some examples may demonstrate.

The first example is actually a series, indeed a whole literary genre, the Spanish picaresque novel. One might begin at the beginning in the middle of the sixteenth century with *Lazarillo de Tormes*, in which the hero (or antihero) serves a succession of masters and in so doing reveals a succession of selves. One day Lazarillo, who was out of work, encountered a nobleman. The man was 'quite well dressed' and 'looked pretty well-off'. He hired Lazarillo and they went home to an empty house, lacking both furniture and food. His new master had sold everything in order to appear in the street as a nobleman should.[26]

Lazarillo began a Spanish tradition which lasted for four hundred years (the latest example known to me is Camilo José Cela's *La Colmena*, published in 1951). It was particularly important in the age of the baroque, the age of Mateo Alemán and Francisco Quevedo, a time of particularly acute concern with the gap between appearance and reality, *ser* and *parecer*, or in other languages *être* and *paraître*, *Sein* and *Schein*. Is it too much to suggest that this concern was encouraged by the rise of the anonymous city? The picaresque genre also appealed to writers and readers in the Netherlands, Germany and Britain, with Defoe's *Moll Flanders* as a vivid illustration of the fluidity of female identity in the city.

---

[25] Park, p. 3.

[26] *La Vida de Lazarillo de Tormes* (1554), edited by Julio Cejador y Frauca, Madrid 1962, pp.148–59; Francisco Rico, *The Spanish picaresque novel and the point of view* (1969), English trans., Cambridge 1984.

My principal witness, however, is not Spanish but French. He is Antoine Furetière, best known as the compiler of a French dictionary, and his novel *Le roman bourgeois* (1666). Even the title of this text is revealing, since it seems to be the first instance of the term *bourgeois* used as an adjective to describe the style of life of a social group. However, this group is not that of merchants or shopkeepers. The novel is set in the world of the lawyers in or near Place Maubert, not far from the *quartier* of the nobility.

In this novel Furetière tells a story about a certain Nicodème, 'un homme amphibie, qui estoit le matin advocat et le soir courtesan; il portoit le matin la robe au Palais pour plaider ou pour écouter, et le soir il portrait les grands canons et les galands d'or pour aller cajoler les dames. C'est un de ces jeunes bourgeois qui, malgré leur naissance et leur éducation, veulent passer pour des gens du bel air' (an amphibious man, who was a lawyer in the morning and a courtier in the evening; in the morning he wore the long robe and went to the Palace of Justice to plead or listen to cases, and in the evening he wore large *canons* [decorative cloths attached to the *culotte*] and gold trimmings in order to chat up the ladies. He was one of those young bourgeois who, despite their birth and education, wanted to pass for people of fashion).

The key word is 'passing', a subject which has attracted a good deal of recent interest.[27] However, as this text suggests, the phenomenon is much older. *Le roman bourgeois* might be described as the first social novel, in the sense of a 'how-to-do-it' book concerned with the details of dress, furniture, gesture, vocabulary and accent as so many social indicators. When he wants to pass for noble, Nicodème puts on a blonde wig. 'Son collet de manteau estoit bien poudré, sa garniture fort enflée, son linge ornée de dentelle ... Enfin, il estoit ajusté de manière qu'un provincial n'auroit jamais manquée de le prendre pour modelle pour se bien mettre' (his cloak collar was well powdered, its trimmings rich, his linen ornamented with lace ... In other words, he was turned out in such a way that a provincial would certainly have taken him as

---

[27] On literature, Elaine K. Ginsberg (ed.) *Passing and the Fictions of Identity*, Durham, NC 1996; on life, Maria Carla Sánchez and Linda Schlossberg (eds.) *Passing: Identity and Interpretation in Sexuality, Race and Religion*, New York 2001.

a model of dress', although the pretender was given away to those who knew by 'his grimaces and affectations'. Nicodème has to be given away, since the story is a satire, just as Molière's *bourgeois gentilhomme* has to be unsuccessful in his attempts to act like a nobleman.[28]

[the tradition continued. In Rousseau's *Nouvelle Héloïse* (1761) Saint-Preux describes Paris as 'ce vaste désert', where he feels lonely and dislikes the fact that 'chaque coterie a ses règles' and that people pretend to be what they are not]

IV

Of course an empiricist historian wants to ask whether there is hard (or at any rate harder) evidence that this kind of behaviour took place in the cities of early modern Europe. Dr Johnson certainly thought so. He observed that in London you can 'play tricks with your fortune ... Here a lady may have well-furnished apartments, and elegant dress, without any meat in her kitchen'.

The judicial records of the major cities of early modern Europe, records which are far from having given up all their secrets, have revealed a few early modern individuals who tried to pass for what they were not. There were poor and humble adventurers who eloped with heiresses after presenting themselves as rich and well-born. A sodomy trial in Paris 1726 reveals a certain Deschauffours changing names whenever he changed addresses (which was often). He tried to pass for noble and called himself the 'Marquis du Preau' or 'Sieur Des Fourneaux Bellair' – an inspired choice of name but one that did not protect its owner from eventual unmasking.[29]

The anonymity of the city also offered a certain freedom to women chafing under the pressure of social conventions, whether of rank or gender. In an eighteenth-century French comedy, Florent Carton de Dancourt's *Les Agioteurs* (1710), Mademoiselle Ur-

---

[28] Antoine Furetière, *Le roman bourgeois* (1666) rpr in *Romanciers du 17e siècle*, edited by Antoine Adam, Paris 1958, pp. 900–1104, at pp. 906–8.

[29] *Les procès de sodomie aux 16e, 17e et 18e siècles*, edited by 'Ludovico Hernandez', Paris 1920.

bine, who is described as a coquette, explains that she moved from one *quartier* of Paris to another because 'dans le Fauxbourg comme dans le Marais les rangs sont si heureusement confondus, que l'on y fait telle figure que l'on veut, sans apprehender la médisance' (in the suburb as in the Marais, the social order is so happily mixed up that one can play whatever role one pleases without fear of gossip).[30]

As for gender, it is best not to become entangled in the problem of the veil and whether it is a symbol of male oppression or a means of female liberation. All the same, it is worth noting that in the early eighteenth century, Lady Mary Wortley Montagu, living in Edirne (or 'Adrianople', as she and other English people called it at the time), noted the 'liberty' of women in the Ottoman Empire thanks to this 'perpetual masquerade'. Her remark tells us something about Britain, if not about the Turks. In the nineteenth century, we have the famous testimonies of two female writers, Flora Tristán and George Sand. In Peru Flora sometimes wore the *manto*, which covered most of the face, while in London, where she visited Parliament, she sometimes put on men's clothes. In her autobiography, George Sand records feeling 'lost in the crowd' when she was dressed as a man, anonymous and so virtually invisible. Vita Sackville-West also records that she 'never felt so free' as when she was dressed in men's clothes.[31]

In early modern cities, there is both literary and archive evidence concerning women who dressed as men (cases of men dressing as women, from Horace Walpole to the Chevalier Dion). In London, for example, there was Mary Frith, known as 'Moll Cutpurse' or 'The Roaring Girl', a major figure in the underworld in the 1620s, while in Amsterdam a number of women dressed as men successfully joined the army and the navy.[32]

These dramatic examples of cross-dressing may be viewed as

[30] Florent Carton de Dancourt, 'Les Agioteurs', in *Oeuvres*, 3rd. edn, 9 vols, Paris 1710, vol. 7, pp. 226–30.
[31] Deborah E. Nord, *Walking the Victorian Streets*, Ithaca 1995, pp. 4, 119.
[32] On Firth, Stephen Orgel, *Impersonations: the Performance of Gender in Shakespeare's England*, Cambridge 1996, 139–53; cf. Rudolf M. Dekker and Lotte C. van de Pol, *The Tradition of Female Transvestism in Early Modern Europe*, London 1989.

extreme cases of a much more general phenomenon. In the everyday life of the large anonymous city, people's status was largely defined by their clothes (it still is in certain places, such as expensive hotels and restaurants). Hence the early modern sumptuary laws, but also their lack of success. The city was a stage for self-presentation, not only a stage for public events like royal entries or Lord Mayor's Shows but also for everyday performances of identity. Daniel Roche has described the function of clothes in eighteenth-century Paris, the importance of what he calls 'the culture of appearances'.[33]

However, as Furetière knew so well, to pass for noble it was necessary to know how to wear these clothes, in other words to study performance or deportment. Eighteenth-century Britain has been described by some recent historians as a 'culture of politeness', in other words a society in which good manners were becoming an essential criterion for status.[34] Hence the increasing importance in English culture of the dancing-master, who often taught deportment as well.[35]

Language was another new criterion of status. [the diplomat Callières 1691 etc on *le bel usage,* the distinctions between the *façon de parler* of the *bourgeois* and *gens du monde*] The right vocabulary and accent now took on a new importance and the obsession of the English with accent as an indicator of class dates from the eighteenth century. Elocution masters such as Thomas Sheridan (ironically enough, an Irishman) joined dancing masters as indispensable teachers of the would-be socially mobile. Another linguistic change of the period was the decline of 'thou', replaced by 'you'. To say 'thou' to someone required the certainty that he or she was of lower status. In the anonymous city it was better to play safe and call everyone 'you'.[36]

---

[33] Daniel Roche, *The Culture of Clothing: Dress and Fashion in the 'Ancien Régime'* (1989), English trans. Cambridge 1994.
[34] Paul Langford, *A Polite and Commercial People: England 1727–1783,* Oxford 1989; Lawrence E. Klein, *Shaftesbury and the Culture of Politeness,* Cambridge 1994.
[35] Audrée-Isabelle Tardif, 'Aspects of social dancing among the upper classes of 18th-Century England' (Cambridge Ph. D dissertation 2002).
[36] Anna Bryson, *From Courtesy to Civility: Changing Modes of Conduct in Early Modern England,* Oxford 1998, p. 283.

What I have been describing was a major social change. The evidence is superficial in the sense of coming from surfaces or appearances but the change itself was a change in deep structure, social structure. The eighteenth century, in Western Europe at any rate, was the time of a shift from status based on inheritance and legal privilege to status based on style of life. In this chapter I wanted to draw attention to the perceived anonymity of the city in facilitating and perhaps even in initiating this fundamental social change, linked to the rise of self-fashioning. The history of social structures and the history of the social imagination are not separate enterprises, but part of a common history.

Bibliography

James Boswell (1951) *London Journal*, ed. F. A. Pottle, rpr London 1973.

Peter Burke (1975) 'Reflections on the Pre-Industrial City', *Urban History Yearbook* (1975), 13–21.

Antoine Furetière (1666) *Le roman bourgeois*, in Antoine Adam, ed., *Romanciers du 17e siècle*, Paris, 1958, 900–1104.

Herbert Gans (1962) *The Urban Villagers*, New York.

Erving Goffman (1959) *The Presentation of Self in Everyday Life*, New York.

Ulf Hannerz (1980) *Exploring the City*, New York.

Lewis Mumford (1938) *The Culture of Cities*, New York.

Robert Ezra Park (1925) 'The City: Suggestions for the Investigation of Human Behavior in the Urban Environment', in Park, Ernest W. Burgess and Roderick D. McKenzie, *The City*, Chicago, 1–46.

Jonathan Raban (1974) *Soft City,* London.

Richard Sennett (1977) *The Fall of Public Man,* Cambridge.

Georg Simmel (1903) 'The Metropolis and Mental Life', in *Die Großstadt,* ed. Petermann, trans. Paul K. Hatt and Albert J. Reiss (eds.), *Cities and Society,* Glencoe, Ill., 1959, 635–46.

10: URBAN SENSATIONS: ATTRACTIVE AND REPULSIVE

⁂

One of the ways in which the so-called 'cultural turn' has affected urban history is in encouraging scholars to give more attention to the experience of living in towns, alongside relatively objective data such as the size of cities and the number of townspeople to be found in different occupations, from tailor to servant. The so-called 'sensory revolution' forms part of this wider movement. In this vein, what follows is an attempt to imagine the impact of cities on the senses of both inhabitants and visitors in the course of the three hundred years allocated to this volume, whether that impact was pleasant or unpleasant, what provoked cries of pleasure or admiration or, on the contrary, 'What made eyes water, ears ache, noses wrinkle, fingers withdraw and mouths close' (Cockayne 2007, 21). A first step, for us who live over 350 years later than the end of the period discussed here, is to imagine cities without the sights, sounds or smells to which we have become accustomed; the tall buildings made of glass, the streams of cars and buses in the streets, the smell of petrol fumes, the rumble of lorries, the hooting of drivers, the ear-splitting sounds of electric drills, the sirens of police cars and fire engines and so on. Taking all those sensations away, what should we imagine in their place?

The obvious question to ask at the start of such an investigation concerns the sources for such a reconstruction. The richest of those sources are descriptions of cities by travellers of the period in print or in manuscript: 'travelogues', we may call them. Precisely because they are away from home and confronted with unfamiliar sensations, travellers are unusually aware of what they see or hear. Some sensitive observers might be described as connoisseurs of sensations. One of them, the Englishman Thomas Coryat (1611, 306), declared that the church of San Marco in Venice 'did ravish my senses'. In other words, he was conscious of synaesthesia.

It is tempting and all too easy to produce a chapter that is essentially a mosaic of quotations from sources of this kind. We need to remember, however, that millions of people experienced cities in this period, whether as inhabitants or visitors, while we have access only to hundreds of travelogues. What is more, the authors form a biased sample of travellers, since they were predominantly upper class, male, and northern European.

It is obviously necessary to supplement these rich but biased sources with others, preferably presenting cities from inside and from below. Municipal regulations, for instance, offer a view from within the city, documenting attempts to control dirt, noise, stench and so on. It cannot be assumed that these regulations were effective, but at least they testify to the ideals of the city's rulers. Paintings and engravings offer valuable testimony to the ways in which cities were viewed. The artists sometimes improved the appearance of particular buildings and streets, but these improvements, like regulations, offer valuable evidence of contemporary ideals. Private diaries and published plays, poems, stories and biographies all add precious details. As for the experiences of ordinary people, it can be reconstructed, if at all, only in fragments, preserved in popular songs or letters or in interrogations that survive in judicial archives.

The smell and taste of the city

The idea that smells have a history is a relatively new one that owes a good deal to a pioneering study by the French historian Alain Corbin (1982), concerned with both 'the foul' and 'the fragrant'. To take the good smells first, they included spices such as cinnamon and cloves, and a variety of perfumes such as civet and musk and herbs such as lavender and rosemary. Many of these were displayed for sale in the open air, on Piazza San Marco in Venice, for instance, during the Ascension Fair, the *Sensa*. More common was the smell of baking bread, or the frying of other kinds of food, prepared and sold from stalls in the street. In Cairo, a fifteenth-century Spanish visitor remarked on cooks walking the streets 'carrying braziers, and fire, and dishes of stew for sale' (Tafur 1926, 100). Other smells were more or less neutral. Simon Schama has reconstructed the smell of Amsterdam, especially the part of the city closest close to the river IJ, in the following terms: 'A briny aroma of salt, rotting wood, bilgewater and the tide-rinsed remains of countless gristly little creatures housed within the shells of periwinkles and barnacles' (Schama 1999, 311).

As for bad smells (such as urine, excrement, rotting fruit and fish and decaying corpses, especially in times of plague), Corbin argues that around the year 1750, the upper classes ceased to tolerate stenches that their ancestors had learned to live with, thus provoking a wave of sanitary reforms in Paris, London and elsewhere. He is right about the sanitary reforms, of course, but the frequent complaints to be found in earlier sources suggests that the verb 'tolerate' may be too strong. Montaigne, for instance, remarked that his appreciation of both Venice and Paris was diminished by the 'sharp smell' (*aigre senteur*) of the lagoons in the first case and of the mud in the second (Montaigne 1580–8, Book 1, ch.55). Paris was singled out for its stink in the seventeenth century, especially by British visitors. The writer James Howell claimed that the city 'may be smelt many miles off' (Lough 1985, 53). The virtuoso John Evelyn, who was interested in science, was more specific, writing that the city smelled 'as if sulphure were mingled in the mudd' (1955, vol. 1, 94).

The complaints were extended to other cities. In the early seventeenth century William Brereton, a Cheshire gentleman who was familiar with both London and Amsterdam, described the smell of Edinburgh as strong and 'noisome'. 'I never came to my own lodging in Edinburgh, or went out, but I was constrained to hold my nose, or to use wormwood or some such scented plant' (Brereton 1844, 105). In 1654, an English gentleman who lived in Cambridgeshire, Dudley North, complained of London's 'sooty air', while in 1661 Evelyn published a pamphlet offering advice about ways to reduce the amount of smoke in the capital, an increasingly severe problem as wood supplies ran out and people turned to coal for their fires and furnaces (Jenner 1995). Outside Europe, the situation was no better. The Italian missionary Matteo Ricci, for instance, remarked on the foul smell of Beijing. The remark might be dismissed as the prejudice of a 'foreign devil', but it is corroborated by the Ming dynasty official Xie Zhaozhe (who came from a small town in the South) in his *Fivefold Miscellany* (1608), noting 'a lot of excrement and muck in the markets' (Elvin 2004, 404). At this point one appreciates all the more the claim – whether it was correct or not – made about Florence by the humanist Leonardo Bruni, that the city 'is unique and singular in all the world' because 'you will find here nothing that is ... offensive to the nose (*nichil tetrum naribus*)', since whatever mess was produced during the night would be taken away in the morning (Bruni 2000, 5).

The complaints were all the more serious because it was commonly believed that bad air spread disease. What was to be done? One measure, offered by Evelyn among others, and sometimes enforced, was to confine trades such as butchers, dyers, tanners and tallow-chandlers to the edge of the city so that the inhabitants of the centre, especially the upper classes, would be free from these 'horrid stinks'. Smell management, including the removal of meat and cheese stalls from Piazza San Marco, was one of the duties of the health commissioners of Venice, for instance, the *provveditori della sanità* (Wheeler 2007).

Another solution to the problem of stench was of course to clean the city. However, cleaning the streets of rotting vegetables was often left to pigs, who roamed the streets and brought their own odours with them. Serious cleaning was often an emergency measure. In 1580 the Lord Mayor of London ordered street cleaning for 'the Avoydinge of the infection of the plague and the loathsome Stinckes and savours that are in the severall streetes of this Cyttie' (Jenner 2000, 131). In Italy, at times of plague, perfume was used as a means of disinfection. The use of perfume in order to fight one smell with another was even more common at an individual level. The upper classes wore perfumed gloves or carried perfumed balls known as 'pomanders' in their hands, or relied like Brereton on using wormwood or holding their noses. In some northern cities, however, municipal hygiene was coming to be taken more seriously than before. The English gentleman Fynes Moryson, in Lübeck in 1591, noted that 'the citizens are curious to avoid ill smells' (Moryson 1617, vol.1, 7). In the seventeenth century, the same point would often be made about Dutch cities, often as praise but sometimes as criticism, the cleanliness being described as 'rigid' or 'superstitious'.

There is less to say about taste because explicit comment on the taste of food and drink is relatively rare in the sources; an exception is the English merchant Peter Mundy, taking his first cup of coffee in Istanbul, and comparing its taste as well as its appearance to soot. However a few residents and travellers do at least record what they ate, giving an impression of the quantity and variety of food obtainable in cities (as the Milanese Pietro Casola noted in the case of Jerusalem), as well as references to local specialities such as the 'excellent Sauciges' of Bologna (according to the English gentleman Francis Mortoft). In Macao, Peter Mundy discovered lychees, 'the prettiest and pleasauntest fruit that ever I tasted', and also tea ('a certaine Drinke called Chaa') about which he was less enthusiastic (1907–19, vol.3, 162). The street cries of Paris, London and elsewhere often refer to food and drink: to eel pies, for instance, to herring, to cherries, to peaches, to waffles ('Tartelettes friandes à la belle gauffre') and so on.

For a well-documented case-study one might take **Samuel Pepys**, a man for whom sensuous as well as sensual experiences were particularly important, often records what he ate and drank. In the first month of his diary, January 1660, he refers to drinking ale, wine and sack (including a 'posset' in which wine was mixed with milk and spices), and eating turkey, 'brawn' (boar's meat), venison, rabbit, beef, veal, mutton, goose, 'pullets' (young chickens), larks, marrow-bones, ling (a kind of fish), prawns, anchovies, cabbage and bread and cheese. The high proportion of meat and the low proportion of vegetables scored by Pepys were about par for the period, at least for his upper-middle social class (Pepys, 1970–81, vol.1, 3–35).

As for cooking, in one now notorious trial, in Rome in 1603, the judicial archives inform us about different possible styles. The painter Caravaggio assaulted a waiter in an inn after being served with eight artichokes, four cooked in butter and four in oil. When Caravaggio asked which ones were which, the waiter replied 'Smell them'. Caravaggio's response was to break a plate over the man's head (Friedlaender 1955, 280).

The tactile city

What were the most important tactile experiences in Renaissance cities? They were not necessarily pleasant. Crowded streets, for instance, meant jostling, elbowing, squeezing and other forms of the invasion of personal space. A German visitor to London in 1602 found the Exchange 'so filled with people that only by force are you able to make your way' (Gershow 1602, 11). Evelyn complained that Paris needed 'a redresse of the multitude of Coaches, Laquays and throngs of Mankind' (1955, vol. 2, 107). Mundy noted that in Agra, 'in the Bazare ordinarilye there is such a throng that men can hardly passé without much trouble' (1907–19, vol.3, 207). Violence was common in cities, as indeed it was in the countryside, despite attempts to regulate it. The Englishman William Wey was not the only pilgrim to Jerusalem to record the fact that 'as we entered, boys threw stones at us', doubtless because they looked foreign and might be Christians. On entering Florence in 1546, a German visitor discovered, he was required to hand over his sword, while an Englishman had to hand over his pistols at the gate of Genoa in 1658 (Sastrow 1902, 172; Lough 1985, 41). What was more specific to cities was collective violence on a large scale, the violence of what would later be called the 'mob', whether composed of apprentices trashing brothels (a common practice in seventeenth-century London), of crowds sacking the houses of the rich (as in Lyon in 1529), lynching unpopular officials (as in Naples in 1585) and so on.

At a more superficial level, itching may not have been a specifically urban experience, but it was probably worse in urban environments as a result of polluted air and the prevalence of fleas and lice in zones of high density of population. On the other hand, bath-houses were an urban institution, though a declining one after the 1520s, because they were increasingly seen in both Catholic and Protestant countries as a threat to morals, a step away from brothels, if indeed they were not brothels under another name. The *hamam* survived in the Islamic world (Boyat and Fleet 2010, 249–70), while bath-houses were commonplace in Japan, but public baths would not return to Western Europe until the eighteenth century. No wonder then that Western visitors to Istanbul, such as George Sandys and Jean de Thévenot, both in the seventeenth century, found the *hamam* so fascinating. Meanwhile, commercialized 'sex in the city' continued to flourish, from the up-market courtesans of sixteenth-century Venice down to the poorest streetwalker.

The tactile experience that the travellers noted most regularly, though, was that of movement around cities, especially on foot, leading them to comment on the quality of street surfaces. The Spaniard Pero Tafur was impressed by Venice in this respect, writing that 'The city is as clean for walking as in a gracious chamber, so well paved and bricked it is, without the usual mud and dust (Tafur 1926, 167). Ricci by contrast complained that in Beijing 'Very few of the streets ... are paved with brick or stone and it is difficult to say which season of the year is more objectionable for walking', the summer with its dust or the winter with its mud (Ricci 1953, 310). In similar fashion, the Englishman George Sandys noted that in Cairo 'the streets are unpaved and extremely dirty after a shower', while in Naples, to his relief, 'the streets are broad and paved with brick' (Sandys 1615, 119, 259). Evelyn noted with pleasure the paving in Paris, which 'renders it more easy to walk on then our pibbles of London', though his approval was not shared by another English traveller, Peter Heylyn, who claimed that a little rain made the streets 'very slippery and troublesome' (Evelyn 1955, vol.2, 94; Lough 1985, 53). Bologna received special praise for its arcades, 'so that one may walke here without feeling the heat of the sun or be in danger to be troubled by the raine' (Mortoft 1658, 176).

The sounds of the city

The sources allow much more to be said about the sounds of the city, so various and often so localized that it may not have been difficult for blind persons to navigate the streets by ear. Even for sighted people, it has been suggested, sounds were 'significant in shaping people's sense of urban space' (Garrioch 2003, 14). Although 'we have to contend with much louder sounds', as Bruce Smith reminds us, the soundscape of early modern London, for instance, was 'acoustically dense' (1999, 49, 53). In the background Londoners could hear 'the constant sounds of running water', from fountains, for instance. In Amsterdam, it was 'the slap of canal water against the bridges' (Smith 1999, 57; Schama 1999, 312).

However, these sounds, to which it was easy to become so accustomed as to fail to notice them, were often drowned by inanimate noises such as clanging, clattering, clinking, creaking, grinding, hammering, rapping, rattling, ringing, roaring, rumbling, sawing, scraping, thundering, ticking and tolling. To all these sounds one needs to add animate noises such as dogs barking, birds chirping, cocks crowing, pigs squealing, horses clopping and neighing, cats caterwauling, rats and mice squeaking and humans speaking, shouting or singing. A city was the scene of what the English satirist Edward Guilpin described in 1598 as a 'hotch-potch of so many noyses' (Korhonen 2008, 338). Even in our own age of much greater noise pollution it remains easy to sympathize with the Florentine artist Piero di Cosimo, who could not abide the sounds of 'children crying, men coughing, bells ringing or friars chanting' (Vasari 1550, vol. 4, 69), or even the character 'Morose' in Ben Jonson's play *Epicoene* (1609), set in London, a man who is hypersensitive to what he calls 'the discord of sounds', who 'hath chosen a street to live in so narrow at both ends that it will receive no coaches nor carts nor any of these common noises'.

Like smelly trades, noisy trades were supposed to be exiled to the edges of cities, but the rule was not always enforced (how could it be, as cities continually expanded? In any case, this common regulation displaced the problem rather than solving it. Dante, who died in 1321, was already complaining of the noise coming from the Arsenal in Venice, where ships were under construction. In Bologna in the fifteenth century, Tafur noted the existence of a hundred watermills grinding wheat, sawing wood and so on, and in Milan, he visited a street where armourers were at work Tafur (1926, 31). It was not desirable to live next to the workshop of an armourer, as some Londoners complained in 1378 – to no avail (Cockayne 2007, 115). Morose, on the other hand, is represented as powerful enough to prevent an armourer from setting up shop in his parish. Like the sixteenth-century antiquary John Stow, he hated the 'loathsome noise' of metal-working in the city, the sounds evoked by the writer Thomas Dekker (a Londoner himself): 'hammers are beating in one place, Tubs hooping in another, Pots clinking in a third' (Smith 1999, 54). The chains of prisoners made a similar sound to the pots: not for nothing was a medieval prison on London's south bank known as 'The Clink'. The noise of traffic must not be forgotten, especially the sound of horses' hooves and wooden wheels on cobblestones. Visiting Venice in the early 1640s, Evelyn was struck, as tourists still are today, by the quiet. They notice the absence of cars, while he found the city 'almost as silent as a field', without the usual 'rattling of coaches' and 'trampling of horses'.

To the noises of work in Christian Europe it is necessary to add the sound of chiming clocks and of church bells, marking the passage of time or drawing attention to major events, such as a papal election or the canonization of a saint, when cannon might be fired and bells ring all night. Bells rang, pealed or tolled, distinctions in early modern English that reveal contemporary sensitivity to the different messages that bells could transmit. The tocsin, for instance, was a special bell that sounded the alarm, while the muffled sound of a bell that tolled denoted a death. Tafur described the Campanile in Venice and its different bells with different meanings, 'one for Mass, one for Vespers, one to summon the Council ... and one when they arm the fleet', omitting the famous *marangone*, the great bell that told listeners when to begin work and when to stop (Tafur 1926, 164–5). The Dutch historian Johan Huizinga noted that in late medieval France and Flanders, individual bells were given names such as Fat Jacqueline or Bell Roelant and that 'everyone knew their individual tones and instantly recognized their meaning' (Huizinga 1919, 2). Clocks on town halls, increasingly common from the fourteenth century onwards, could usually be heard as well as seen. The Prague clock, for instance, which is still active, was installed in 1410. In China, bells were also in use but urban time was often marked by drums, located in the drum towers of Beijing, Nanjing and elsewhere.

Competing with these inanimate sounds and the cries of animals and birds was a babble of human voices. In the Islamic world, the call to prayer five times a day from the minaret of every mosque replaced the bell as a means of telling time. In some places, main squares for instance, or the exchanges of London or Amsterdam, one might hear the buzz of many conversations. The English writer John Earle, obviously a connoisseur of sound, noted that in 'Paul's Walk' (the central aisle of St Paul's cathedral in London, still the old St Paul's in this period) the dominant sound was the 'humming or buze, mixt of walking, tongues and feet … a still roar or loud whisper' (Smith 1999, 61). Elsewhere one might hear the shouting of children playing or neighbours quarrelling. Added to the mix were the 'street cries' of many different trades, which the locals were able to distinguish and decode: the signature tunes of tinkers, knife-grinders, men and women selling fruit and vegetables, coopers making barrels ('Have you any work for cooper?) and so on. In the early sixteenth century the cries of Paris inspired the composer Clément Jeannequin to turn them into a song for four voices.

Cities, especially large cities, produced a babel of voices in the literal sense of a mixture of languages, dialects and accents. In Venice, for instance, one might hear not only Venetian but also German, Spanish, Greek and Turkish, as well as the dialect of nearby Bergamo. In Amsterdam, besides Dutch (or the Flemish of immigrants from the South) one might hear French, German, English and the Scandinavian languages. In Central Europe, even small towns might be multilingual. Sárospatak in Hungary, for instance, was described in the 1650s by the Czech scholar Comenius (Jan Komenský) as a place in which five modern languages could be heard (presumably Hungarian, Czech, Slovak, German and Ukrainian) so that 'one person understands another no more than in the Tower of Babel' unless Latin was used as a lingua franca (Bérenger 1969, 5). What linguists call 'the urbanization of language' should not be forgotten'. Foreigners apart, to a visitor from the countryside the accents of townspeople would have sounded strange or even unintelligible (Wright 2007).

The city was among other things a stage where a variety of performances could be heard. Drums rolled when soldiers marched into or out of the city, and also at public executions. Announcements were made by town criers, often accompanied by trumpeters or drummers in order to draw attention to their message in a noisy environment. In Florence, the main square and seat of government, Piazza della Signoria, included a platform called the *ringhiera* from which announcements and speeches ('harangues') could be made. Public squares such as Piazza San Marco in Venice served as stages for charlatans, who drew crowds by acting out their cures, and for singers of tales, *cantimbanchi* ('singers on benches'). In the late Middle Ages, religious plays were performed in churches or in the open air on the occasion of major festivals such as Easter or Corpus Christi, while purpose-built playhouses were constructed in major cities from the sixteenth century onwards. Sermons were another form of performance, dominated by the friars in the fourteenth and fifteenth centuries and by the Protestants in the sixteenth and seventeenth. A new form of church, the *Hallenkirche,* was constructed in the late Middle Ages to allow the congregation to see and hear preachers better. However, churches were not large enough to accommodate the most popular preachers, such as the Franciscans San Bernardino of Siena and Olivier Maillard, who performed in the open air, with some of their listeners perched on roofs or trees. In the Protestant world, the Dutch pastor Jacobus Borstius was famous for the sermons he preached at Dordrecht and elsewhere. The crowd was sometimes so dense that babies fainted in their mothers' arms (Francken 1942, 210–11).

Late medieval or Renaissance cities were also the sites of many musical performances, as recent studies in urban musicology remind us, noting what one scholar calls 'the sonic expressions of urban identity' (Kendrick 2002, 3; cf. Strohm 1985, Getz 2005, Fenlon 2007). Many cities employed musicians to play on special occasions, while individual pipers and fiddlers performed every day in the streets and in taverns. Ballads were sung rather than recited, by professionals and amateurs alike. Some London taverns had the texts of ballads pasted on the walls to encourage drinkers to join in performances, the sixteenth-century equivalent of today's *karaoke*. However, in this period, which ends with the rise of opera-houses and concert-halls, the best music, especially singing, was usually to be heard in churches. Visitors to cities often commented on the quality of the performances. The Dutch barber-surgeon Arendt Willemsz, for instance, who visited Venice in 1525, noted that 'The canons of St Mark's perform beautiful song, year in, year out', 'intoning the psalms very pleasantly and magnificently' (quoted in Fenlon 2007, 75, and Howard and Moretti,). One English gentleman in Rome remarked that 'the best voices I ever heard are in the Pope's chappell', while another, visiting the church of San Apollinare, found the music 'so rare and sweet that it would have Inchanted any man's Eares that heard it' (Somerset 1993, 233; Mortoft 1658, 118). The Protestant patrician Sastrow, visiting the Catholic city of Trent at Easter 1546, confessed to hearing 'most delicious singing' in the churches (Sastrow 1902, 143). The English merchant Robert Bargrave, an adventurous traveller, entered a church in Iași, in Moldavia, and found the 'anthems', as he called them to be 'rather like the Turkish', while in L'viv, in the Ukraine, he found the church music to be 'much sweeter and more regular' (Bargrave 1999, 136, 145).

Not all music was perceived as sweet or smooth, however. Judicial records contain complaints about street music as well as about hammering and shouting. 'Rough music' (*Katzenmusik*), in other words a serenade played on pots and pans, was a not uncommon event in cities in this period in many parts of Europe, especially when an old man married a young woman, and the event usually took place at night (Cockayne 2002). Readers who think of preindustrial cities as sonic utopias because they are free from sirens, horns and drills may be well advised to think again.

Viewing the townscape

The rise of the painted or engraved townscape in Italy, the Netherlands and elsewhere took place for the most part after 1650, although Vittore Carpaccio, for instance, portrayed the streets of Venice in some detail around the year 1500 in paintings ostensibly devoted to religious subjects. However, in our period literary sources reveal an increasing interest in the appearance of cities on the part of insiders and outsiders alike, especially a concern with uniformity and symmetry. Needless to say, both insiders and outsiders looked at other people as well as at the urban fabric, even if travel diaries say little about this. The age of the *flâneur* may not have dawned, depending as it did on the rise of the arcades and boulevards of nineteenth-century Paris and elsewhere, but to see and be seen were already strong motives for both men and women to walk or ride through the streets of the city. In London and elsewhere, 'beauty', both of the body and its clothing, 'was an essential ingredient of street culture', while Paul's Walk has been described as 'the early modern catwalk' of fashionable London (Korhonen 2008, 336, 339). Male visitors from other countries remarked on the freedom of women in England. As Platter noted, 'they often stroll out or drive by coach in very gorgeous clothes' (Quoted in Korhonen 2008, 345). The Italian priest Pietro Casola, on pilgrimage to Jerusalem, complained about the use of veils there, so that 'I was never able to see a beautiful woman' (1494, 257). Rich, colourful and shiny materials impressed some visitors. Visiting the Corpus Christi procession at Venice, Casola declared himself to have been dazzled by the brocades and jewels of the priest's vestments. At the Uffizi in Florence, what most impressed Mortoft was the furniture, especially tables made of jasper and decorated with jewels.

An interest in the 'sights' of the city goes back a long way, witness the discussions in classical antiquity of the Seven Wonders of the World, all of them urban. Following this model, a mid-sixteenth-century painting attributed to Pieter Claessens represented the 'Seven Wonders of Bruges' (*Septem Admirationes Civitatis Brugensis*). Guidebooks to cities, notably Rome, to countries, notably Italy, and also to travel in general already existed in this period.

They told readers what to see and even, on occasion, how to see it. Some travel diaries of the period, although written by eyewitnesses (Evelyn, for example), reproduce passages from these books, suggesting that literature shaped perceptions. For example, one account after another of visits to Milan draws attention to the cathedral, the Castello Sforzesco and the hospital.

In certain cities, such as Florence and Genoa, visitors were impressed by the height of the buildings, a reminder that in this period most people lived in houses of one or two storeys. 'Do not look up at the heights like a man from the country', the thirteenth-century Florentine Brunetto Latini warned his readers. Tafur probably did so all the same, for his description of Genoa noted that 'all the houses are like towers of four or five storeys or more'. Visitors also paid attention to the material from which cities were constructed. Tafur once again makes an eloquent witness, commenting on the 'beautiful white stones' of the Temple of Solomon in Jerusalem, and the marble, porphyry and jasper to be seen in Santa Sofia in Constantinople. Again, Somerset called Genoa 'one of the stateliest built townes of Italie', thanks to its use of marble (Tafur 1926, 27, 61, 139; Somerset 1993, 177–8). A number of travellers were concerned with cleanliness and dirt: one might contrast the Portuguese Jesuit João Rodrigues on Kyōtō, 'extremely clean', 'the streets are swept and sprinkled with water twice a day', with Somerset on Paris: 'the streetes are at all times almost of the year verie durtie and mirie' (Rodrigues 2001, 168; Somerset 1993, 87).

Travellers not infrequently commented on the beauty of town squares. Like tourists today, they were impressed by Piazza San Marco. Again, Moryson found what he called the 'market place' in Leipzig to be 'large and stately', Brereton admired what he called the 'fairest' and 'most spacious' marketplaces of Delft and Harlem, while Bargrave described the main square of the new town of Zamość in Poland as 'very handsome and uniforme' (Moryson 1617, 9; Brereton 1844, 19, 50; Bargrave 1999, 147). The breadth of the streets in certain cities also impressed some visitors, indicating what they were accustomed to at home. Thomas Platter the Younger, for instance, who came from Basel, found the streets of Perpignan to be 'extremely beautiful and wide' (*mechtig schön unndt breit*:

Platter 1968, 323). Bridges were often considered to be worthy of note. Platter remarked, as people still do, on the 'beautiful bridge' at Avignon, and Evelyn on its 'very fair bridge', as well as the Pont Neuf of Paris, 'a stately bridge'. The Englishman Thomas Coryat also noted the 'faire bridges' of Paris, while the Rialto at Venice was the 'fairest bridge' that he ever saw. 'Fair bridges' were one of the attractions of Rotterdam for Brereton (Platter 1968, 114; Evelyn 1955, vol.2, 161, 92; Coryat 1611, vol.1, 170, 306; Brereton 1844, 7).

Houses too attracted attention. As might have been expected, some travellers enthused over what Coryat called the 'sumptuous and magnificent palaces' on the Grand Canal. Moryson was impressed by the 'beautie and uniformitie of the houses' in Lübeck. Samuel Pepys, on a brief visit to The Hague, found 'The houses so neat in all places and things as is possible', though Bargrave found those of Amsterdam 'so superstitiously neat, as is fitter for sight than use' (Coryat 1611, vol. 1, 306; Moryson 1617, 7; Pepys 1970–83 vol.1, 138; Bargrave 1999, 167). Brereton even praised the gallows at Leiden, 'the daintiest curious gallows that ever I saw' (1844), 38; also 49, on Harlem).

The references to uniformity by both Moryson and Bargrave deserve comment. They are not alone. Robert Dallington (1604, C4b), described the buildings of Paris as 'fayre, high and uniforme', while Evelyn found some streets 'incomparably fair and uniform' (1955, vol.2, 108). Somerset admired Antwerp because it was 'one of the first townes built for uniformitie, that a man shall lightly see in Christendome; it hath marvellous fayre streets, and all the houses built answerable one to the other' (1993, 283). Brereton admired Dutch cities for the same reason. In Dordrecht he noted 'uniform and complete building', while the Keizergracht in Amsterdam impressed him because it was 'most uniforme … built alike on both sides' (1844, 13, 68).

By this time, towards the end of our period, the concern with regularity and symmetry was widespread. At the beginning of the period, though, this concern can already be found among the patricians of Florence, as some of the urban regulations of the time testify. In 1330, for instance, it was declared that Piazza della Signoria 'ought to be more elegant and regular than anywhere else (*magis deberat esse decora et equa, quam aliqua alia*), while in 1363 shacks (*domunculae*) were to be removed from Piazza San Giovanni (Piazza Duomo) because they 'spoil the appearance and the beauty of the whole square (*deturpant faciem et pulchritudinem totius plate*: Braunfels 1959, 104, 253). Later regulations required the facades of houses to be harmonious. No wonder then that Leonardo Bruni praised Florence as unique not only for its lack of bad smells but also for having 'nothing that is disgusting to the eye' (*nichil fedum oculis*: Bruni 2000), 5). One might have expected this concern in the age of Bruni, Filippo Brunelleschi and Leon Battista Alberti; what may be more surprising is to find it in urban regulations in the fourteenth century, when the Gothic style was still dominant.

The concern with symmetry went with an increasing interest in views or 'prospects. Late in our period, travellers often described climbing towers in order to see a city as a whole. Moryson wrote of Lübeck as providing 'a faire prospect', while he regularly noted cities 'of a round forme', as if he had viewed them from above or had been looking at engraved plans. In Dordrecht, Brereton entered a turret that 'gives you a full view of the whole town', while in Edinburgh he went up to the castle, where 'you may take a full view of the situation of the whole city'. In Milan, Coryat viewed the city from the roof as found it to be 'a most beautiful and delectable shew'. In Danzig (now Gdańsk), Bargrave found that 'From the Topp of the Steeple is a fair Prospect of the City' (Moryson 1617, 6, 9, etc; Brereton 1844, 13, 102; Coryat 1611, 244; Bargrave 1999, 151). The Dutch poet Constantijn Huygens climbed the tower of Strasbourg cathedral and wrote about the experience, though his verses say more about the danger of the climb than about the beauty of the view.

Alternatively, the city could be viewed from afar or from the sea. Visiting Siena, Evelyn noted that 'The Citty at a little distance presents the Traveller with an incomparable Prospect', including the many brick towers. In Genoa, he appreciated 'the streetes and buildings so ranged one above the other, as our seats are in Playhouses'. In similar fashion a little later, Richard Lassels described Genoa as 'like an amphitheatre to those who behold it from the sea' (Eveyln 1955 vol.2, 201, 172; Somerset 1993, 178n).

In short, the city was becoming 'a visually appreciated entity' (Strohmeyer 2007, 75, 80). The taste for wide views encouraged urban planning, and in its turn the results of planning reinforced the taste for views.

Conclusions

Reading these different accounts of cities gives the impression that visitors at least, especially visitors who did not live in cities themselves, suffered from as well as enjoying the hyper-stimulation of the senses in an urban environment. One wonders whether visitors and citizens alike needed some kind of retreat and where they found it. Green spaces were common in cities at this time but they usually took the form of private gardens. Churches were a possible safe haven, at least outside the times of services, though as Dutch paintings of church interiors remind us, barking dogs as well as beggars might disturb the peace of anyone who wished to escape from the sounds of the city.

In any case, as I remarked at the beginning of this chapter, urban experiences were not the same for everyone. Men and women, old and young, rich and poor, immigrants from the countryside and upper-class foreign travellers are unlikely to have experienced cities in the same ways. For example, the sense of insecurity is likely to have been greater for women, the elderly and visitors than it was for men, for the young and for locals. Cities that were small by the standards of the twenty-first century were bewildering for visitors who came from villages. As a Russian traveller remarked in 1349, 'Entering Constantinople is like a great forest' (Majeska 1984, 44).

It is also necessary to distinguish the experiences of night and day, summer and winter, working days and holidays. In this period the streets of cities were still dark at night, so that the stars were visible, while walkers and riders needed individual torches or lanterns. Given this norm, it is not difficult to imagine the effect on spectators of masses of lighted candles in theatres or in churches for the Forty Hours devotion, or the fireworks that celebrated happy events such as victories or the birth of a sun to the local ruler. As for the sounds of the city, the night was not necessarily quiet. For example, 'Shouting, yelling and screaming'(*jauchzen, jählen und schreien*) in alleys and houses at night was condemned in a Strasbourg ordinance of 1651 (Koslofsky 2011, 160, 337).

For a major event such as the feast of the patron saint (San Giovanni in Florence, for instance) or the entry of a ruler the city would wear its best clothes, with triumphal arches erected in the streets and carpets hanging from balconies. Fireworks would light up the night sky and the soundscape would be transformed by music. When the emperor Charles V entered Milan in 1533, for instance, he was accompanied by singers and by musicians playing instruments. When Margaret of Austria entered the same city in 1598, she heard the trumpeters playing 'antiphonally' at the Porta Romana, as well as the Te Deum sing by four choirs in the cathedral. When King Henri III of France visited Venice in 1574, for instance, he was accompanied everywhere by trumpets and drums and frequently serenaded (Kendrick 2002, 4; Fenlon 2007, 193–216).

The Ascension Fair in Venice was 'as much about viewing, touching, tasting and hearing as it was about making a profit' (Welch 2005, 183, 189). Carnival too was a feast for all the senses. It was a time of fancy dress. In Italy, for instance, people dressed as characters from the *commedia dell'arte*, such as Arlecchino, Dottore or Pulcinella, while elsewhere people dressed as devils, wild men or fools. There was much singing and dancing, in which the usual musical instruments were joined by special ones such as the Dutch *Rommelpot*, made from a pig's bladder and squealing like a pig. Insults flew about like confetti on an occasion when many people felt that anything was permitted, while wearing masks gave them a sense of invisibility. Participants might throw eggs at one another, eggs filled with rose-water (or a liquid with a less pleasant odour), or they might throw oranges (in Provence), or flour, or stones. The streets were crowded and harassment (especially of women, of Jews and of animals) was commonplace. Carnival was also a time of eating on a grand scale, especially meat, which Catholics were about to give up for Lent, as well as special Carnival food such as pancakes and waffles. Those who could not afford to buy such items had to content themselves with the smell of roasting, baking, frying and boiling. There was also heavy drinking, especially during the days leading up to Shrove Tuesday, with beer and wine first sharpening the perceptions of the drinkers and then dulling them (Burke 1978, 259–71). In similar fashion Peter Mundy, visiting Agra, noted that the Holi festival was 'used in the same manner as Shrovetide is in France, by eating, drinckeing, feasteinge, playing, throweing sweete oyles and water with red powder', as well as what he called 'affrontive Gambolls to those that passé by' (1907–19, vol.3, 219).

Different kinds of visitor with different purposes came to the city with different horizons of expectations and hence they viewed it in different ways. Pilgrims, for instance, saw cities such as Jerusalem, Constantinople or Rome as assemblages of churches, relics and images that were if possible to be touched as well as to be seen. For the English pilgrim Richard Guylforde, the sights of Venice included a golden chalice and two golden candlesticks from the treasury of San Marco, though he was also a knight and was equally impressed by the artillery at the Arsenal (Guylforde 1506, 7). Young men like Pepys (and there were probably many such, if few who were quite so frank in writing about his experiences) moved through the city on the lookout for pretty women. Visitors from abroad were naturally impressed by the contrasts with the townscape at home. In a dialogue by the Englishman Thomas Starkey, in the reign of Henry VIII, one speaker remarks that 'Methought when I first came into Flanders and France, that I was translated, as it had been, into another world, the cities and towns appeared so goodly, so well builded, and so clean kept' (Starkey 1871, 92). Friar Felix Fabri, who came from Zurich, recorded his amazement when he entered Cairo at night, impressed by the density of the crowds in the streets, the shouting, bright lights and so on (Fabri 1483, 400–1).

As Constance Clasen has suggested, one reason that the senses have a history is that they are informed by cultural values, which change over the long term. The art historian Michael Baxandall wrote about what he called the 'period eye' in fifteenth-century Italy, though the practices he described were, as Herman Roodenburg suggests, examples of synaesthesia, including haptic visuality and kinaesthetic empathy (Clasen 2012, 12; Baxandall 1972, Roodenburg 2012, 4). One might equally well speak about the period eye in other places and times as well as about the period ear or nose. We have already seen how travellers in this period increasingly noticed and praised the regularity of certain townscapes, another case of the 'Renaissance eye' or the classical sensibility. One might add that this regularity was appreciated all the more because it was still rare. By the time that it had become common, in the eighteenth century, observers were taking more pleasure in irregularity and other features of what would later be christened the 'romantic sensibility'.

One major cultural event affecting the perception of cities was the Reformation, bringing with it, in the Protestant parts of Europe, the taming of Carnival and the disappearance of many images from churches (often following bouts of iconoclasm). Among the most obvious and important changes taking place as this period gave way to the following one around the middle of the seventeenth century were more lighting in cities at night, more paved streets, more traffic (especially the rapid rise of coaches in the seventeenth century), and more pollution (a result of increasing reliance on coal for heating). The rise of coffee-houses brought with it a new taste and a new aroma. Using London judicial records, one scholar has detected 'a rise in the perceived levels of noise nuisance' after the year 1600, including increasingly negative reactions to street music (Cockayne 2007, 129). The soundscape of churches changed as Protestant ministers encouraged their congregation to sing hymns rather than to listen to them. Opera-houses, beginning in Venice in the 1630s, spread through Europe in the course of the following century or so.

Turning to the history of the eye, the seventeenth and eighteenth centuries were the age of the rise of townscapes, especially Dutch and Venetian, by artist such as Berckheyde and Canaletto, both expressing and encouraging an interest in the appearance of streets and squares, an aesthetic or 'picturesque' gaze. The style of travel writing changed, with later travellers paying more attention to the manners and customs of the inhabitants of the places they visited. A vivid example of the new style is the travelogue written by a young Englishman, Philip Skippon, who visited the Netherlands, Germany, Italy and France in the 1660s. In Italy, for instance, Skippon (1732) made vivid observations on the local food ('they strew scraped cheese on most of their dishes'), clothes (with a sketch of a doge's cap), flagellants, funerals, blasphemies, silk production, a guillotine used in Milan, the voting system in Venice (complete with a diagram of a ballot-box), and even the ways in which three gentlemen walked together (with a diagram) or the manner in which the washing was hung out to dry on iron bars across the streets. For all these reasons, the years around 1650 make a convenient – if approximate – ending for this chapter.

Bibliography

Bargrave, R. (1999) *The Travel Diary of Robert Bargrave, Levant merchant (1647–1656)*, ed. Michael G. Brennan, London: Hakluyt Society.

Baxandall, M. (1972) *Painting and Experience in Fifteenth-Century Italy*, Oxford: Oxford University Press.

Béranger, J. (1969) 'Latin et langues vernaculaires dans la Hongrie du 17e siècle', *Revue Historique* 242, 5–28.

Boyat, E. and K. Fleet (2010) *A Social History of Ottoman Istanbul*, Cambridge: Cambridge University Press.

Braunfels, W. (1959) *Mittelalterliche Stadtbaukunst in der Toskana*, Berlin: Mann.

Brereton, W. (1844) *Travels in Holland, the United Provinces, England, Scotland and Ireland M.DC.XXXIV.-M.DC.XXXV*, Manchester: Chetham Society.

Bruni, L. (2000) *Laudatio Florentine Urbis*, ed. Stefano U. Baldassarri, Florence, SISMEL.

Burke, P. (1978) *Popular Culture in Early Modern Europe,* 3ʳᵈ edn Farnham: Ashgate.

Casola, P. (1494) *Pilgrimage to Jerusalem,* English translation Manchester: Manchester University Press, 1907.

Cockayne, E. (2002) 'Bad Music in Early Modern English Towns', *Urban History* 29, 35–47

Cockayne, E. (2007) *Hubbub: Filth, Noise and Stench in England,* New Haven: Yale University Press

Corbin, A. (1982) *The Foul and the Fragrant: odor and the French social imagination,* English translation, Leamington Spa: Berg.

Coryat, T. (1611) *Coryat's Crudities,* rpr 2 vols., Glasgow, MacLehose, 1905.

Cowan, A., and J. Steward (eds., 2007) *The City and the Senses: urban culture since 1500,* Aldershot: Ashgate.

Dallington, R. (1604) *The View of Fraunce,* facsimile edn London: Oxford University Press, 1936.

Elvin, M. (2004) *The Retreat of the Elephants: an environmental history of China,* New Haven: Yale University Press.

Evelyn, J. (1955), *Diary,* ed. G. De Beer, 6 vols., Oxford: Clarendon Press.

Fabri, F. (1483) *Voyage en Egypte,* French translation ed. Jacques Masson, 3 vols., Paris: Institut français d'archéologie orientale, 1975.

Fenlon, I. (2007) *The Ceremonial City,* New Haven: Yale University Press.

Francken, A. W. (1942) *Het Leven Onzer Voorouders in de Gouden Eeuw,* The Hague: Stols.

Friedlaender, W. (1955) *Caravaggio Studies,* Princeton: Princeton University Press.

Garrioch, D. (2003) 'Sounds of the City: the soundscape of early modern European towns', *Urban History* 30 (2003), 5–25.

Gerschow, F. (1892) 'Diary of the Journey of Philip Julius through England in the Year 1602', *Transactions of the Royal Historical Society* 6, 7–53.

Getz, C. S. (2005) *Music in the Collective Experience in Sixteenth-Century Milan,* Aldershot: Ashgate.

Guylforde, R. (1506) *Pilgrimage to the Holy Land,* ed. H. Ellis, London: Camden Society, 1851.

Howard, D. and L. Moretti, *Sound and Space in Renaissance Venice,* New Haven: Yale University Press.

Huizinga, J. (1919) *The Autumn of the Middle Ages,* English translation Chicago: University of Chicago Press, 1996.

Jenner, M. (1995) 'The Politics of London Air', *Historical Journal* 38, 535–51.

Jenner, M. (2000) 'Civilization and Deodorization? Smell in Early Modern English Culture', in P. Burke, B. Harrison and P. Slack (eds.) *Civil Histories,* Oxford: Oxford University Press, 127–44

Jonson, B. (1609) *Epicoene, or the Silent Woman.* Ed. R. V. Holdsworth, London: Black, 1979.

Kendrick, R. L. (2002) *The Sounds of Milan, 1585–1650,* Oxford: Oxford University Press.

Kent, F. W. (ed., 2000) *Street Noises, Civic Spaces and Urban Identities in Italian Renaissance Cities,* Melbourne.

Korhonen, A. (2008) 'To See and be Seen: beauty in the early modern London street', *Journal of Early Modern History* 12, 335–60

Koslofsky, C. (2011) *Evening's Empire: a history of the night in early modern Europe,* Cambridge: Cambridge University Press.

Lough, J. (1985) *France Observed in the Seventeenth Century by British Travellers,* Stocksfield: Oriel Press.

Majeska, G. P. (1984) *Russian Travelers to Constantinople in the Fourteenth and Fifteenth Centuries,* Washington, D.C.: Dumbarton Oaks Library.

Montaigne, M. de (1580–8) *Essais,* ed. Maurice Rat, Paris: Gallimard, 1962.

Mortoft, F. (1658) *Travels through France and Italy, 1658–1659,* ed. M. Letts, London: Hakluyt Society, 1925.

Moryson, F. (1617) *An Itinerary,* rpr. 4 vols., Glasgow: MacLehose, 1907.

Mundy, P. (1907–19) *Travels,* ed. R. C. Temple, 3 vols, London: Hakluyt Society.

Pepys, S. (1970–83) *Diary,* ed. R. Latham and W. Matthews, 11 vols., London: Bell.

Platter, T. (1968) *Beschreibung der Reisen durch Frankreich, Spanien, England und die Niederlande 1595–1600,* ed. R. Keiser, Basel: Schwab.

Ricci, M. (1953) *China in the Sixteenth Century: the journals of Matteo Ricci 1583–1610,* translated from the Latin by L. J. Gallagher, New York: Random House.

Rodrigues, J. (2001) *Account of Sixteenth-Century Japan,* ed. M. Cooper, London: Hakluyt Society.

H. Roodenburg (2012) 'A New Historical Anthropology? A Plea to take a Fresh Look at Practice Theory', http://hsozkult.geschichte. hu-berlin.de/forum/type=diskussionen&id=1826, accessed 9 August 2012

Sandys, G. (1615) *A Relation of a Journey begun an: Dom: 1610,* London: Barret.

Sastrow, B. (1902) *Social Germany in Luther's Time,* English translation London: Constable.

Schama, S. (1999) 'The City in Five Senses', in *Rembrandt's Eyes,* London: Allen Lane, 311–22

Skippon, P. (1732) 'An Account of a Journey made thro' part of the Low-Countries, Germany, Italy and France', in A. Churchill and J. Churchill (eds.) *A Collection of Voyages,* 6 vols., 1704–32, vol.6 (London: Churchill), 647–87.

Smith, B. (1999) *The Acoustic World of Early Modern England,* Chicago: University of Chicago Press.

Somerset, C. (1993) *The Travel Diary (1611–1612) of an English Catholic,* ed. M. G. Brennan, Leeds: Leeds Philosophical and Literary Society.

Starkey, T. (1871) *A Dialogue between Pole and Lupset,* London: Early English Text Society.

Strohm, R. (1985) *Music in Late Medieval Bruges,* second edn Oxford: Oxford University Press, 1990.

Strohmeyer, U. (2007) 'Engineering Vision in Early Modern Paris', in Cowan and Steward, 75–92.

Tafur, P. (1926) *Travels and Adventures, 1435–1439,* translated and edited by M. Letts, London: Harpers.

Vasari, G. (1550) *Le vite de'più eccellenti pittori, scultori, e architettori,* ed. P. Barocchi, 4 vols 1966–76, Florence: Sansoni.

Welch, E. (2005) *Shopping in the Renaissance: consumer cultures in Italy 1400–1600,* New Haven: Yale University Press.

Wright, L. (2007) 'Speaking and Listening in Early Modern London', in Cowan and Steward, 75–92.

11: COMMUNICATION

The media of communication – orality, writing, print, radio and so on – are technologies, but they are not neutral. They are not pure 'conduits' of information. In the words of Marshall McLuhan, exaggerated for rhetorical effect but containing an important insight, 'The medium is the message' (it is more exact though less ear-catching to say that the medium is part of the message).[1] Such an emphasis on the media does not necessarily imply technological determinism. We might look at different media as presenting different opportunities that individuals or groups may grasp.

As for cultures, we might view them as distinctive packages of technologies and 'communicative resources'. In contrast to a normal package, though, the contents interact. Cultural history is the story of both tradition and innovation (innovation as resistance to tradition and tradition as resistance to innovation). A simple model of the 'replacement' of one medium or genre by another does not do justice to the tradition side of the equation. It is more illuminating to work with a model of the cultural 'co-existence' of orality and writing, manuscript and print, print and radio, radio and television, television and the Internet. When new media are introduced, old ones survive, although their place in the package and the functions that they perform are generally more limited or specialized than before.[2]

---

[1] Marshall McLuhan, *Understanding Media: the extensions of man* (London: Routledge, 1964).

[2] Asa Briggs and Peter Burke, *A Social History of the Media from Gutenberg to the Internet* (3rd edn, Cambridge: Polity, 2009), introduction.

Communication in history

To write a chapter about communication in human history is a challenge. The origins of language go back a minimum of 50,000 years and a maximum of five or six million years. The cave paintings of Lascaux are about 20,000 years old, while writing has a history of five thousand years or more. In order to present such a long history and to discuss many parts of the world in a few pages, it will obviously be necessary to be somewhat schematic.

Any history of communication is inevitably concerned with what the American political scientist Harold Lasswell described as 'Who says What to Whom through What Channel with What Effect'.[3] In what follows I shall privilege the 'channels', in other words the 'media' of communication. The schema chosen to organize this chapter, the red thread through the labyrinth of communication, is that of the successive dominance of four media, which may be described for the sake of brevity as the oral, the written, the printed and the electric systems. There are of course others: communication by *qipu,* for instance, in Peru under the Incas (discussed below), or by *chapatti* from village to village in Hindustan in 1857, the year of the great 'Mutiny', a rebellion against British rule, as well as communication by gesture and especially by ritual.

The Epic of Milman Parry

As a reminder of the importance of interaction between media it seems appropriate to begin this account with a story, the story of a scholarly adventure. For centuries, scholars had engaged in debate about the Homeric poems. Among the questions that they debated, two were particularly important: were the *Iliad* and the *Odyssey* the work of the same poet? Were they composed in writing or were they originally sung? In the 1930s, a young Harvard professor of

---

[3] Harold D. Lasswell, *Politics: who gets what, when, how* (New York: Mcgraw-Hill, 1936).

classics, Milman Parry, who was to die tragically young, had the idea of testing the oral hypothesis in the field.

Obviously unable to visit ancient Greece, he decided to work in Bosnia, knowing that oral poets were still active in that region and that they continued to compose epics about battles between Christians and Turks and heroes such as Marko Kraljević. Like an anthropologist, Parry went to live in the region, armed with a phonograph recorder and accompanied by an assistant, Albert Lord. Analysing the poems they heard in coffee-houses, at weddings and elsewhere, recited to the accompaniment of the *gusle*, a one-stringed fiddle, Parry and Lord discovered that the epics were never sung in exactly the same way twice, especially when the poet was as gifted as one of their informants, Avdo Međedović.

More exactly, the epics were semi-improvised, full of recurrent 'formulas' (stock lines or half-lines) and recurrent incidents or 'themes' such as the arming of the hero, the sending of a letter and so on. With the aid of these formulas and themes, a *guslar* was able to improvise a narrative for hours at a time. Comparing the poems recorded in Bosnia with the Homeric poems, equally full of formulas and themes, the two scholars concluded that the *Iliad* and the *Odyssey* were originally oral poems, semi-improvised at each performance, so that the texts that have come down to us must record special 'command performances' for scribes.

This memorable story has itself an epic quality and indeed one of the Bosnian poets narrated it in verse as 'the epic of Milman Parry'. The conclusions, published in French in Parry's doctoral thesis and in English, by Albert Lord, in a book called *The Singer of Tales* (1960) cast a good deal of light on the creative process by which narratives are produced, combining or developing schemata and thus producing something new.[4]

All the same, some of the conclusions of these remarkable works remain debatable. Some later scholars have noted, for example, that in other parts of the world, such as Rajasthan in India, sung

---

[4] Albert B. Lord, *The Singer of Tales* (Cambridge MA: Harvard University Press, 1960).

stories keep much closer to fixed texts.[5] The weakest point in the argument is the authors' emphasis on purity. Parry and Lord were in search of an oral culture that was uncontaminated by writing or print. They found what they wanted to find. They ignored evidence to the contrary. Bosnia in the 1930s still had a low literacy rate but it was not a purely oral culture. Printed versions of epics were in circulation, and they were known to some at least of the oral poets. The two scholars failed to notice interaction between media, perhaps less obvious in Bosnia in the 1930s than in (say) the Northeast of Brazil, but present all the same. Today, scholars are familiar with the Parry thesis via print and some of them study the Bosnian epics by listening to the old phonograph recordings, thus illustrating once again the interaction between media.

The Oral System

At first sight, it might be thought that oral communication has no history, as it is a permanent feature of life in society. It is indeed difficult to imagine any culture in which conversation, rumour and gossip does not play an important role. But at different times and in different places, oral communication has been supported by different institutions, performed different functions and played more or less important parts in the media system.

Until relatively recently, about five thousand years ago, writing did not exist. The system of communication was predominantly oral, although speech was supplemented by ritual and by image-making. The great problem of studying the period before writing is the lack of sources. We can still view the cave-paintings but we are ignorant of the cultural context that would allow us to interpret the images of hands, wild beasts and so on. The oral culture of that long period can only be reconstructed indirectly, by analogy with later oral communications recorded in writing or in post-scribal media such as discs and tapes.

---

[5] J. D. Smith, 'The Singer and the Song: a re-assessment of Lord's "oral theory"', *Man* 12 (1977), 141–53.

What we can say, thinking of the last five thousand years, is that oral communication has never lost its importance but only its former centrality. In the sphere of religion, for instance, besides Christian services, prayers and sermons, one might mention the Hindu Vedas, which were transmitted orally long before they were written down, and also the regular recitation of the Qur'an in the Muslim world (the Arabic word 'Qur'an' means 'recitation'). Indeed, Muhammad himself was illiterate, and must have dictated the text to a scribe.

The number and the variety of institutions and forms of material culture that supported oral communication in different cultures, even in the ages of writing and print, deserve to be noted. Think for instance of the pulpits constructed in churches for the use of preachers, or of the balconies of town halls from which speeches were made (the Town Hall of medieval Bologna was called the *Arengo* or 'Speech' for this reason). Think of taverns, barber's shops and pharmacies, all three notorious – among early modern elites – as places where ordinary people discussed the affairs of the world and criticized the authorities. Think of theatres, built specifically for the purpose of performing plays: a few in the sixteenth century, more in the seventeenth century, many more in the eighteenth. Again, one of the functions of coffeehouses, clubs and *salons,* three institutions that flourished in Europe in the eighteenth and nineteenth centuries, was to facilitate different kinds of oral communication, especially conversation. Bookshops too were centres of oral communication, illustrating the interaction of talk and print – like coffeehouses, where newspapers were often available to clients.

These examples come mainly from Europe, but the Islamic world also had its pulpits and its coffee-houses – after all, coffee-drinking originated in the Middle East. Traditional China and Japan had their tea-houses, while in nineteenth- and twentieth-century Bengal, *adda* – a place for conversation, often accompanied by food – was an important cultural institution.[6]

---

[6] Dipesh Chakrabarty, '*Adda:* a history of sociality', in his *Provincializing Europe* (Princeton: Princeton University Press, 2000), 180–213.

Ancient Greece and modern Africa have been selected as case-studies of cultures in which an oral system of communication was dominant.

In the ancient Greek city-states, politics – the very word is derived from 'polis' – depended to an unusual extent on public oral communication. Discussing the optimum size of the *polis*, Aristotle argued that it had to be small enough for all the citizens to be able to hear public speeches. Speeches in assemblies such as the Athenian *ekklesia* (open to all male citizens over the age of eighteen) were essential to the functioning of the ancient Greek public sphere. So were plays, raising fundamental moral problems and seen and heard by large number of people in open-air amphitheatres. So was the reciting in public of poems such as the *Iliad* and *Odyssey*, long viewed not as mere entertainment but as guides to conduct. Today, ancient Greece is studied on the basis of texts by poets, playwrights and philosophers, but those texts were the products of a largely oral culture in which writing interacted with speech.[7]

A similar point might be made about African cultures after the introduction of writing and printing, often by Muslim or Christian missionaries, in the nineteenth century. Even today, when writing and print have been overtaken by the electric media, oral performances remain unusually important. Storytellers continue to entertain the public, allowing them to participate by using opening and closing formulae to which audience will reply. In West Africa, oral poets, known as *griots,* are still active. For a long time, knowledge about the past was handed down orally. In Ashanti, there was a special genre known as drum history, in which the drums simulated speech, making use of formulae to avoid the ambiguity of drum language, with its relatively small 'vocabulary'.

It would be a mistake to view these oral cultures as poor in communicative resources, like the oral cultures of the modern West that have been impoverished by competition from alternative media. To describe the African situation, including the diasporic cul-

---

[7] Eric A. Havelock, *Preface to Plato* (Oxford: Oxford University Press, 1963); Rosalind Thomas, *Literacy and Orality in Ancient Greece* (Cambridge: Cambridge University Press, 1992).

tures of African-Americans, we therefore need to use terms such as 'verbal art' or the oxymoron 'oral literature', drawing attention to the complexity and sophistication not only of individual perform-ers, African equivalents of Avdo, but also of a variety of 'speech genres'.[8]

This oral system has been modified by three revolutions in com-munication: the rise of writing, printing and finally of what we might call for convenience the electric media, including radio, tel-evision and the internet.

The Writing Revolutions

Oral performances, especially lengthy ones like sermons, speeches or the singing of epics, require a good memory. Hence the so-called 'art of memory', associating the things to be remembered with viv-id images located in an imaginary structure such as a theatre or a palace, flourished in medieval and Renaissance Europe.[9] More generally, there was a search for mnemonics. The formulae and themes discussed by Parry and Lord may be regarded as a form of mnemonics. Another form is that of the *qipu* of Peru, the Quechua term for 'knot', referring to coloured strings with knots in them. These 'talking knots' were used to keep accounts of transactions concerning a variety of days, numbers of people, goods, donors, receivers and so on.[10]

It has also been argued that some at least of the world's writing systems originated as forms of mnemonics. For example, the cu-neiform writing system of ancient Babylonia seems to have begun in this way, the marks on the clay tablets being used, like the *qipu*, to record the giving or receiving of various goods. Writing, in the

---

[8] Ruth Finnegan, *Oral Literature in Africa* (Oxford: Clarendon Press, 1970); Karin Barber, *The anthropology of texts, persons and publics: oral and written culture in Africa and beyond* (Cambridge: Cambridge University Press, 2007).
[9] Frances Yates, *The Art of Memory* (London: Routledge, 1966); Mary Carruthers, *The Book of Memory: A Study of Memory in Medieval Culture* (2nd edn, Cambridge: Cam-bridge University Press, 2008).
[10] Marcia Ascher and Robert Ascher, *Code of the Quipu: A Study in Media, Mathematics, and Culture* (Ann Arbor: University of Michigan Press, 1980).

strict sense of signs employed to represent language, developed later.[11]

The first writing systems, in this more precise sense, developed in the Middle East before 3000 BCE and include both Babylonian cuneiform and Egyptian hieroglyphics. They were followed by Chinese ideograms, in use before 1000 BCE, and the pictograms of the Mayas, which date from round 500 BCE. Since that time the number and variety of writing systems has vastly increased, as well as the material on which they have been written (palm leaves, birch bark, animal skins and bones, silk, papyrus, parchment, paper, wax, clay, stone or metal, using styluses, brushes, reed, quill or metal pens and so on).

Writing systems used to be divided into two groups, the first, (including hieroglyphics, ideograms and pictograms) remaining closer to the mnemonic origins of script and representing ideas or things, while the second, alphabets, represent words or sounds. However, recent research has undermined the importance of this binary distinction and scholars now speak in terms of the predominant organizing principle of a given script.[12]

For historians, the great question or questions to answer is surely that of the manifold effects of writing on culture and society in different parts of the world. Two answers to these questions have become particularly famous, one of them being associated with the Canadian economic historian Harold Innis, in the 1950s, and the other with the British anthropologist Jack Goody, from the 1960s onwards.

Innis suggested that the use of heavier and more durable materials led to what he called a 'cultural bias' towards time and so to religious organisation. The clay tablets used in Assyria, for example, were difficult to transport but they were well suited to the keeping of permanent records in an archive. On the other hand the lighter media, such as paper and papyrus, which are relatively ephemeral but may be moved quickly over long distances, led to

---

[11] Jerrold S. Cooper, 'Babylonian Beginnings: the origin of the cuneiform writing system in comparative perspective', in Stephen Houston, ed., *The First Writing: script invention as history and process* (Cambridge: Cambridge University Press, 2004), 71–99.
[12] Stephen D. Houston, 'Overture', in Houston, *The First Writing*, 3–15.

a bias towards space and political organisation. In a sense, then, Innis anticipated the idea associated with his younger colleague at the University of Toronto, Marshall McLuhan, that 'the medium is the message'.[13]

The Goody thesis (originally formulated in collaboration with the literary historian Ian Watt) emphasized the social effects of writing in general and the alphabet in particular. Contrasting ancient Greece in the age of 'alphabetic culture' with the fundamentally oral culture of West Africa (where Goody had carried out his fieldwork), the two scholars argued that writing encouraged abstract thought, a critical attitude to ideas and the development of political democracy. The thesis has been criticised for paying insufficient emphasis to the various contexts in which different literacies have developed, while Goody himself has revised his views, qualifying but not abandoning them.[14]

Other consequences of writing, and especially of the spread of literacy, have been identified, especially in two domains, religion and politics. In the case of religion, attention has focussed on the rise of authoritative 'scriptures': Buddhist, Jewish, Christian or Muslim. Writing aided the spread of Mahayana Buddhism, for instance, around the first century CE.[15] Again, in Western Europe in the thirteenth and fourteenth centuries, writing assisted the spread of Christian heresies among what have been described as 'textual communities', groups of literate laymen and laywomen meeting to discuss a book, perhaps the Bible (and so illustrating the interaction between speaking and writing). The Lollards, followers of John Wyclif, are a famous example of such groups.[16]

In the domain of politics, the consequences of literacy were at least equally profound. The famous contrast drawn by the Ger-

---

[13] Harold Innis, *Empire and Communication* (Oxford: Oxford University Press, 1950).

[14] Jack Goody, *The Domestication of the Savage Mind* (Cambridge: Cambridge University Press, 1977); id., *The Interface between the Oral and the Written* (Cambridge: Cambridge University Press, 1987); Brian V. Street, *Literacy in Theory and Practice* (Cambridge: Cambridge University Press, 1984).

[15] Richard Gombrich, 'When the Mahayana began', in Tadeusz Skorupski, ed., *The Buddhist Forum*, vol.1 (London: School of Oriental and African Studies, 1990), 21–30.

[16] Brian Stock, *The Implications of Literacy* (Princeton: Princeton University Press, 1983).

man sociologist Max Weber, between traditional 'patrimonial' or personal government on one side and modern bureaucratic or impersonal forms on the other, depended on the issuing of written orders and the keeping of written records.[17] 'Paperwork', which we associate (like the 'red tape' used to tie the papers into bundles) with bureaucracy, depends on endless supplies of cheap paper. Paper had long been regularly employed in China, it was in use in the Islamic world from about 800 CE, and it was increasingly available in Europe around 1400. Hence it was in the early modern world that the effects of writing on the practices of government became particularly visible, in Europe and the Ottoman and Mughal Empires as well as in China under the new dynasty of the Qing.

There were two sides to this rise of writing, two opposite consequences. On one side, it made information about the society they were administering available to ruler and the central government. This was why Jean-Baptiste Colbert, for instance, one of the most powerful ministers in the service of King Louis XIV of France, spent so much energy collecting, arranging and retrieving information.[18] Qing China was another example of what has been described as the 'archive state'. The flow of information from the provinces to the centre was carefully organized, with two tracks, the routine track and the confidential track (leading from high provincial officials to the emperor himself, who would add his comments in vermilion ink).[19] Cosmopolitan written languages such as Sanskrit, Latin and Arabic have long helped to hold multilingual empires together.

There was also a negative side to the rise of writing. King Philip II of Spain became known as the "paper king" (*el rey papelero*), chained to his desk and so missing the opportunity to become as well acquainted with his empire at first hand as his father, the constantly itinerant Charles V. From Spain to Sweden, critics spoke and wrote of 'the rule of the secretaries' rather than that of the

---

[17] Max Weber, 'The Three Types of Legitimate Domination', in *Essays in Economic Sociology* (Princeton: Princeton University Press, 1999), 99–108.

[18] Jacob Soll, *The Information Master: Jean-Baptiste Colbert's Secret State Intelligence System* (Ann Arbor: University of Michigan Press, 2009).

[19] Philip A. Kuhn, *Soulstealers: the Chinese Sorcery Scare of 1768* (Cambridge, MA: Harvard University Press, 1990), esp. 122–4.

monarchs for whom they supposedly worked. In similar fashion, in the early modern Mughal Empire, the regime of Akbar was known as 'government by paper' (*kaghazi raj*) and the administration became more and more 'paper-bound' in the late seventeenth and early eighteenth centuries.[20]

Medieval Europe and the Islamic world have been chosen as two short case-studies of cultures of writing. In medieval Europe, one of the major social distinctions was that between the clergy, defined as able to read, and the laity. The church and the state kept records, generally written on expensive parchment. They were less extensive than they would be in the age of the 'paper state', but the chancery, the place where secretaries wrote and filed letters to and from the prince, was already an important organ of government.[21]

The knowledge of the learned was collected into treatises, available in their hundreds in libraries, especially the libraries of monasteries. Monks copied manuscripts, and so did students in universities, but the multiplication of manuscripts took place above all (at least in the late Middle Ages) in commercial *scriptoria*, where groups of scribes would write down the same words from dictation and thus allow the 'publication' of a text before the age of print.

Medieval Europe may also be described as a 'notarial culture' in which, especially in the cities of the Mediterranean region, a substantial proportion of the population had recourse to notaries in order to record wills, contracts, transfers of property and so on (thus providing what archivists describe with a mixture of pride and complaint as 'kilometres' of sources for today's historians). It was not necessary for the client to be literate: in the Middle Ages, and indeed much later, people who could not themselves write or even read made use of writing through intermediaries.

In later centuries too, in major cities there were particular places where clients knew they could find public writers who would

---

[20] Martin Moir, 'Kaghazi Raj: Notes on the Documentary Basis of Company Rule: 1783–1858', *Indo-British Review* 21, No. 2, 185–193.

[21] Carla Bozzolo and Ezio Ornato, *Pour une histoire du livre manuscript au moyen âge: trois essais de codicologie quantitative* (Paris: CNRS, 1980); Michael T. Clanchy, *From Memory to Written Record: England, 1066–1307* (2nd edn, Oxford: Blackwell, 1993): Stock, *Implications of Literacy.*

both compose and write out letters and other documents for them. In eighteenth-century Paris, there was the cemetery of the Saints-Innocents, where graves were used as desks, and in Mexico City, even today, there is the Plaza de Santo Domingo in the old city centre, where the scribes now use electric typewriters.[22] In villages, priests or pastors might perform this function for their parishioners. The importance of what is known as 'mediated literacy' should not be forgotten.

In the Islamic world, until about the year 1800, printing was generally banned, so that scholars have spoken of the 'calligraphic state'.[23] One might even speak of 'calligraphic culture' since in response to the prohibition of the public display of images, writing, in a variety of scripts, angular or cursive (Kufi, Naskhi, and so on) was used on a variety of surfaces, stone, metal, wood, wool or ceramics, to decorate walls, weapons, pulpits, rugs, plates and so on. Good handwriting in the Arabic alphabet (also used to write texts in Persian, Turkish, Urdu and other languages) was a much appreciated skill. It was necessary for the scribe (*warraq*), who spent his working life producing magnificent manuscripts of the Qu'ran and other texts for wealthy patrons. It was equally necessary for the secretary (*katib*), working in the chancery (*diwan*), who both composed and wrote letters on behalf of sultans and shahs. Libraries of manuscript books were founded by rulers in Baghdad, Córdoba and elsewhere and the numbers of books in them, even if the estimates were exaggerated, far surpassed the holdings of medieval libraries in the West.[24]

However, even more stress was placed on written communication in medieval Europe than in the Muslim world at the same

---

[22] Christine Métayer, *Au tombeau des secrets: les écrivains publics du Paris populaire, Cimetière des Saints-Innocents (XVIe-XVIIIe siècle)* (Paris: Albin Michel, 2000); Judy Kalman, *Writing on the plaza: mediated literacy practice among scribes and clients in Mexico City* (Cresskill, NJ: Hampton Press, 1999).

[23] Brinkley Messick, *The Calligraphic State: Textual Domination and History in a Muslim Society* (Berkeley: University of California Press, 1993).

[24] Abdelkebir Khatibi, Mohammed Sijelmassi, *The Splendour of Islamic Calligraphy* (London: Thames and Hudson, 1976); George Makdisi, *The Rise of Humanism in Classical Islam and the Christian West* (Edinburgh: Edinburgh University Press, 1990); Houari Touati, *L'armoire à sagesse: bibliothèques et collections en Islam* (Paris: Aubier, 2003).

time, at least in the domain of higher education. Muslim students literally sat at the feet of the master, listening to his words.[25] In Europe too universities were centres of oral communication – as indeed they still are – but speech was supplemented by writing. Lectures, for example, expounded texts, while students often took written notes and copied texts in manuscript. The coming of printing would add another element to the mix.

The Print Revolutions

It has become commonplace to refer to the invention and spread of printing with moveable type as a revolution, even though it was still presented as 'the unacknowledged revolution' thirty years ago, by the North American historian Betty Eisenstein in 1979.[26] However, in this context it might be wiser to use the term 'revolution' in the plural, referring to separate revolutions in China, Korea and the West.

In China, in the seventh century, the age of the Empress Wu, recently described as 'The Woman who discovered Printing', it was already possible to print on a massive scale, using wood-blocks carved with ideograms, a block for each page. The technique was used at this time to print short Buddhist spells, but it would later be employed to print images and also a wide range of texts from the Confucian classics to novels such as *The Romance of the Three Kingdoms*.[27]

Printing with moveable type made of clay, wood or metal was also in use in China and Korea in the thirteenth and fourteenth centuries, but it does not seem to have been taken up widely for

---

[25] Jonathan Berkey, *The Transmission of Knowledge in Medieval Cairo* (Princeton: Princeton University Press, 1992); Michael Chamberlain, *Knowledge and Social Practice in Medieval Damascus* (Cambridge: Cambridge University Press, 1994).
[26] Elizabeth Eisenstein, *The Printing Press as an Agent of Change* (2 vols., Cambridge: Cambridge University Press, 1979), 3–42. Cf Eisenstein, 'An Unacknowledged Revolution Revisited', *American Historical Review* 107 (2002), 87–105, and Adrian Johns, 'How to Acknowledge a Revolution', *ibid.*, 106–25.
[27] Timothy H. Barrett, *The Woman Who Discovered Printing* (New Haven, Yale University Press, 2008).

obvious reasons. For alphabetic cultures, moveable type makes printing simpler and possibly cheaper (though this point has been contested), but for China, with about 2,000 basic ideograms (and another 30,000 in use by educated people), its advantages are, to put it mildly, not obvious. It is surely no accident that the development of printing in Korea coincided with the invention of an alphabetic script in the middle of the fifteenth century.[28]

The similarities between Korean printing with moveable type and Gutenberg's 'invention' are obvious enough, and it is quite possible that Gutenberg had heard about the Korean technique (just as Galileo had heard about a Dutch telescope before constructing his own). What was new in Europe was the development of this technique for commercial purposes, thanks in part to the arrival of relatively cheap paper and also to the spread of literacy among the laity (including some women) in the late Middle Ages. In contrast to the West, where printing was commercialized from the start, in both China and Korea printing was controlled by the government. Books were given away rather than sold. By the sixteenth century, however, commercial printing was flourishing in China too, and by the seventeenth century in Japan as well.[29]

Printed images were an important form of communication in all these parts of the world, whether they were used to illustrate texts or sold by themselves. In the West, from the Renaissance onwards, leading artists such as Sandro Botticelli and Albrecht Dürer produced 'prints', originally woodcuts, then copperplates, and later etchings, mezzotints, aquatints, lithographs and so on, using different techniques to create images that could be reproduced by machine. In China and Japan by contrast, the woodcut continued

---

[28] Roger Chartier, 'Gutenberg Revisited from the East', *Late Imperial China* 17 (1996), 1–9; Cynthia Brokaw and Kai-Wing Chow (eds.) *Print and Book Culture in Late Imperial China* (Berkeley: University of California Press, 2005); Pow-Key Sohn, *Early Korean Typography* (2nd edn, Seoul: Po Chin Chai, 1982).

[29] Cynthia Brokaw, 'Commercial Publishing in Late Imperial China: the Zou and Ma family businesses of Sibao, Fujian', *Late Imperial China* 17 (1996), 49–92; Peter Kornicki, *The Book in Japan: a cultural history from the beginnings to the nineteenth century* (Leiden: Brill, 1998); Mary Elizabeth Berry, *Japan in Print: information and nation in the early modern period* (Berkeley: University of California Press, 2006).

to dominate production, using the same method as wood-block printing but refining it to produce colour prints, as in the famous Japanese genre of *ukiyo-e*, 'pictures of the floating world' [the world of the urban pleasure quarters] to which artists of the calibre of Hokusai, Hiroshige and Utamaro all contributed.[30]

Gradually, the new medium took over the world. Presses were established in Spanish America in the sixteenth century, in both Mexico and Peru. By contrast, only four printers were at work in North America before 1680, while presses were forbidden to be established in Brazil before 1808, so that books had to be imported from Portugal.

The years around 1800 are a watershed in the history of printed communication in many parts of the world. It was in 1810 that the German printer Friedrich Koenig patented a new invention, a press operated by steam power and so capable of printing many more pages per hour than was possible for a press operated by hand.

In Brazil, permission to print in 1808 was followed by the rise of short-lived political and polemical journals such as *O Maribondo* (1822), *Bússola da Liberdade* (1832), and others, mainly from Recife.[31] The *Mercurio Peruano* was founded in 1791, and a famous Mexican newspaper, *El pensador mexicano,* in 1812. Following the revolt against Spain, the first printing houses were established in Buenos Aires and a newspaper in English, the *British Packet and Argentine News,* was founded in 1826.

In Africa, writing and printing arrived at more or less the same time in the nineteenth century, along with missionaries (both Muslim and Christian). The *Cape Town Gazette* and the *Sierra Leone Royal Gazette* both date from the year 1800.

In the Islamic world print, long banned (apart from an abortive experiment in Istanbul at the beginning of the eighteenth century) began to be permitted. In 1795, for instance, the French em-

---

[30] David Landau and Peter Parshall, *The Renaissance Print 1470–1550* (New Haven: Yale University Press, 1994); Muneshige Narazaki, *The Japanese print: its evolution and essence* (Tokyo: Kodansha International, 1966).

[31] Everardo Ramos. *Du marché au marchand. La gravure populaire brésilienne* (Gravelines: Musée du Dessin et de l'Estampe, 2005).

bassy in Istanbul was allowed to print a newspaper, the *Bulletin des nouvelles*, followed in 1825 by the *Spectateur oriental*, edited by the Frenchman Alexandre Blacque, a merchant in Izmir. Blacque was subsequently asked by the sultan to edit the official Ottoman gazette, the *Takvim-i-Vekayı* (1831). Meanwhile, in 1821, in Cairo, a newspaper in Turkish and Arabic, *Jurnal ül-Khidiv*, had begun publication.[32]

Like writing, the introduction of printing had important consequences, both intended and unintended, for the cultures that adopted it. For one thing, it encouraged the spread of the 'paper state', including its multitude of official forms. Literacy campaigns were organized by churches (in Protestant Germany and Sweden in the eighteenth century, for instance), so that ordinary people would become better Christians by reading the Bible. Similar campaigns were organized by the state in twentieth-century Russia, Cuba and elsewhere, in order to make ordinary people better citizens, or at least more receptive to official propaganda.[33] Some democratic governments, from the United States to Brazil, have made voting in elections conditional on literacy.

One might say that these governments agreed with the German philosopher-sociologist Jürgen Habermas, who has argued that the rise of what he calls *Öffentlichkeit*, usually translated as the 'public sphere', was encouraged by changes in communication such as the reading of newspapers in coffee-houses in the eighteenth century and led – like literacy, according to Goody – to the rise of critical attitudes and democratic culture.[34] This insight is a valuable one. All the same, it might be more useful to employ the term 'public sphere' in the plural than in the singular, distinguishing between male and female, bourgeois and working-class or religious and secular spheres. It would also be illuminating to distinguish dif-

---

[32] Francis Robinson, 'Technology and Religious Change: Islam and the Impact of Print', *Modern Asian Studies* 27 (1993), 229–51.

[33] Gerald Strauss, 'Lutheranism and Literacy', K. von Greyerz, ed., *Religion and Society in Early Modern Europe, 1500–1800* (London: German Historical Institute, 1984), 109–23; Robert F. Arnove and Harvey J. Graff, eds., *National literacy campaigns: historical and comparative perspectives* (New York: Plenum Press, 1987).

[34] Jürgen Habermas, *The Structural Transformation of the Public Sphere* (English trans. Cambridge: Polity, 1989).

ferent media of communication, noting the importance of the traditional oral public sphere, associated with public squares, taverns and other centres of sociability, as well as the newer spheres associated with radio, television and the Internet.

Despite earlier literacy campaigns, reading remained a minority skill in most countries until the twentieth century. Around the year 1850, half the adult population of Europe could not read (around 75% in Italy and Spain, and over 90% in the Russian Empire), while 84% of the Brazilian population was officially described as illiterate in 1890.[35] These illiterates were often familiar with books at second hand, listening to others read aloud. The importance of the oral communication of printed texts must not be forgotten. To take a striking example from Cuba in the nineteenth and early twentieth centuries, workers in tobacco factories, where hands are busy but ears have little to do, used to club together to pay the wages of a colleague who did not work but instead read aloud to the others from a pulpit constructed for the purpose.

The unintended consequences of the arrival of the printing press have probably been even more profound. Print helped to standardize and fix the formerly fluid vernacular languages – especially in their written forms – in order to sell books outside a single region. The press also undermined monopolies of knowledge, allowing readers to share the secrets of many crafts, from mining to cooking. As the rise of advertising in seventeenth-century European books vividly illustrates, communication gradually became more and more commercialized.

Both the religious and the political consequences of printing were profound. Printed pamphlets attacking the Catholic Church, printed translations of the Bible and printed catechisms all played an important role in the Protestant Reformation, confirming the fears of Catholic clerics that literacy led to heresy and leading to the publication of the notorious *Index of Prohibited Books,* an attempt to fight printing with its own weapons. In the domain of politics, as in that of religion, print, especially printed newspapers, encour-

---

[35] Carlo Cipolla, *Literacy and Development in the West* (Harmondsworth: Penguin, 1969).

aged criticism and even revolution, as in the case of England in the 1640s and France in 1789.[36] Benedict Anderson has argued that what he calls 'print capitalism', and especially the printed newspaper, aided the construction of 'imagined communities', especially the nation, though it should be remembered that only a minority of the population had access to newspapers before the second half of the nineteenth century.[37]

Slowly but surely, printed texts reached wider and wider circles of readers in Europe, Asia, Africa and the Americas, especially in the form of the booklets known in English as 'chap-books' because they were retailed by 'chapmen' or pedlars. France, for instance, had its *Bibliothèque Bleue*, booklets with blue covers that were distributed in the countryside as well as the towns by itinerant pedlars from the seventeenth century onwards. Spain had its *literatura de cordel*, so-called because the booklets were sold in market-places hung on a string. Japan had its *kana-zōshi*, stories written in a simple syllabic script (rather than the Chinese characters used by the elite) and sold in the street.[38]

Brazil had its *folhetos* from the later nineteenth century to the late twentieth (or even later, though this form of literature is in decline), texts that illustrate once again the central theme of this essay, the interaction between media. *Folhetos* were short texts, ranging from eight to thirty-two pages, printed in small numbers on hand presses in small-scale establishments in a style that is amateur rather than professional (for example, the typeface might change from one page to another). There was often a woodcut illustration on the cover. The texts were traditionally divided into genres such as prophecies, 'stories of suffering' and 'bold exploits',

---

[36] Briggs and Burke, *Social History of the Media*, 61–90. Cf R. W. Scribner, *For the sake of simple folk: popular propaganda for the German Reformation* (Oxford: Clarendon Press, 1994); Joad Raymond, *The invention of the newspaper: English newsbooks, 1641–1649* (Oxford: Clarendon Press, 1996); Robert Darnton and Daniel Roche, eds., *Revolution in Print: the press in France, 1775–1800* (Berkeley: University of California Press, 1989).

[37] Benedict Anderson, *Imagined Communities* (3rd edn London: Verso, 2006).

[38] Robert Mandrou, *De la culture populaire aux 17e et 18 siècles: la Bibliothèque Bleue de Troyes* (Paris: Stock, 1964); Roger Chartier, *The Cultural Uses of Print in Early Modern France* (Princeton: Princeton University Press, 1987), 240–64; Julio Caro Baroja, *Ensayo sobre la literatura de cordel* (Madrid: ediciones de la Revista del Occidente, 1969).

associated with heroes ranging from medieval knights to modern bandits, notably Lampião.

However, these printed texts remained close to oral performances. They were written in verse in a traditional form, *sextilhas,* verses of six lines with seven or eight syllables to the line. The poets, known as *cantadores* or *trovadores,* not only wrote the texts, but also performed them, reciting the verses aloud (often accompanying themselves on a guitar or other stringed instrument), usually at weekly markets, before selling copies of the text to the audience. The printed text was not able to produce many features of the performance, but it may well have functioned as a kind of mnemonic, facilitating re-enactments by the buyers and their friends.

This hypothesis helps explain the paradox that the public for *folhetos* was most extensive in an area of particularly low literacy, the rural North-East. The *folheto* was in a sense a book for the illiterate, a text which they bought so that literate friends or relatives could read it to them. Towards the end of the twentieth century, the *folhetos* were modernized. They discussed contemporary themes, from AIDS to Brazil's foreign debt. The woodcut on the cover was replaced by a coloured photograph. The poets used microphones for their recitations, and sold not only texts but cassettes as well. Where the booklet used to function as a souvenir of the performance, the performance turned into a commercial for the cassette.[39]

Elsewhere in the twentieth century, the rise of 'comics' in the West and *manga* in Japan both continued and transformed the tradition of the chap-book, while Nigeria in the 1950s and 1960s developed a 'market literature', entertaining or improving stories with appealing titles such as 'Mabel the sweet honey that poured away'. The booklets were sold in markets, especially in the town of Onitsha, until the Nigerian civil war.[40]

Scholars have often linked commercialization to mass-production and even to 'mass culture'. However, the rise of journals and

---

[39] Candace Slater, *Stories on a String: the Brazilian literature de cordel* (Berkeley: University of California Press, 1982).

[40] Emmanuel N. Obiechina, *An African Popular Literature: a study of Onitsha market pamphlets* (Cambridge: Cambridge University Press, 1973).

magazines produced for different groups of people with different interests suggests that the market for print has long been diverse. The first magazines for women date from the late seventeenth century, the *Mercure Galant* in France, for instance, and their editors had already discovered the combination of fashion information, romantic stories and competitions that long remained a key to commercial success. Individual variety is also demonstrated by letters to newspapers and magazines, another tradition that goes back to the years around 1700 (to the *Athenian Mercury* and the *Spectator*) and is not yet exhausted.[41]

What we call 'print culture' is actually a mix of oral, written and printed communication. The interaction of orality and print may be illustrated by the *folhetos* discussed above and their equivalents in other cultures. Manuscript and print also interacted. Printers produced hybrid books with blank spaces for readers to add information and comments, thus personalizing the text.[42] The production of hand-written texts continued in the age of print but a certain division of labour was established, with intimate and clandestine communication becoming the domain of the manuscript. Handwritten newsletters, for instance, continued to provide the news that was not allowed to be printed.[43]

The Electric Revolutions

'Electric culture', a convenient shorthand phrase to refer to a sequence or package of nineteenth- and twentieth-century media, is actually 'oral, written, printed and electric culture'. The phrase is something of a mouthful – but a mouthful with the advantage of reminding us of the variety of cultures of communication in

---

[41] Helen Berry, *Gender, Society and Print Culture in Late-Stuart England. The Cultural World of the Athenian Mercury* (Aldershot: Ashgate, 2003).

[42] David McKitterick, *Print, Manuscript and the Search for Order, 1450–1830* (Cambridge: Cambridge University Press, 2003), 37–8.

[43] Harold Love, *Scribal Publication in Seventeenth-Century England* (Oxford: Oxford University Press, 1993); François Moureau, ed., *De bonne main: la communication manuscrite au 18e siècle* (Paris and Oxford: Universitas and Voltaire Foundation, 1993).

which we continue to live. The age of globalization and cultural homogenization is also an age of fragmentation and heterogenization.[44]

The electric age may be divided into stages dominated by the telegraph, the film, radio, television and the Internet, but the earlier stages have survived into the later ones and once again interact with them, as in the case of the technological 'convergence' that has recently produced mobile phones that are also cameras and give access to the Internet.[45]

To begin with the telegraph, in 1850, a German journalist, Paul Reuter, who lived in Aachen, began using the new telegraph line to send news to Berlin. This marked the beginning of what became Reuter's Telegram Company, founded in 1865 and based in Britain. The consequent acceleration of the transmission of information about crops, prices and so on made a considerable impact on the economy. The telegraph also made an impact on politics: the outbreak of the Franco-Prussian War in 1870, for instance, followed Bismarck's publication of an edited form of a confidential telegram, deliberately provoking the French to declare war.

Where the telegraph might be seen as an ally of print, assisting the newspaper, film and radio have undermined the print revolution, encouraging the return of the image and also the return of the oral. However, the cultural and social effects of film and radio have been very different.

The film can of course be used to present news. In France, Pathé Frères began to issue 'newsreels', as they came to be called, in 1908, while in London a news cinema opened in 1909, the Daily Bioscope. All the same, the future of the film was in drama, especially popular dramas of the kind produced in Hollywood and later in 'Bollywood' in Bombay. This future also turned out to be international, especially after the rise of dubbing and sub-titling. Hollywood made an unexpected contribution to the globalization of culture, making Third World audiences aware of North American patterns of clothing and behaviour (from kissing to eating with a

[44] Arjun Appadurai, *Modernity at Large: Cultural Dimensions of Globalization* (Minneapolis: University of Minnesota Press, 1996).
[45] Briggs and Burke, *Social History of the Media,* 121–302.

knife and fork) and encouraging imitation thanks to the 'glamour' of the 'stars'.[46]

The new medium helped to create these stars. Some actors and singers had achieved fame in earlier periods, but film allowed far more people in many places to develop enthusiasms for a relatively small number of performers, creating fanatics or 'fans' as well as stars. One unexpected consequence of the star system has been its impact on politics. Glamour, or charisma, can be translated into votes, launching the political careers of actors such as Ronald Reagan and Arnold Schwarzenegger as well as a number of Bollywood actors in India such as Sunil Dutt and Vinod Khanna, who joined the Bharatiya Janata Party and became Minister of Culture and Tourism in 2002.

In contrast to film, radio turned out to be an ideal medium for presenting the news, especially at the level of the nation. Indeed, one important effect of communication by radio was to encourage the standardization of spoken language, just as print had encouraged the standardization of written language. In Italy, for instance, when the country was united in 1861, less than ten per cent of the population spoke Italian (as opposed to regional dialects). It was only in the age of radio that the majority came first to understand and then to speak the national language.

By the 1930s and 1940s, a number of governments had become aware of the value of the new medium as a means of generating popular support. Leaders as different as Adolf Hitler and Winston Churchill, with their radio speeches, and F. D. Roosevelt, with his 'Fire Side Chats', grasped the opportunity. Lázaro Cárdenas of Mexico, with his annual New Year broadcasts, and Juan Perón – not to mention his wife Eva – also made use of the radio for political purposes. Again, in the Brazil of Gétulio Vargas, who became a dictator in 1937, there was a daily hour of radio propaganda, the *Hora do Brasil*, from seven till eight in the evening, which all channels were obliged to broadcast.

All the same, the importance of radio as a medium of entertain-

---

[46] Daniel Lerner, *The Passing of Traditional Society: Modernizing the Middle East* (Glencoe, IL: Free Press, 1978), 196.

ment should not be forgotten. In England in the middle of the twentieth century, for instance, popular programmes included serials such as *Mrs Dale's Diary* (which ran for more than twenty years, 1948–69), and *The Archers,* featuring a farm family, which began to be broadcast in 1950 and is now the longest-running serial in the world.

Television, invented before the Second World War but launched commercially afterwards, soon overtook both film and radio, combining their advantages, since the medium is well adapted both for spreading the news and for telling stories, for domestic and foreign markets. It brought the world into the living-room and saturated everyday life with images. One of its central genres, the 'soap opera' or *telenovela,* imitated serials on the radio (which had in turn imitated the serials in magazines), but enjoyed much more popular success in countries as different as the USA and Egypt. *Novelas* produced in Mexico and Brazil (most famously *The Slave Isaura,* 1976) have been particularly successful internationally, not only in other parts of Latin America but in Europe and China as well. Like films, they have contributed to globalization by making different styles of life better-known all over the world, even if a soap opera such as *Dallas* has been 'read' or interpreted in very different ways by audiences who are culturally as well as geographically distant from Texas.[47]

In our age of accelerating technological innovation, television has in turn been overtaken by audio- and video-cassettes, by DVDs and above all by the rise of the Internet from the early 1990s onwards, when a network originally developed in order to support academic research was opened to a wider public.

Some at least of the many economic, political and cultural consequences of this rapid sequence of changes in the media are visible enough. One of the more obvious trends might be described as the end of the paper state (dominant for the last five hundred years or so) as governments come to keep more and more information on disc. The survival of the newspaper is also threatened, although

---

[47] Ien Ang, *Watching Dallas: soap opera and the melodramatic imagination* (London: Routledge, 1985); Tamar Liebes and Elihu Katz, *The Export of Meaning: cross-cultural readings of Dallas* (second edn, Cambridge: Polity, 2004).

at the moment paper versions and electronic versions of the same newspaper continue to coexist. The printed book is often said to be an endangered species, but at the moment at least it is holding its own, with something like 200,000 new titles a year published in Britain today, far more than a generation ago.[48]

Another highly visible trend is the tendency to 'unfix' communication, thus reversing the five-hundred-year trend that followed Gutenberg. The new interactive media do not resemble print so much as the oral and manuscript modes of communication, when singers responded to the wishes of their listeners or scribes modified the text they were copying for their own purposes.

In the case of other social and political consequences of the recent round of changes in the media, there are forces pulling in different directions and it is far from clear which, if any, will be victorious. On the one side, the ownership of newspapers and television networks by multinational corporations encourages globalization. On the other, it is now possible for an increasing number of diasporic communities not only to keep in almost daily contact with relatives thousands of miles away but also to conserve their separate culture, for example by viewing television programmes from their country of origin via satellite.[49]

Again, on one side, governments have more access to information about their citizens than ever before, fuelling fears of dictatorial rule by a 'Big Brother' state. Media 'moguls' who control empires of communication are no new phenomenon: they go back at least as far as the Englishman Alfred Harmsworth (1865–1922) and the American William Randolph Hearst (1863–1951), but they have acquired more and more influence on what people see and hear every day from their screens, including the way in which the news is presented. We therefore have some reason to fear what might be called 'Cyberdictatorship'.

On the other hand, leaks of information are increasingly common. Hackers reveal economic, political and military secrets, while investigative journalists are able to bring down governments, as in

---

[48] John B. Thompson, *Books in the digital age: the transformation of academic and higher education publishing in Britain and the United States* (Cambridge: Polity, 2005).
[49] Appadurai, *Modernity*, 21–2.

the case of 'Watergate', when President Richard Nixon was forced to resign in 1974. In the Islamic world, videocassettes have not only allowed Osama bin Laden to publicize his denunciations of the West, but also permitted a debate about the principles of Islam that some scholars have compared to the Protestant Reformation, with the cassette taking the place of the printing press.[50]

Most spectacular of all, the rise of the Internet, a centrifugal medium, is widening the public sphere and supporting civil society and democracy. Like earlier letters to newspapers or telephone calls to television stations, 'blogs' or web-logs, which became popular at the beginning of the twenty-first century, allow individuals to express their opinions in public, but on an even wider scale. The spread of Email has encouraged networking and the activism of groups of citizens, especially important when a political regime is authoritarian and controls other media, as in the case of China today (though the Golden Shield project, inaugurated in 2003, is intended to erect a great wall against the Internet). For these reasons – although bloggers in some countries risk prison if they criticize the government – there is hope for what some commentators call 'Cyberdemocracy'.[51]

In short, new media bring new opportunities with them as well as new dangers. If anything future is certain, it is that people will have to learn to adjust still more rapidly to changes in the media of communication than they are trying to do today.

[50] Dale F. Eickelman, 'Inside the Islamic Reformation', in Donna Bowen and Evelyn A. Early, eds., *Everyday Life in the Muslim Middle East* (2nd edn Bloomington: Indiana University Press, 1997), 246–56.
[51] Mark Poster, *What's the Matter with the Internet?* (Minneapolis: University of Minnesota Press, 2001).

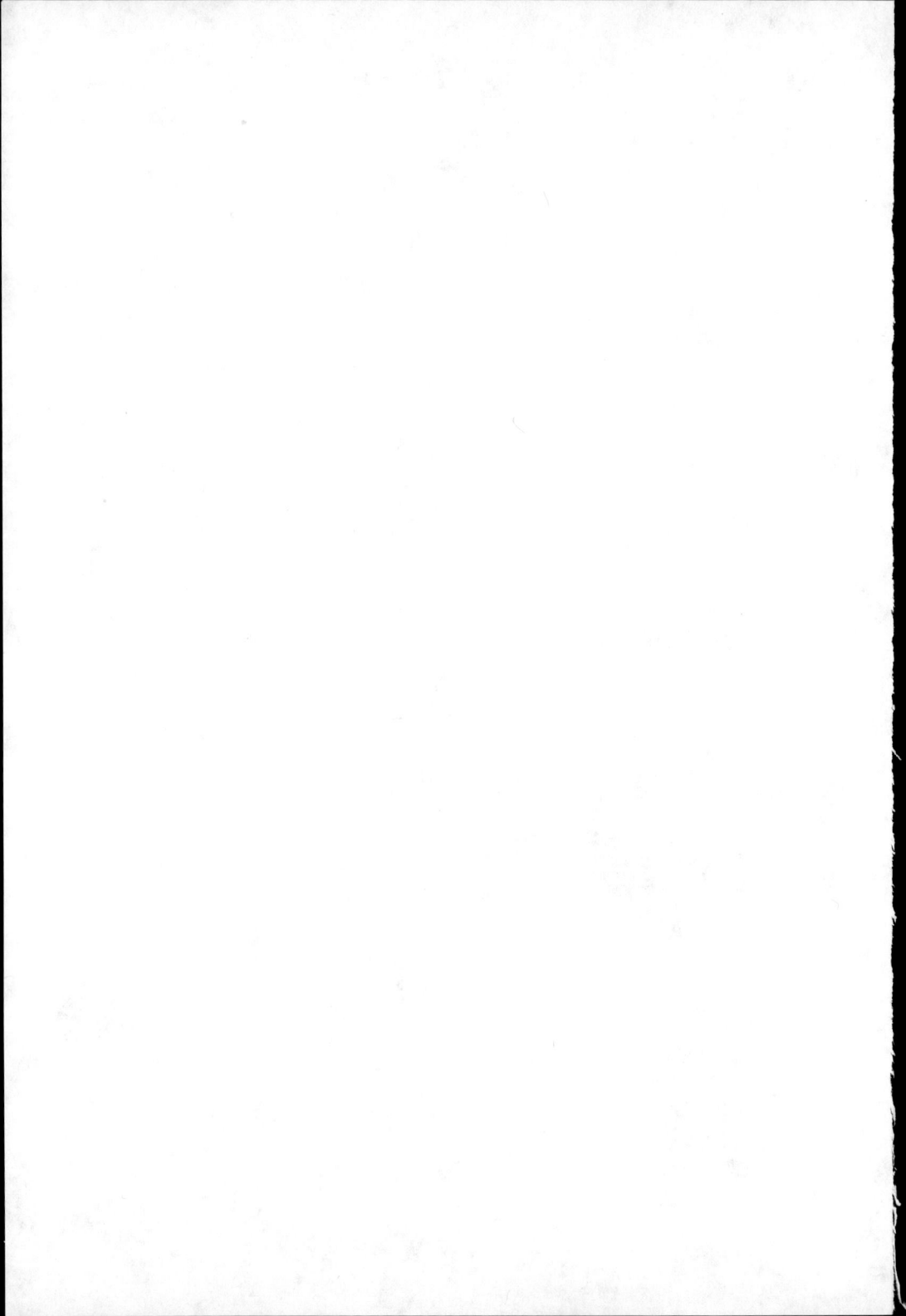

www.ingramcontent.com/pod-product-compliance
Lightning Source LLC
Chambersburg PA
CBHW070611270326
41926CB00013B/2505